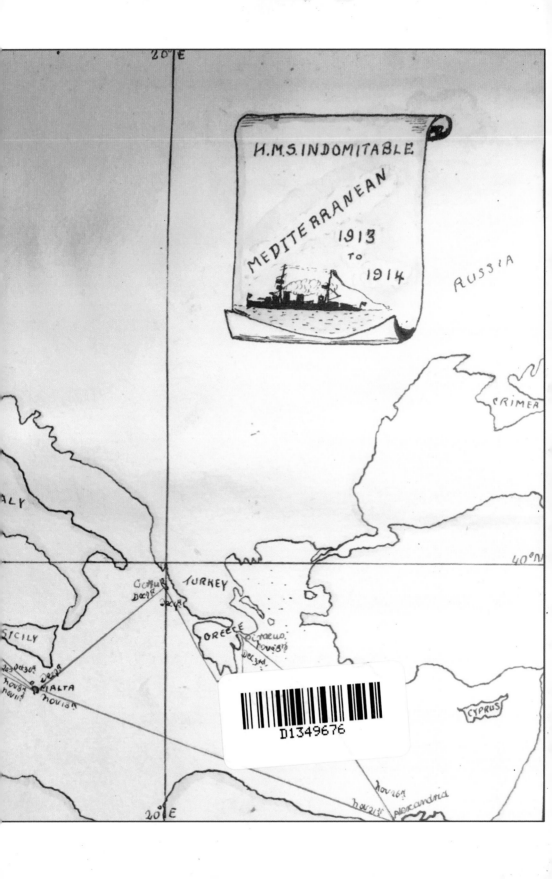

With the Royal Navy
in War and Peace

By the same author:

The Royal Navy Today
The Russian Convoys
British Sea Power
The Rescue Ships (with L.F. Martyn)
Loss of the Bismarck (republished in *Stringbags in Action*)
The Attack on Taranto (republished in *Stringbags in Action*)
Operation Neptune
The Arctic Convoys
The Story of HMS Dryad

With the Royal Navy in War and Peace

O'er the Dark Blue Sea

By

Vice Admiral B.B. Schofield CB CBE

Edited by

Victoria Schofield

Pen & Sword
MARITIME

First published in Great Britain in 2018 by
Pen & Sword Maritime
An imprint of
Pen & Sword Books Ltd
Yorkshire – Philadelphia

Copyright © The Estate of the Late Vice Admiral B.B. Schofield 2018

ISBN 978 1 52673 647 5

The right of Vice Admiral B.B. Schofield to be identified as Author of this work
has been asserted by him in accordance with the Copyright, Designs and Patents
Act 1988.

A CIP catalogue record for this book is
available from the British Library.

Printed and bound in the UK by TJ International Ltd, Padstow, Cornwall.

Pen & Sword Books Limited incorporates the imprints of Atlas, Archaeology,
Aviation, Discovery, Family History, Fiction, History, Maritime, Military, Military
Classics, Politics, Select, Transport, True Crime, Air World, Frontline Publishing, Leo
Cooper, Remember When, Seaforth Publishing, The Praetorian Press, Wharncliffe
Local History, Wharncliffe Transport, Wharncliffe True Crime and White Owl.

For a complete list of Pen & Sword titles please contact
PEN & SWORD BOOKS LIMITED
47 Church Street, Barnsley, South Yorkshire, S70 2AS, England
E-mail: enquiries@pen-and-sword.co.uk
Website: www.pen-and-sword.co.uk

Or

PEN AND SWORD BOOKS
1950 Lawrence Rd, Havertown, PA 19083, USA
E-mail: Uspen-and-sword@casematepublishers.com
Website: www.penandswordbooks.com

Contents

Maps

All maps are pre-1945; in general boundaries and country names indicated are those following the First World War.

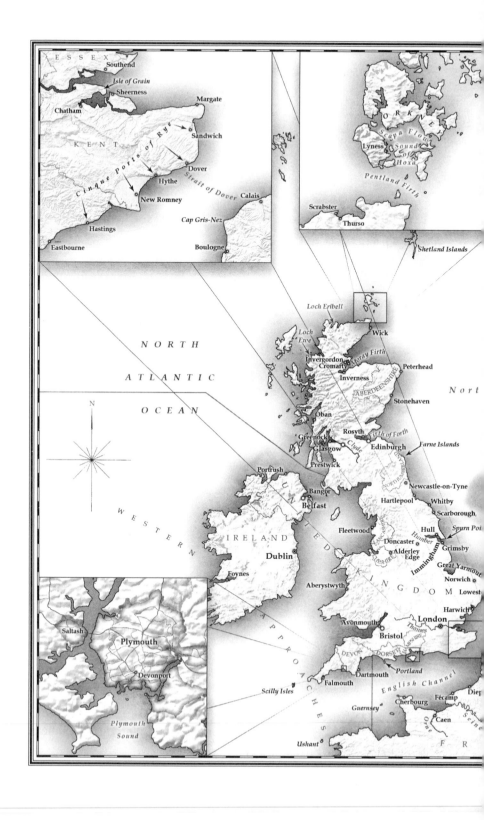

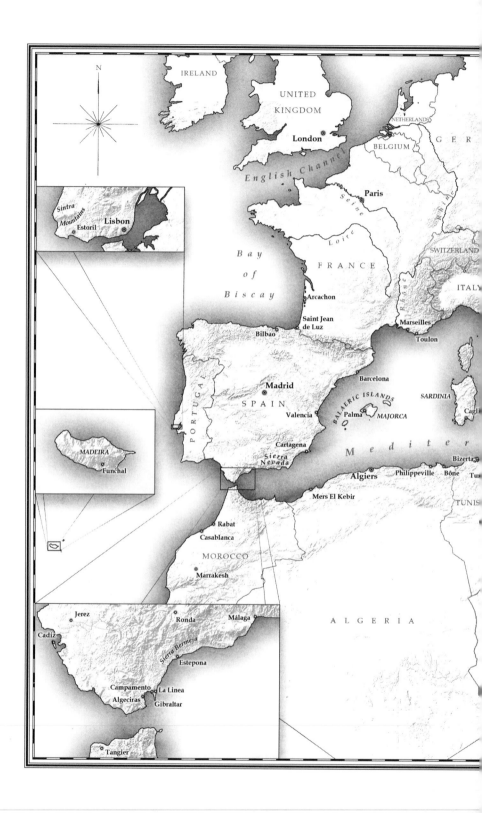

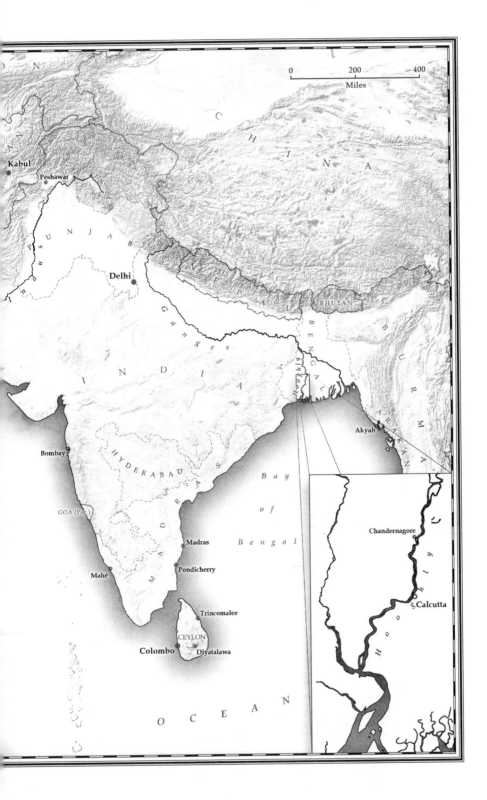

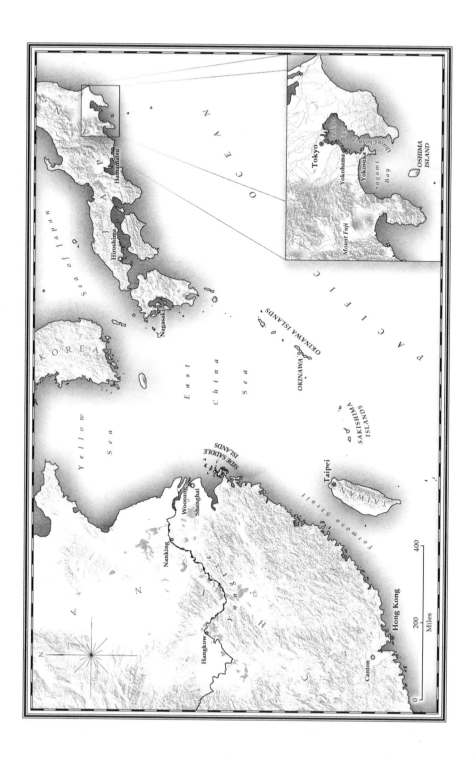

List of Illustrations

Unless otherwise stated, all illustrations are in the Schofield family possession.

End papers: map of HMS *Indomitable*'s passage 1913-1914 drawn by Schofield in his Midshipman's Journal, Imperial War Museum.

Jacket cover: Captain Schofield on board HMS *King George V* leaving Melbourne, November 1945.

Foreword

There is a history in all men's lives
Figuring the natures of the times deceased,
The which observed, a man may prophesy
With a near aim of the main chance of things.[1]

The naval career of Vice Admiral Brian Betham Schofield CB CBE spanned the first half of the twentieth century, encompassing two world wars. When, in retirement, he chose to record his service in the Royal Navy, he did so in 1956, while his memory was fresh, and before embarking on a second career as a naval historian. What is reproduced here is that memoir, in his own words; as he makes clear, in recollecting the past he was greatly assisted by his letters to his parents. Only one has survived (together with some personal correspondence in 1946) and so what would have been first hand accounts are subsumed into recollections. My task, as editor, has been to put the events he describes in context as well as adding some background information, which was common knowledge at the time of writing, but is less so to the twenty-first century reader.

As a late Victorian, the era of Schofield's birth dictated his life: having joined the Royal Navy in 1908, he was already serving as a midshipman at the outbreak of the First World War. By the time the Second World War began he had achieved the rank of captain which, together with his training as a navigator, provided the opportunity of taking command of what were called 'first class ships'. The portrait he paints is of a bygone era, when Britain's naval strength was at its zenith. It was a time when officers and men spent long periods at sea, the ship's log repeatedly recording 'hands employed cleaning ship', 'hands employed painting', 'hands employed sweeping decks', 'hands to mend clothes', 'hands employed preparing for sea', not forgetting 'leave to bathing parties' and 'Divine Service'.

Like the service careers of so many thousands, risk and chance played their part. That he was relieved of his command of HMS *Galatea* in 1941 a few months before the ship was torpedoed off the coast of Egypt meant that instead of Captain Brian Schofield it was Captain Edward Sim who went down with his ship. That, for personal reasons, he relinquished command of HMS *Duke of York* just before her action against the *Scharnhorst* in 1943 meant that his successor, Captain (later Admiral Sir) the Hon Guy Russell, had the opportunity of taking part in an historic sea battle. Yet, as all those who join the Armed Forces know, service is a commitment whose outcome can neither be foretold nor preordained.

Despite being a man of action, in common with many of his times, Schofield had an extensive knowledge of literature, which included the works of Plutarch, Hesiod, Lucian and, of course, Shakespeare and Rudyard Kipling. Only someone familiar with Dante's *Divine Comedy* would think to compare the dense and hazardous fog in which he was caught in the East China Sea with verses from a canto in *Il Purgatorio* or to cite Hesiod's *Theogony* when battling a storm off the south-east coast of England! What emerges from the narrative, notwithstanding the very challenging times and the loss of many friends, is how he combined duty with genuine enjoyment of his work and of his surroundings as well as gratitude at his good fortune. His personal life receives little mention; his first marriage, to Doris Ambrose, ended after nineteen years in 1941; his second marriage to a widow, Norah Handley (née Beatty), ended with her death in 1946; at the age of fifty, he married a former WRNS officer, Grace Seale.

In body and spirit Brian Betham Schofield was a sailor all his life, never more content, as he once said to me, than when he could feel the deck beneath his feet. His eightieth birthday was spent on board a passenger ship, returning once more to the West Indies from where, as a young lieutenant in 1919, he had first crossed the Equator and become 'a Son o' Neptune'.

> *And this our life, exempt from public haunt,*
> *Finds tongues in trees, books in the running brooks,*
> *Sermons in stones, and good in everything.*[2]

Victoria Schofield

Chapter One

Disciplina, Fide, Labore

There is nothing the Navy cannot do.[1]

1908–13

'You see, Sir', a member of the well-known naval outfitter, Gieve Matthews & Seagrove Ltd (later Gieves Ltd) said to my father as, in fun, he placed an admiral's cocked hat on my twelve-and-a-half-year-old head, 'it fits him very well.' Although cocked hats were no longer in fashion by the time I reached flag rank, I am glad that my father lived to see the outfitter's prediction theoretically fulfilled. In those days the total cost of purchasing a naval cadet's uniform was £41.11s.6d; the most expensive item was the sea chest costing £5.10s.0d, while my winter working jacket, vest and trousers cost £3.3s, or, as we used to say, three guineas.

Before purchasing my uniform I had to pass my interview with the Board of Admiralty in London. Again accompanied by my father, Thomas Dodgshon Schofield, I was dressed in an Eton suit with a large white turndown stiff collar and bow tie and felt very nervous. We were shown into an ante-room where several other boys and their parents or guardians were sitting and who were no doubt all as nervous as I was. Such conversation, as there was, was muted and ceased altogether each time the door at the far end of the room opened and a young man in a black coat and pin-striped trousers called a candidate's name. After what seemed an eternity, my name was called and I followed the young man into a large room in the centre of which was a long, polished mahogany table at which a number of elderly gentlemen were sitting. I was directed to a chair beside the thick-set swarthy man seated at the head of the table and who was wearing a double-breasted nautical jacket with black horn buttons. He bade me sit down and then the members of the board asked me a number of questions. At one stage the president of the board stood up and asked me to follow him to a map hanging on a wall. He then asked me to indicate the positions of various European capital cities. After a few more questions I was dismissed.

It was not until some time later that I discovered that the president was the formidable First Sea Lord, Admiral Sir John (Jacky) Fisher. He was apparently interested in seeing what sort of boys were joining the Royal Navy under the Selborne scheme, which combined the military and engineering branches of the Royal Navy and which he had done so much to promote. Also known as the Selborne-Fisher scheme, it had been approved in 1903 by the First Lord of the Admiralty, William Palmer, Earl of Selborne.[2]

Although my father was in no way connected with the Royal Navy nor the sea, from the moment I passed my entrance examination that summer of 1908 he became the most avid reader of naval literature and so we were always able to discuss together the problems in which I was interested. Writing a lifetime later, I believe that any measure of success which I may have achieved is primarily due to the great and enduring interest which he took in my career and to the strong bond of affection which united us all as a family. As each step in rank came along, my greatest happiness was knowing the pleasure it gave to my devoted parents. When my father died on 8 December 1952 at the great age of 93 (followed by my mother aged 92 in 1953), I found that he had carefully treasured every letter I had ever written to him (and we were regular correspondents). He had also kept all the newspaper cuttings, appointments and certificates connected with my career, which had reached him over a period of forty-five years. These have proved invaluable in refreshing my memory of events which occurred many years ago.[3]

Osborne

The title of this chapter, *Disciplina, Fide, Labore,* is the motto which appeared on the cover of the termly magazine while the Royal Naval College was based in the Isle of Wight at Osborne House, the former summer residence of Queen Victoria until her death in 1901. Built between 1845–51 it served as the Royal Navy's junior officer training college from 1903 until 1921. The motto was chosen, I believe, because those three words express the essence of a naval officer's training. The object of education should be to discipline the mind in the use of its own powers of assimilation; self-discipline is also essential to anyone who is going to command his fellow men. Whilst religious faith is of primary importance, there is also the faith necessary in the building of character. 'For they conquer who believe they can,' observed Virgil.[4] Lord Nelson interpreted this truth when he wrote 'There is nothing the Navy cannot do.' This motto was written up in big brass letters on a beam in the college assembly hall, which was named after that most famous of Britain's sailors. Many men have discovered that it is necessary to work hard to capture the prizes to which ones aspires. 'It is for want of application rather than of means that men fail of success,' observed the French writer, François de la Rochefoucauld. The Royal Navy teaches the same thing in different words: 'Difficulties are made to be overcome.'[5]

Turning over the pages of the Osborne and Dartmouth College magazines in which the happenings of the next four years are chronicled, I am pleasantly surprised to find how green my recollection is of the names and faces recorded therein. After the accounts of cricket, rugger, soccer and hockey matches, of assaults at arms, sports, sailing and pulling regattas, of meets of the Beagles, there follows on the last page the term order giving the numerical position of each cadet in his own term as a result of the end of term examinations. With what concern these lists were scrutinised and with what indignation did one learn that that little blighter 'Bloggins' had gone over one's head. And there was old 'Tomkins', bottom again and he had been warned last term that if he did not 'buck up' he would be sent down. Yet he survived to reach flag rank and earned great distinction as a destroyer commander.

The cadets were organised into six terms based on the date of entry into the college. These were called Exmouth, Blake, Drake, St Vincent, Hawke and Grenville. We were privileged to include among our contemporaries His Royal Highness Prince Edward (known to his family as David and later His Majesty King Edward VIII), who was a member of the Exmouth term, four terms senior to me. 'Priority,' he wrote, describing our curriculum, 'was not unnaturally given to mathematics, navigation, science, and engineering. Instead of Latin and Greek we learned to tie knots and splice rope, sail a cutter, read and make signals, box the compass, and master all the intricacies of seamanship.' During his last term he was joined by his younger brother, His Royal Highness Prince Albert (later His Majesty King George VI), who was a member of Grenville, one term my junior.[6]

In early 1909 their parents, Their Royal Highnesses the Prince and Princess of Wales, took up residence at Barton Manor, a royal residence near Osborne House. During their four-day stay they made daily visits to the college, inspecting the classrooms, watching the sports and, on Sunday, inspecting the cadets and afterwards attending church in the big assembly hall, Nelson. In those days the weather could be as fickle as we believe it to be now, for the official chronicler records: 'by 8pm [on Saturday] the rain was again coming down in torrents and continued without intermission until 5pm on Sunday'. One of the classrooms they visited was that of Monsieur L. Lassimonne where Prince Albert was at his French lessons. The French master was a kind-hearted but rather awe-inspiring man and a short time previously had reduced the prince to tears, his exasperated comment on that occasion: 'Albert, Albert, vat are you crying for?' going the rounds of the college, and had doubtless reached the ears of the royal parents, who wished to see for themselves what manner of man Monsieur Lassimonne was.[7] The thoroughness and extent of the royal visit shows not only the natural interest of parents in the education of their children but also the Prince of Wales's particular concern for the progress of naval education. Dubbed the Sailor King, Prince George – the future George V – was renowned for his abiding interest and pride in the service in whose life and work he had already actively participated for thirty-three years. This knowledge was a source of inspiration to all of us who had the honour of serving in the Royal Navy during his reign. It was a matter of great pride to me in later years when I was nominated to command the battleship which bore his name.

On 6 May 1910 King Edward VII died. The senior terms at Osborne and Dartmouth were among those selected to attend his funeral which took place on Friday 20 May. I was fortunate in being one of the Osborne contingent. It was a very memorable experience, albeit trying for us youngsters. The night before the funeral we were accommodated in a hotel in Norwood outside London, whence we departed at a very early hour the next morning to take up our appointed station on Horse Guards Parade. It was a hot and sunny day and we appeared to be marching for miles and miles so that by the time we reached our destination we were rather weary. Then followed a two-and-a-half hours' wait, falling in and standing at ease and a number of my companions fainted. When the cortege arrived, since we were right out in front, we had an uninterrupted view of the procession, especially of the crowned heads (of which there were many in those days) who rode behind the coffin. I remember quite well seeing the German Emperor and King of Prussia, Kaiser Wilhelm II, the eldest grandchild of Queen Victoria, ride past on his white charger.

On Sunday 3 July in the same year I and fifty-eight members of my term were confirmed by the Bishop of Southampton. Three weeks later we were again honoured by a royal visit. The new King and Queen, accompanied by their fourth son, Prince George (later the Duke of Kent) and Princess Mary took the salute at a march past of the cadets and afterwards attended church in Nelson. It was our last term at Osborne; in the autumn of 1910 we moved to the RN College at Dartmouth. I was not yet fifteen.

Dartmouth

The atmosphere of Devon is redolent of the sea and the centuries old traditions of the sea service. I sensed it the moment I first set foot there and I have been conscious of it, not only when stationed there, but also when serving in any west country manned ship. The spirit of Drake is firmly implanted in the people of Devon and it was a happy circumstance that led to the establishment of the principal naval college on the rich loam of that county. From being the senior term at Osborne we found ourselves once again the junior one, but there was a difference. We knew most of the cadets in the terms above us.

Although the location and the buildings themselves were far superior to those of Osborne, the latter had a distinct advantage in the matter of playing fields. At Dartmouth there was not enough level ground around the college for all the playing fields required and so for many of our games we had to climb to the top of the hill on the side of which the college stands, near Dartmouth's mother church, St Clement's, Townstal. The great attraction of Dartmouth is the River Dart and some of my best recollections of the next two years were connected with the 'blue boats' and 'black cutters', as the pulling and sailing boats attached to the college were named. And I shall never forget the peerless delicacy of 'jam, bun and cream' which we devoured in enormous quantities at the canteen, nor the wonderful teas consumed at the surrounding farmhouses on Sunday afternoons. My two years at Dartmouth passed quickly enough; for my sixteenth birthday my parents gave me a Bible which I kept all my life. At the end of the summer term of 1912 we took the first of a series of exams, the results of which were to count towards our seniority as lieutenants.

At Sea

After a period of leave we joined the training cruiser, HMS *Cornwall*. Launched in 1902, she had recently run aground off Nova Scotia but had been re-floated and repaired. On 25 September we set sail from Devonport for a cruise which was to take us to Newfoundland, Nova Scotia, the West Indies, Bermuda and the Mediterranean. The cruise, however, did not go according to plan for we had only spent four days at St Kitts, the northernmost of the Windward Islands, when, in early November, we received orders to proceed to Bermuda where we spent ten weeks waiting for further instructions from Whitehall. We were all disappointed at seeing so little of those historic waters about which we had learnt so much in our naval history lessons but our chagrin at the change of programme was soon forgotten. The people of Bermuda received us with open arms and entertained us so hospitably that if we had had any say in the matter, we would have cheerfully settled down in these enchanted islands and roamed no further.

The pattern of naval education has changed to meet the changed conditions in which we live, but I shall always maintain that the best training an embryo naval officer can get is on board a ship at sea. There is no better way to learn a job than to have to do it yourself and to make mistakes and to profit by them. In a ship wholly devoted to training, mistakes are allowable whereas in ships of the fleet they are not kindly tolerated, hence a training squadron or flotilla is a paramount necessity. On one occasion during the cruise when we were battened down I unwisely opened up one of the gunroom scuttles with the usual result in a bad sea. I was then obliged to spend the next hour catching bits of waves in a bucket, so I learnt my lesson the hard way!

On 20 January 1913 we left Bermuda for Gibraltar, ceded to Britain 'in perpetuity' under the terms of the Treaty of Utrecht in 1713 and an important naval base for the Royal Navy. During the journey we had our first encounter with an Atlantic gale and with tragedy which is never far away in heavy weather. A young stoker, Sidney Cuthbert, whose duty it was to feel the bearings of the great reciprocating engines with which the ship was fitted, lost his balance when the ship lurched and was thrown into the crankpit where he received fatal injuries before the engines could be stopped. I have since witnessed many burials at sea, but the committal of the stoker's body made a deep impression on me.

It took us ten days to cross the Atlantic, travelling at a slow speed owing to a shortage of coal. Except for short visits to Malaga on the southern coast of Spain and the island of Madeira, we spent the rest of the cruise at Gibraltar. I was fortunate since my uncle, Canon Richard Shiers-Mason, was the chaplain to the Missions to Seamen at Gibraltar which had been established by the Anglican diocese of Gibraltar in the last century.[8] He and my aunt, Ethel – my father's younger sister – lived in a house which they had built near the village of Campamento at the head of the bay across the frontier in Spain. In those days there was no road around the bay to Algeciras and the only way of reaching my uncle's house was by walking or preferably riding along the sea shore from La Linea. My uncle was something of a character. He rode in and out of Gibraltar on a white horse which contrasted noticeably with his black clerical garb. His was a muscular type of Christianity, as befitted one whose calling required him to carry the gospel to the sailors on board the many ships which called at the port in the Mission's launch *The Flying Angel*. He sprinted up the Jacob's ladders (which was all some masters saw fit to lower during their brief stay) with the agility of a cat.

For many years he had to be content with a pulling boat, which was all the Mission could afford, but at length this was replaced by a motor boat which enabled him to get around to many more ships with less discomfort. Even when he was over seventy he still visited his floating parish in all weathers with no thought for himself and the drenching which was often his lot. He was a very keen cricketer and played regularly for the garrison team. Fishing for bass off the harbour moles was another of his hobbies in which he tried to interest the soldiers of the garrison for whom, as he used to say, drink and the devil were always lying in wait. Although we had never met before, my uncle and I took to each other at once. He was a little disappointed to find that I was no cricketer, but he forgave me when he found that I could ride.

Riding picnics were one of the many delightful entertainments which Gibraltar had to offer. Besides the usual sports such as cricket, football, hockey and tennis there was swimming at Rosia Bay, climbing the Rock, and, over the Spanish border, visits to the bull ring at La Linea and the orange groves at Estepona. Whosoever has not tasted a luscious 'nina pipina' straight off the tree and still warm from the rays of the Andalusian sun has missed a lucullan dish. For those able to go further afield there were visits to Algeciras, the mountaintop city of Ronda, with its old Roman and Moorish buildings, Cadiz and the famous sherry town of Jerez de la Frontera. I sampled all of them more than once during the next forty-three years, but I still recall with pleasure those first early rides amongst the cork trees with the pungent smell of charcoal burners scenting the air. On some of these rides I was accompanied by a charming girl called Isseult to whom my aunt had introduced me. When I next visited the Rock I was told that she had married a Greek millionaire!

The cruise ended at Devonport on 31 March 1913, having sailed 11,480 miles.[9] Our time as cadets was over and we could now don the coveted white patch of a midshipman. We went on leave and, in due course, received our first appointments. Mine directed me to join HMS *Indomitable* in Cromarty Firth on the east coast of Scotland. Alas, time and two world wars have taken their toll of those who were my companions during those four years of training at the naval colleges. Out of the seventy-two of us of the Hawke term who joined Osborne in September 1908, only twenty-two were still on the active list when the Second World War began (not counting five who had transferred to the Royal Air Force). Of these, seven had reached the rank of captain and five subsequently attained flag rank. Our doyen was George Creasy, two days my junior, who was promoted to Admiral of the Fleet in 1955.[10]

As I embarked on a life of service in the Royal Navy, one of my valued possessions was a silver napkin ring on which, as time passed,

I had engraved the names of all the ships in which I served and the establishments I attended, beginning with Osborne 1908 and Dartmouth 1910.

During the first decade of the twentieth century, the United Kingdom's military establishment had been overhauled. Plans had been made for a British Expeditionary Force to be deployed to Europe in support of France in the event of war against Germany. Between 1904 and 1910 while Admiral Fisher was First Sea Lord, the Royal Navy had undergone a number of reforms, which included scrapping obsolete ships to enable new ones to be built. The launching of HMS Dreadnought, *the first of the all big-gun ships, propelled by steam turbine, in 1906, marked a turning point. The following year Admiral Alfred von Tirpitz reformed Germany's Home Fleet into the German High Seas Fleet, which was to be powerful enough to challenge the Royal Navy's supremacy. Subsequently, in an attempt to maintain maritime parity, other countries developed prototype 'dreadnoughts' and later 'super-dreadnoughts'. Those ships built before 1906 were classed as pre-dreadnoughts.*

Chapter Two

Pare Bellum

The greater the danger, the greater the coolness required.[1]

1913–15

HMS *Indomitable* was an Invincible-class battlecruiser of 17,250 tons; armed with eight 12-inch guns, she was one of the new and more powerful ships laid down in 1906. When, 'by command of the Commissioners for Executing the Office of the Lord High Admiral', I joined her at Cromarty on 13 May 1913, I was pleased at being appointed to serve in a ship which already had a distinguished record: in 1908, when Quebec celebrated the 300th anniversary of its founding, she had carried the then Prince of Wales – the future King George V – across the Atlantic. On the return voyage she had made the passage from the Strait of Belle Isle in eastern Canada to the Fastnet light south of Ireland at an average speed of just over 25 knots, beating by one and a half knots the record of the eastward passage held by RMS *Lusitania*.[2] During this record-making run, the prince had descended to one of the boiler rooms and helped in firing up some of the boilers. In commemoration, the shovel he had used, suitably polished and inscribed, was kept in a glass case in the wardroom. Together with her sister ship, the *Invincible* and a newer Indefatigable-class ship, the *Indefatigable*, she formed part of the 1st Battle Cruiser Squadron, commanded by Rear Admiral David Beatty in his flagship, HMS *Lion*.[3]

The *Indomitable's* captain was Francis 'Cuts' Kennedy, one of the last captains of the old sailing brigs. A strict disciplinarian, he had earned his nickname from the way in which he dispensed that particular form of corporal punishment officially described as 'cuts with the cane', but a finer type of naval officer it would be hard to find. Coming from County

Kildare, with twinkling blue eyes, he had all the fire and enthusiasm of his native land.[4]

After the customary twenty-four hours in which to sling our hammocks, the captain sent for us. We trooped into his cabin in fear and trepidation, the senior midshipmen having taken good care to prime us with stories about the 'old man's' ferocity. He was sitting writing at his desk when our 'nurse', as the lieutenant in charge of midshipmen was known, reported us present. For what seemed an age he went on writing, then he suddenly spun around in his chair and barked at us: 'Well young gentlemen, do you know what you have joined this ship for?' He paused, as if waiting for an answer, but getting none, he gave it himself. 'War,' he thundered.

I suppose we all reacted with the expected degree of surprise, for he went on more quietly to explain to us how, by the Naval Laws passed regularly by Germany since 1898 (and, most recently, in 1912), the German Empire had thrown down the gauntlet in a challenge to the British Empire's supremacy at sea and that a war between the two countries was inevitable. There were not many people who, in May 1913, would have made a similar pronouncement with such certainty. As we soon realized, the prospect of the approaching conflict was always uppermost in his mind, so that when the storm broke sixteen months later we were prepared for it.

Although, as midshipmen, we were not well-versed in naval tactics, Captain Kennedy never missed an opportunity to instruct us. While being proud of the ship under his command, he was not blind to the weaknesses of her design. There was a transverse magazine amidships serving the two 12-inch turrets en echelon, P and Q, above which the diesel dynamo room was sited. This was ventilated by a large air trunk to the upper deck across which was fitted an armoured grating, so there was nothing to stop a plunging shell from penetrating the magazine, the explosion of which would inevitably break the ship in half. This fact may well have accounted for the fate of the *Invincible* at the Battle of Jutland in 1916. Such thoughts, however, were far from our minds when on 15 May we weighed anchor and went to sea.

With the Mediterranean Fleet

As soon as the summer manoeuvres were over, we were under orders to join the Mediterranean Fleet, under the command of Admiral Sir

Berkeley Milne.[5] An immediate priority was exchanging our British stewards and cooks for Maltese ones from a ship recently returned from the station. The gunroom messman (to whose mess I belonged) was a well-dressed individual with toothbrush moustache, who, while we were in home waters, fed us mainly on promises of the delicacies which would be ours on arrival in Malta, headquarters of the Mediterranean Fleet. Although these never materialised, we forgave him because, towards the end of the month, he was always good for an advance of ten shillings, which was of great importance to an impecunious midshipman drawing one shilling and nine pence a day. During the weeks before our departure, through the agency of the messmen, the canteen manager and other Maltese on board, contracts were awarded to their various relatives in Malta for the privilege of doing our laundry when we arrived on the station; another 'privilege' was the right to lie off ship in their gaily painted *dghaisas* – small boats resembling gondolas – and take officers and men ashore when required. This latter concession included the highly-prized 'gashing' rights which entitled the holder to collect all the left-over food from the appropriate mess, a large number of Maltese families living entirely on what the fleet discarded.

At last the great day came and, on 27 August 1913, we slipped our moorings. Making our way down the Channel, we rounded the south-westerly island of Ushant and set course for Gibraltar, entering the harbour at the beginning of September. Since Admiral Milne, in his flagship, the *Inflexible*, was at Gibraltar, we spent the next two months cruising and exercising in the Western basin as well as taking part in the annual Mediterranean Fleet Regatta. Towards the end of October we proceeded to Malta, stopping at Cartagena and Valencia, with its neoclassical style bullring, built like a Roman amphitheatre. Our last port of call was Cagliari in Sardinia.

Long before Gozo Light came up over the horizon, all the Maltese on board crowded on the fo'c'sle sniffing the air; when we entered Malta's Grand Harbour their excitement was intense. That the names of all the successful applicants for jobs had long been known in the island did not deter the unsuccessful ones from turning up to welcome us as well. There were always one or two undistributed 'plums' to be picked up, like the chief and petty officers' laundry and the 'gashing' rights on their messes. So, on this fine October afternoon as the bugler sounded the 'G', at which signal the booms swung out and the gangways were lowered with clockwork precision, an indescribable clamour arose from the floating populace gathered to greet us. Dozens of *dghaisas* surged forward, impelled by the powerful strokes of the two standing oarsmen. As they converged on the ship and lack of sea-room prevented any further movement, tongues wagged instead of oars, giving the impression of a wordy battle of unparalleled ferocity. Quite unmoved by the commotion around them, a number of 'would-be' washerwomen or sellers of lace sat quietly in the sternsheets under their black faldettas, awaiting their chance to come on board. It took the officer of the watch, assisted by the gangway staff, all his time to check the credentials of the invaders as they sought to take possession of the latest addition to the fleet.

For a young midshipman – I was just eighteen – it was an interesting and exciting glimpse of the old Europe. Turkey held sway down the Palestinian coast, Egypt was under British tutelage and the aged Emperor Franz Josef still sat on the throne of the Austro-Hungarian Empire. In November we visited Alexandria and I obtained leave to visit Cairo and the pyramids. During our stay Field Marshal Lord Kitchener – famed for his victory at Omdurman in 1898 and currently serving as British Agent and Consul-General in Egypt – gave a ball at the Citadel to which members of the fleet were invited. The fact that he omitted to remove his sword meant that the officers had to adhere to protocol by following his example and keeping theirs on, much to the discomfort of their dancing partners, until an ADC summoned up enough courage to inform the great man, who was a non-dancer, of the trouble he was causing!

Christmas Day 1913 was spent on board ship, my journal recording: 'Fine but cloudy...we had a short stand up service on the quarter deck... the mess decks were elegantly decorated with green and coloured papers.'

By late January 1914 we had returned to Sheerness for a change of crew before returning to Gibraltar. During the spring and summer months we steamed across the Mediterranean, stopping at various ports along the way. The cruise which I enjoyed most was at the beginning of May when we went up the Adriatic to Venice, the water so shallow that we had to anchor some seven-and-a-half miles from the city. The customary salutes were exchanged, an Italian aeroplane flying over the fleet as we anchored.

Having obtained leave to go ashore, my first sight of St Mark's Square, the Rialto and the Bridge of Sighs remains in my memory. I knew little of Titian and his fellow artists, but the seeds of appreciation were sown which, with increased knowledge, ripened into deep affection. I have since returned to Venice many times and it retains all the enchantment of when I first discovered its many treasures.

At Trieste the Austro–Hungarian Navy entertained us most hospitably. In accordance with custom, the SMS *Viribus Unitis* had been detailed to be our host ship (we called host ships 'chummy' ships) for the duration of our visit and we junior officers became very friendly with our opposite numbers. The first of a class of four dreadnought battleships to be built for the Austro-Hungarian Navy, the *Viribus Unitis* had just been commissioned in 1912. A feature which interested us was her triple 12-inch turrets since, in those days, triple turrets were something of an innovation. Another unusual feature was that they were painted dark green. One memorable excursion was travelling inland to visit the famous stables at Lipizza, where the beautiful grey horses which drew the emperor's carriage were bred.

We then set course for Pola (Pula) on the Adriatic's eastern coastline. A large number of Austrian ships were in harbour including the *Prinz Eugen,* another of Austria-Hungary's new dreadnoughts and we were again well looked after. At a brilliant ball at the Marinekasino – the Officers' Club – I encountered my first experience of 'cutting in'. I can well remember my disappointment at having to surrender a charming partner to a magnificently attired young army officer who approached and, with a short, stiff bow and a click of his highly polished boots, indicated his desire to dance with her. I naturally ignored his first approach but when the lady explained that it was the custom of the country I regretfully had to comply. Returning via Brioni (Brijuni), where we visited the Zoological Gardens, by mid-May we were back in Malta.

Our visit had ended with many *auf wiedersehens* but barely a week later the Austrians arrived in Malta on a return visit, their squadron consisting of the *Viribus Unitis, the Tegetthoff* and a pre-dreadnought battleship, the *Zrinyi.* We were overjoyed to find ourselves in a position to return some of their hospitality. We wined and dined them and thoroughly enjoyed ourselves in youthful exuberance and extravagance, little thinking that we were entertaining men who would soon become our enemies.

Our last cruise in early July took us to Marmarice (Marmaris), a delightful landlocked harbour on the southern shore of Asia-Minor and subsequently the setting of Major William Drury's famous 1933 story *The Passing of the Flagship*, where the *Indomitable's* crews excelled themselves in another regatta.[6] From there we visited Larnaca in Cyprus, Tripoli and Beirut on the Mediterranean coastline before returning to Malta.

Despite the political uncertainty in Europe following the assassination of the Archduke Ferdinand and his wife Sophie, Duchess of Hohenberg, on 28 June in Sarajevo (our friends on the *Viribus Unitis* transporting their bodies from Sarajevo to Trieste), on 24 July we went into the dockyard to start a refit which, as the captain noted 'was especially badly wanted on account of our electric wiring being in such a very rotten state'. Three days later we commenced the refit, but, during the day, news was received that Austria had declared war on Serbia, since the Serbians had failed to comply with Austria's demands concerning the recent assassinations. Our refit was therefore postponed and we prepared for sea.

'The situation in Europe is becoming very grave,' I noted on 29 July, 'Great Britain and France are expected to support Russia, and Russia' (who had already indicated her support for Serbia) 'has mobilised.' On Sunday 2 August after divine service on the quarterdeck, Captain Kennedy addressed the ship's company 'on the subject of being prepared for action both morally and physically'. At 2.30pm news was received that Germany had declared war on Russia. Shortly afterwards we were given orders to recall all men and raise steam for full speed; during the night a signal was received from Admiral Milne that the situation was extremely critical and that a surprise attack might be expected. However nothing was sighted and we sailed towards Malta. At 10pm we received orders to proceed at high speed towards Gibraltar to intercept the German battlecruiser *Goeben* which had been sighted in the Mediterranean.

In addition to the three battlecruisers, Inflexible, Indomitable *and* Indefatigable, *the First Cruiser Squadron, under Rear Admiral Ernest Troubridge, comprised four armoured cruisers, while there were also four light cruisers, including HMS* Gloucester *commanded by Captain Howard Kelly, (who was to play an important role in shadowing the* Goeben *when she eventually headed towards Cape Matapan) and HMS* Dublin, *commanded by his brother, Captain John Kelly. Having received intelligence that the German ships had reached the harbour at Messina in order to coal, Admiral Milne's assumption was that they would attempt to break out and reach the Atlantic. After dispatching* Indomitable *and* Indefatigable *towards Gibraltar, Milne, in his flagship, the* Inflexible, *remained near Malta to coordinate operations, while Troubridge watched the Adriatic.*[7]

War Routine

On the morning of 4 August smoke was sighted on our starboard bow and 'Action' was sounded off. In a few minutes we realised this was the German cruiser *Breslau*; shortly afterwards the *Goeben* appeared about 10,000 yards on the starboard beam, both ships having been engaged in bombarding the fortified ports of Bône and Philippeville in North Africa following France's declaration of war on 3 August. Since Great Britain had not yet declared war we could not engage the *Goeben* and could only follow orders to shadow her. It was an exciting moment and an entry in my journal records the fact that we loaded all guns, keeping them trained fore and aft, 'being fully prepared to fire on her if she fired on us'. Captain Kennedy also had to determine whether the flag of the German Admiral – Rear Admiral Wilhelm Souchon – was flying, since, according to the Regulations and Customs of the Sea, we should have saluted it, even though there was a risk of the Germans replying by shot and shell. But, he observed, 'there was no such luck for there was not a flag up'.[8] We continued to shadow her until about 4pm when, although both the *Indomitable* and the *Indefatigable* were going full speed, she drew away from us. The cruiser, HMS *Dublin* was then dispatched to shadow her but at 6.30pm she returned reporting that the *Goeben* had outdistanced her and appeared to be steering to the south-west. We took a north-easterly course hoping to meet her. At 10pm we received orders to join Admiral Milne in his flagship, the *Inflexible*, off Cape [Cap] Bon. At 11pm we received news that an 'ultimatum' had been issued to Germany on account of her trying to force Belgium to give her free access for movement of her troops in Belgian territory.

Having outrun the British battlecruisers, the German ships returned to Messina to re-coal. Unknown to Admiral Milne, following an alliance with Ottoman Turkey on 2 August, Souchon had been instructed to head for the Dardanelles.

My journal on 5 August began: '1.20am, a signal was received from the Admiralty "War is declared. Commence hostilities against Germany."' But, I continued, 'Italy intends to maintain her neutrality and we are not at war with Austria.' By 10am we were off Cape Bon: 'nothing having been seen during the night. Flagship & *Chatham* & *Dublin* also joined & several destroyers'. Since no news had been received of the *Goeben* or *Breslau*, we made for Bizerta on the northern coast of Tunisia, where we were detailed to coal. With news spreading of our declaration of war against Germany, we entered the harbour amidst prolonged cheers from all the French ships and inhabitants.

By the afternoon of 6 August we had finished coaling and again prepared for sea. The following day (7 August), with both the *Inflexible* and *Indefatigable* ahead of us, we set course for Malta. Having again taken on coal and oil fuel, the next day we were once more at sea, travelling eastward, the *Goeben* and *Breslau* now having been reported to have passed Cape Matapan 'late yesterday'. But on the same day a rather questionable order was received from the Admiralty to 'commence hostilities against Austria' which meant that we altered course up the Adriatic. As I recorded in my journal it was not until 3pm on 9 August that a signal was received: 'Not at war with Austria, Battle cruisers continue chase of *Goeben* & *Breslau*.' So we turned and set course for Cape Matapan ordering the two cruisers, *Weymouth* and *Chatham*, to join us. The following day we parted company with the *Inflexible* and spread out to patrol. Finally, at noon on 11 August we heard from the Admiralty: 'Urgent. *Goeben* and *Breslau* arrived Dardanelles' whereupon the three battle cruisers proceeded to the Dardanelles and began patrolling 17 miles from the mouth, while the *Weymouth* and *Chatham* were stationed at the mouth. The next day came the information that the German ships had been sold to Turkey and that the crew was going to return to Germany!

As we now know, had the right dispositions been made, they would never have escaped from the trap into which they had ventured. Captain Kennedy felt very strongly about this and committed his views to paper, a copy of which he sent to his bank in case he should not survive the war. 'Had the C-in-C started from where he was, to the West of Sicily, when he first heard that the *Goeben* had left Messina, even he might have caught her up before she got to the Dardanelles and knocked her about a good bit.' Instead, he complained, we three big ships had 'dawdled to Malta' and waited there for the *Indefatigable* to complete with coal. He was firmly of the opinion that the ships should never have got away and certainly if the size of the hunting force, which comprised three battle cruisers, heavy and light cruisers and a number of destroyers, is taken into consideration, it would seem that when the two German ships stopped at Messina for fuel we ought to have been able to bring them to action when they left. 'Had these German ships been prevented from getting to the Dardanelles', he concluded 'there would hardly have been any chance of the Turks joining in the war.'[9]

Our lack of success was in part due to poor intelligence. It seems to have occurred to no one that they might make for a Turkish port; yet at the end of June the Commander-in-Chief, Admiral Milne, had visited Constantinople (Istanbul), by which time German influence in Turkey was well-established. The *Goeben* was also faster than any ship in the British fleet so a stern chase could avail us nothing. Not since Nelson's famous search for the French fleet before the Battle of Trafalgar had there been such a remarkable game of hide and seek.

Both Admiral Milne and Rear Admiral Troubridge came under severe criticism for having allowed the German ships to escape. In November Troubridge was court-martialled for failure to engage the enemy. Later he was honourably acquitted on the grounds that instructions from the Admiralty were unclear regarding engaging a 'superior force'.[10]

On 13 August, at about 3.30am, a signal was received: 'Commence hostilities against Austria.' This was fully anticipated. While the *Inflexible* and a number of the cruisers returned to Malta, we stayed in the Dardanelles together with the *Indefatigable* and the *Gloucester*, taking up a position off Tenedos Island. Admiral Milne then returned to England, since it had been agreed that the supreme command of the Allied Forces in the Mediterranean would be vested in the Commander-in-Chief of the French Navy in the Mediterranean, 62-year-old Vice Admiral Augustin Boué de Lapeyère.[11]

We remained patrolling off Tenedos Island throughout September and October. On the 29th the Turks carried out a surprise attack on Russia's Black Sea coast leading to Russia's declaration of war against the Ottoman Empire. Two days later, at 9.30pm, we received a signal: 'Commence hostilities against Turkey at once.' On 3 November, in our first action against the Turks, we proceeded towards the Gallipoli Peninsula in order to bombard the forts on Cape Helles at the entrance to the Dardanelles. While British ships opened fire on Sedd el Bahr on the left and northern side of the entrance, the French ships fired at Kum Kale on the southern side. 'After the first two salvos the forts replied to our fire but all their shots were miles short. One ricocheted about 30 yds ahead of us,' I recorded, noting that 'one of our shots raised a huge column of smoke ashore & presumably exploded a magazine & silenced a battery'. After just over two hours we steamed away back towards Tenedos.[12]

Our action was the prologue to the great drama which was to be played out on the Gallipoli Peninsula a few months later, but in which we were not destined to take part, when, following a failed attack by sea in March 1915, Allied troops, including the 'Anzac' forces of Australia and New Zealand, landed on the peninsula on 25 April in order to secure the route to Russia from the Crimea. After eight months and thousands of casualties they had to withdraw, having made no headway against the strongly entrenched Turks.

By the end of November we were back in Malta for our refit. Soon afterwards we were ordered home to join the Grand Fleet under Admiral Sir John Jellicoe's command.[13]

The Grand Fleet and Dogger Bank

We arrived home on a dull and windy Christmas Day, passing through the Firth of Forth at about 4.30pm. 'It was very cold & blowing hard & the ship, especially the messdecks were swimming with water which made a rather unpleasant day for the sailors', I recorded. Our orders were to join the Grand Fleet the next day at 8am at a rendezvous 150 miles due east of the Firth of Forth. Everyone in the ship, from the captain downwards, was glad to get back to the main theatre of operations and to rejoin our old squadron under the command of Vice Admiral Beatty, whose battlecruisers, including the *Invincible*, had already given proof of their prowess in late August at the Battle of Heligoland Bight in the North Sea when they attacked German patrols off the north-west coast of Germany. They were now impatiently waiting for another chance to come to grips with the enemy.[14]

On 23 January 1915 we sailed from the Firth of Forth. The following morning we intercepted a German squadron under Rear Admiral Franz Hipper's command. It comprised the battlecruisers, *Derfflinger, Seydlitz* and *Moltke* and the heavy cruiser *Blücher,* with attendant destroyers, on their way to bombard one or other of our coastal towns of Hartlepool, Scarborough and Whitby. Captain Kennedy, who had carefully studied the reports of the 1904–05 Russo-Japanese war, relating to the benefits of improved hygiene and sanitation to prevent the spread of disease, insisted that everyone should have a sterilised, clean battle suit into which he was to shift before action. Mine consisted of a pair of white duck trousers and a white sweater which was hardly adequate to withstand the rigours of a cold January day in the North Sea. Fortunately, my action station was in one of the 12-inch turrets and, once inside, I was fairly well protected. I can still remember the excitement of seeing my guns loaded and fired in action for the first time. (I did not count the bombardment of the Turkish forts in November which was a very tame affair.) Vice Admiral Beatty's flagship, HMS *Lion*, bore the brunt of the action and had to haul out of line. We, being the oldest ship present, had some difficulty in keeping up with our consorts; when the *Blücher's* speed was reduced and her consorts abandoned her to her fate, we concentrated our fire on her.

'Dearest Father & Mother,' I wrote to my parents, 'I have no doubt you are anxiously expecting to hear from me, and you can be sure I am taking the first opportunity...The morning watch, which was gradually drawing to a close on Sunday 24th found me at Night Defence on the fore lower bridge. Something was expected but no one knew what, and as the grey dawn slowly broke in the East the horizon was eagerly scanned in the hope the approaching day would reveal something. The sea was like a mill pond and it was a cold clear crisp day.' I continued:

Action sounded (0845) grab everything, including notebook and pencil and up on deck and into my turret (Q turret). Test loading

21

gear and everything correct and then up on top of turret to look round and this is what I saw: on our starboard bow the *Lion*, *Tiger*, *Princess Royal* and *New Zealand* cleaving the water at full speed like greyhounds straining at a leash. On our port bow the distant smoke of light cruisers, ahead the black and heavy smoke of the enemy in full retreat followed by three light cruisers leading a host of destroyers. At 9 o'clock the *Lion* opened fire but we could not see how her shots fell and at 0912 the enemy replied. We slowly gained on them and then our other ships began to fire and the shots began to fall faster and thicker. At 0945 three of the enemy ships appeared to be on fire and the last ship in their line, the *Blücher*, was seen to be dropping behind. Flash, flash, flash – bang, bang, bang the battle raged and then, through the navy phone, came 'A turret open fire!' It was now our turn and so down I went into the turret.

At 1031 the enemy altered to port and so did we and this brought my turret into action against the *Blücher*. In and out recoiled the guns as we pounded the German ship. 'Left gun ready' shouted someone and another 850lbs of explosive went hurtling towards the *Blücher*. About 1045 a Zeppelin joined the action and dropped a bomb about twenty yards on our starboard bow with a bang like a gun going off. It paid for its temerity however as it fell a prey to the guns of a light cruiser. At 1115 the other ships had chased the enemy as near to his coast as was deemed safe and so joined us against the *Blücher* which, by 1145, was totally disabled and burning fiercely. Just as we finished a high sheet of flame leapt up forward in the *Blücher* and stayed for about thirty seconds and I should think must have roasted all of them in their fore turret....At 1207 when we were still watching her astern she suddenly listed over to port, a cloud of steam and she was no more. Light cruisers and destroyers surrounded the spot and picked up about 150, I believe, out of a crew of 800 odd. It was a pathetic sight to see that huge ship a mere wreck lying helpless as we steamed by with our guns hot from the fury of battle and just waiting for her to go down.

Imbued with a firm belief – like so many others – that God was on our side, I concluded my letter: 'In the joy of victory we must not forget the Lord who is able to lift up or cast down and so I shall go to early service next Sunday if possible "to give thanks unto the Lord for his many and great mercies.""[15] Although the rest of the German squadron escaped we subsequently learnt that they had suffered considerable damage, a fact which was headlined in a London daily paper as 'Beatty's Battle-cruisers Batter the Baby-killers!' I must admit that I thought the caption rather inapt at the time, but such is or even was, journalese.

When the action was over Vice Admiral Beatty ordered us to take his damaged flagship, the *Lion,* in tow. The weather was beautiful and calm and Captain Kennedy's seamanship superb; we proceeded safely, keeping a sharp look out for submarines, the gun crews having orders to open fire on a periscope at once if they spotted one. About 11am the following day, 26th, we passed under the Forth Bridge amidst the cheers of the forts and ships in harbour and towed the *Lion* up to her berth, where we slipped her and she anchored and we then anchored ourselves. In token of their appreciation Captain Ernle Chatfield and the officers of HMS *Lion* presented the captain and officers of HMS *Indomitable* an extremely handsome silver statuette of a guardian angel, with a silver lion on either side, inscribed 'To commemorate a very excellent 6-and-a-half-inch hawser'.[16] When the ship was broken up after the war it was given to Captain Kennedy and apparently kept on his dining table for many years. We also received congratulations from Admiral Beatty on our fine steaming during the action.

Our engine room men had strained every fibre and every nerve in their bodies to keep the ship so well stoked with the result that we had steamed along at just under 27 knots! Anyone brought up on the oil fuel age can have no idea of the physical effort required of the stokers of a coal-fired ship when steaming at high speed. With the fans in the boiler room revolving at full speed, the boilers devoured coal almost as fast as a man could feed it into the furnace. Black, begrimed and sweating men working in the bunkers on the ship's side dug the coal out and loaded it into skids which were then dragged along the steel floor plates and emptied in front of each boiler in turn. No hygienic sterilised suits for these men. If the ship was rolling or pitching, there was always the danger that a loaded skid might take charge with resultant damage to life and limb.

Looking down from above, the scene had all the appearance of one from Dante's *Inferno*. 'For flames I saw and wailing smote mine ear.'[17] Watching the pressure gauges for any indication of a fall in pressure, the chief stoker walked to and fro encouraging his men. Every now and then the telegraph from the engine room would clang and the finger on the dial move round to the section marked 'More Steam!' The chief would press the reply gong with an oath. 'What do the bastards think we're doing?' To the men he would say: 'Come on boys! Shake it up. Get going!' Then the ship would shudder and above the roar of the fans could be heard the deep boom of the guns as another salvo sped on its way. No wonder that occasionally a man went beserk. To loosen the clinker from the bars of the furnace an iron bar known as a 'slice', 12 feet long and flattened at one end, was used. One day a young stoker, with an imagined grudge against one of the officers, picked up a slice and, raising it above his head, was about to bring it down on the crouching form of the officer who was examining one of the furnaces. A burley chief stoker shot out his arm and deflected the blow, thereby saving the overstressed young man from what might well have been a murder charge.

Coaling ship was an occupation from which no one was excused unless he were sick. The number of tons embarked by each ship per hour, i.e. the rate of coaling, was made known by general signal. Much to the surprise of our sister ships, the *Indomitable* always had the highest rate. Admiral Beatty even visited us to find out the reason why. In fact, it was simple: the squadron always returned to harbour when it was dark and coaling was scheduled to commence at first light. As soon as we anchored one of the picket boats, plus the pinnace, was lowered and part of the watch (a quarter of the seamen complement) was sent to where the colliers lay. The master of the collier from which we were to coal allowed our men to climb on board and begin uncovering the hatches and filling as many bags as possible. When, at daylight, coaling officially began, we already had a head start of more than 100 tons almost every time; spread out over the coaling period, this gave us a higher average than any other ship. The idea had come from Commander J.A. Moreton – known in the gunroom as JAM – who seemed to know all the tricks, especially at general drill in pre-war days. We midshipmen were greatly in awe of him; once he stopped my shore leave because, having thrown his telescope at me for some misdemeanour, I had dodged it with the result that, much to his annoyance, it went over the side![18]

Apart from the fact that coaling was a particularly dirty job and therefore the sooner done the better, in wartime it was essential to replenish bunkers as quickly as possible on return to harbour in case the enemy should sally forth and catch us on the wrong foot. A recent lesson was the experience gained in the South Atlantic. In November 1914 the German squadron commanded by Admiral Maximilian Graf von Spee had attacked a British squadron off the coast of South America at the Battle of Coronel, whereupon a more powerful force of ships, under the command of Vice Admiral Sir Doveton Sturdee, had been sent to search him out. The squadron, which included both the *Invincible* and *Inflexible*, had just finished coaling at the Falkland Islands, when the German squadron appeared and so they were able to sail and encompass its destruction.

The action was known as the Battle of the Falkland Islands. Spee, and his two sons, went down with their ships along with over 2,000 German sailors.[19]

In the weeks following the 'Dogger Bank action' (called the Battle of the Ems River) we made innumerable sorties but I saw nothing more of the German High Seas Fleet during the rest of my time in the *Indomitable*. Meanwhile, troubling news from the Dardanelles filtered through. In May the First Lord of the Admiralty, Winston Churchill, announced that one of our pre-dreadnought battleships, HMS *Goliath*, which was supporting the troops on the Gallipoli Peninsula, had been sunk by a night destroyer attack. About 120 officers and men were saved and about 500 drowned. This was the first record of a night attack made by destroyers during the war. The belligerents in the war were also increasing. At midnight on 23 May Italy declared war against Austria and Germany declared war against Italy.[20]

In September I got my first gold stripe as an acting sub lieutenant. My next appointment was to HMS *Seagull*, a small minesweeper based on Harwich. I took my leave of Captain Kennedy with regret. He had taught me a great deal which was to stand me in good stead throughout my career. One of his sayings, which I have often had occasion to call to mind, was 'the greater the danger, the greater the coolness required'.

Minesweeping

On 19 October 1915 I joined HMS *Seagull,* which was temporarily at Avonmouth, before returning to Harwich. An ancient old tub built in 1889 and originally classed as a torpedo gunboat, in 1909 she had been converted into a minesweeper. As I soon discovered, it was only the coal in the bunkers which kept the water out, since her sides were rusted through and perforated like a colander. Lieutenant Commander Harold de Gallye Lamotte was in command, while the navigating officer, Lieutenant A.J. Lever-Naylor, was a Royal Naval Reserve (RNR) officer from New Zealand. There was also a commissioned gunner, a tough old Irishman, who was forever talking about the white heather of Glengariff in County Cork and Johns, the commissioned engineer.[21] For all my juniority, aged just 20, I was dubbed the first lieutenant.

Minesweeping during the Great War was a comparatively simple affair of towing a wire hawser between two ships, the wire being kept at the required depth by a heavy wooden contraption known as a kite. Our sister ship was another converted gunboat, HMS *Spanker,* and our task was to sweep the channels in the approaches to Harwich through which the force of cruisers and destroyers based there passed on their sorties against the Germans. In February 1916, the light cruiser, HMS *Arethusa,* flotilla leader of the Harwich Force, struck a mine on returning from operations off the German coast and became a total loss and so we were kept very busy. The German submarines were constantly laying small groups of mines in these channels and in the strong tidal steams which pertain to that part of the world, careful calculations were necessary to avoid the danger of being caught at low slack water when the mines were only a foot or two below the surface. On one occasion we were stopped because a sweep wire became foul of one of our propellers. I was aft on the quarterdeck superintending the clearing when I looked up and saw the horns of two mines just awash about 50 yards away on the port beam and we were slowly drifting down on top of them! I shouted to the bridge and the RNR lieutenant rushed to the telegraphs and put them both to full speed. We parted the sweep and damaged the propeller but we missed those mines by a few feet.

On another occasion, in similar circumstances, HMS *Spanker* decided to let go an anchor, whereupon there was a loud explosion and a huge column of water obscured her from view. When she reappeared, and we had ascertained that she was not in any immediate danger, Lieutenant Commander Lamotte reported to the senior officer at the base: '*Spanker* dropped anchor on a mine. No damage to *Spanker* save the loss of her anchor.' A closer inspection, however, revealed that about 2,000 rivets had fallen out of her hull and she had to go in for a refit. Since we had quite a long defect list, we were also sent up the Thames for a refit at Messrs Green and Silley Weirs at the Royal Albert dock.

After six months of this necessary but monotonous minesweeping, I was longing for something more exciting. I envied the fellows in the sleek, black, oil-fired destroyers who dashed out of harbour on mysterious errands and frequently had skirmishes with the enemy, so, taking my courage in both hands, I decided to visit the Admiralty. I had been told that if an officer presented himself at the office of the Second Sea Lord (who was also Chief of Naval Personnel) in person he would be given an interview. I arrived at the entrance leading off the Mall and filled in a form, giving my name and ship. I paused before filling in the space marked 'nature of business'. Noting my perplexity, the kindly porter suggested: 'To discuss appointment', which seemed quite non-committal so I wrote that down. He took the form into one of the offices opening off the corridor in which I was waiting with my heart in my mouth. Returning a minute or two later, he said: 'The Commander will see you, Sir'. I was ushered into a small uncarpeted room with a desk across one corner at which sat a genial-looking man in uniform.

'Well, what do you want?' he asked cheerfully.

'I wondered if there was any chance of a destroyer at Harwich, Sir,' I ventured. He smiled and, picking up a pen on his desk, he asked: 'How soon can you be ready to go?'

'At once, Sir – that is provided my captain will let me go,' I added, feeling rather guilty that I had not consulted him before he went on leave.

'I'll send a telegram directing you to join HMS *Manly* at Harwich forthwith,' he replied. 'The Sub there has gone sick and they've asked for an immediate relief.' I could hardly believe my ears. It was all as simple as that. The *Manly* was one of the destroyers of the 10th Flotilla of the Harwich Force. I could not have wished for anything better. Thanking the commander profusely, I returned to my ship and packed. As soon as the Admiralty telegram arrived, I left. HMS *Seagull* did not survive the war, being sunk in a collision in 1918.[22]

Chapter Three

The Harwich Force

- *We few, we happy few, we band of brothers.*[1]

1916–18

The Harwich Force was a unique command, charged with securing the approaches to the English Channel and preventing any German ships from breaking out into the Atlantic and interfering with our shipping. Composed of the 9th and 10th Flotillas, it included some of our latest destroyers of the L and M classes (of which HMS *Manly* was one) supported by the 5th Light Cruiser Squadron. Most of the officers and men had been together since the beginning of the war and the force possessed a sense of comradeship and a fighting spirit more typical of Nelson's band of brothers than any command in which I have had the honour to serve. The outstanding personality of the Harwich Force was its commander, 45-year-old Commodore Sir Reginald Tyrwhitt, who had already distinguished himself at the Battle of Heligoland Bight; affectionately known to us as 'Com (T)', he welded the whole into a highly efficient fighting unit, every officer and man of which would gladly have followed him into the very jaws of hell itself.[2]

HMS Manly

The commanding officer of the *Manly*, Lieutenant Commander Ernest Kirkby, was one of the junior destroyer captains: a big, jolly man, he was a former navy rugby player and typical destroyer officer and I was to spend three very happy years under his command.[3] Soon after I joined the ship on 21 March 1916, the Germans made another of their tip and run raids on the east coast and bombarded Lowestoft. On 25 April the Harwich Force put to sea and, although very much inferior to the German force, Com (T) led us straight towards them, forcing them to cease firing on the town and turn their attention to us. For a difficult half an hour the Germans gave us everything they had got but Com (T) withdrew in a leisurely manner until, suspecting they were being drawn into a trap, the German ships turned and ran for home. As the great plumes of water thrown up by the bursts of the German shell rose up on all sides, Lieutenant Commander Kirkby walked about the bridge unconcernedly, smoking a cigarette as if he did not have a care in the world. The torpedo coxswain, who always took the wheel in action, was a white-haired chief petty officer from Ireland and once or twice, when a salvo roared overhead he instinctively ducked. 'Now, Coxswain,' said Kirkby with mock solemnity, 'I believe I saw you ducking.' 'Sure you did not, Sir,' replied the coxswain, deeply offended. 'It must have been the pitching of the ship that you were observing'!

On 31 May 1916 the Grand Fleet, under Admiral Jellicoe's command, engaged the German High Seas Fleet off the coast of Jutland in the largest and last full frontal naval battle of the Great War. It was a great disappointment to the Harwich Force that we were not allowed to take part. The Admiralty suspected that one of the objects of the sortie of the German High Seas Fleet might be the reinforcement of the German destroyer flotilla based on the Belgian ports. We were therefore ordered to 'raise steam for full speed' in order to patrol in a position to intercept such an attempt. Among those involved at Jutland was the *Lion*, the damage received during the Dogger Bank action now repaired and the ship once more flying Vice Admiral Beatty's flag in the Battle Cruiser Fleet under his command.

My former ship, the *Indomitable*, together with the *Invincible*, flagship of the squadron's commander, Rear Admiral Horace Hood, and the *Inflexible*, were all present as part of the 3rd Battle Cruiser Squadron, attached to the Grand Fleet. Having come late into the action, it was towards the end of the day that Captain Kennedy saw his next ahead, the *Invincible*, disappear in an angry cloud of smoke and spray, a dreadful explosion having broken the ship in two halves. 'Someone called out "Look at the *Invincible*" but by that time there was no *Invincible* to be seen, only a huge mass of heavy smoke,' he later recorded. 'Trying to see into it, one made out a couple of odd-looking shapes, one like the sharp end of a cigar sticking out of the water and, about fifty yards from it, was what appeared the other end of the cigar... and up above them was the cloud of grey and black smoke. At about fifty yards distance was a circle of wreckage and amongst it could be seen a few very men'.[4]

HMS Invincible *sank with the loss of all but six of the crew of over 1,000 including Rear Admiral Hood who was posthumously knighted. The outcome of the Battle of Jutland was not as decisive as the senior British naval commanders had anticipated. Lasting throughout the night of 31 May–1 June, 151 British and 99 German ships were engaged; fourteen British and eleven German ships were sunk. Over 6,000 British sailors died, twice as many as those lost by Germany, both sides claiming victory.*

With the *Invincible*'s sinking Captain Kennedy found himself in command of Admiral Hood's Battle Cruiser Squadron. Promoted rear admiral, he subsequently flew his flag ashore in command of the base at Peterhead, retiring from the Royal Navy in 1920 with the rank of admiral. He lived to enjoy many happy years of retirement and it was often my privilege and pleasure to visit him and talk over old times in the *Indomitable.*

The Harwich Force was not destined to engage in any further action against Germany, but we had plenty of hard work escorting convoys to and from Holland, patrolling in the Strait of Dover and off the Belgian coast, as well as taking part in periodic sweeps of the Grand Fleet designed to lure the German fleet out of its lair once more. On one occasion a Zeppelin airship appeared and dropped a few bombs in the vicinity of the force and drew upon itself the concentrated fire of the cruiser's 6-inch guns. A lucky hit by a fighter plane set it on fire, whereupon Com (T) made a general signal to the force: 'See Hymn number 224. Last verse.' A hymn book was produced and we read: 'Oh happy band of pilgrims/ Look upwards to the skies/ Where such a light affliction/ Shall win so great a prize.' Although never so devastating as what we were to experience twenty-five years later, the dropping of incendiary bombs by Zeppelins, Harwich being a frequent target, caused numerous fatalities.

On 11 October 1916 we were at Dover. For my 21st birthday I received several copies of the popular red leather-bound *Macmillan's Pocket Kipling*, including *Kim* and *Stalky & Co.* From my sisters, Phyllis and

Peggy, I received *The Day's Work* and from Captain Kirkby, *Captains Courageous*. Subsequently my family and friends added to my collection and the books became as well travelled as I, their red covers stained with sea spray.

HMS Torrid

As the war progressed and new destroyers were being built in increasing numbers, the ships of the Harwich flotillas were replaced by more modern and up-to-date vessels. In early 1917 we steamed the *Manly* up to Newcastle-on-Tyne and, with the exception of the engineer officer and a few key ratings, we turned over to a new destroyer, HMS *Torrid*. She had been built by Messrs Swan, Hunter and Wigham Richardson and the engine constructed by the Walsend Slipsay and Engineering Company.[5] I saw her still going strong seventeen years later in the anti-submarine flotilla at Portland. It was customary in those days for the builders to choose the badges for the ships they built. The *Torrid*'s was a flaming sun similar to that of the Sun Life Insurance Company and underneath was the motto: 'For him dark days do not exist/ The brazen faced old optimist'. Kirkby was delighted with the motto and it was certainly most appropriate for he was always cheerful and optimistic even in the darkest days. The hand carved original now hangs in the Imperial War Museum and I hope still serves to lighten the darker moments of this nuclear age.[6]

When we rejoined the flotilla we found that the frequency of the Dutch convoys had been stepped up and for the next few months we were constantly at sea. The Germans tried in various ways to interfere with these 'beef trips' as we called them, since, in the early stages of the war, the convoyed vessels were mainly carrying meat from Holland to England. German destroyers from Zeebrugge and Ostend would occasionally sneak up under cover of fog or darkness hoping to find a weak spot in our defences, but they were not prepared to risk serious action. They placed great hopes in the use of that most sinister weapon, the mine. On one eventful morning on 25 July while we were at sea, all hands were at action stations at 5am after sighting four German destroyers bearing south; German aircraft were also observed. Having opened fire, the Germans replied with their fire, their leading destroyer appearing to have been hit twice. They then withdrew. But danger was ever present.

On another occasion, on a bitter cold night on 22 December 1917, we were one of eight destroyers escorting a convoy to Holland. As we neared the Dutch coast, the senior officer split the force into two and we, with our division, were ordered to sweep back to the westward whilst he and his division took up a position off the Maas lightship to wait the arrival of the westbound convoy coming out from the Hook of Holland. We were about 20 miles apart when we received news that HMS *Valkyrie*, the senior officer's ship, had struck a mine. Although towed clear, within a matter of minutes we heard to our consternation that the *Torrent*, *Tornado* and *Surprise*, had suffered a similar fate. The surviving ship, the *Radiant*, managed to save only about a quarter of the three ship's companies. It was a grim night and we all felt the loss of so many of our flotilla mates very keenly. Twelve officers and sailors were saved, 252 were never found. Nineteen from the *Valkyrie* also died.

The periodic refits of the destroyers usually took place at Hull or Immingham. The former was by far the more popular. The members of the Hull and East Riding Club made us welcome and we much enjoyed the excellence of their menu until an incendiary bomb from a Zeppelin alighted in their larder. I shall never forget the strange sight of hams, chickens, pheasants and other delicacies still hanging on their hooks but transformed into brittle lumps of charcoal.[7] Grimsby was the nearest centre of amusement to Immingham, but it was at the end of a long ride in a tram or light railway. This difficulty did not prevent the sub lieutenant who had relieved me on my promotion to lieutenant (I having remained on as first lieutenant) from becoming engaged to a young lady whom we first sighted on the stage of the local variety theatre.[8] The sub lieutenant was the son of a Canadian parson and by coincidence, after the war, I had the opportunity to visit Canada before he was able to return there with his bride. It thus fell to my lot to tell his good parents about their new daughter-in-law and to set at rest any fears they may have had. I am glad to say the marriage was happy and successful.

For the rest of the war the Harwich Force continued its operations in the North Sea. Meanwhile the great land battles along the Western Front had taken a devastating toll on life, with offensives fought in 1915 at Neuve Chapelle and Loos – at which a cousin, Lieutenant Cuthbert Schofield, was killed while serving with the Royal Fusiliers (City of London Regiment) – and, in 1916, at Aubers Ridge and the Somme. In 1917 Germany instituted unrestricted submarine warfare, sinking the RMS Lusitania, *this action contributing to the United States' entry into the war. So damaging were Germany's submarine attacks on Allied shipping that an attack was planned against the German submarine shelters on the Belgian coast. First, an advance in the Ypres Salient had to be made on land. But the attempt, in what was known as the Third Battle of Ypres, failed to break through the Western Front, culminating in the disastrous Battle of Passchendaele.*

On the Eastern front, Russian resistance had collapsed in the wake of the 1917 Revolution which brought to power the Bolshevik leaders who signed the Treaty of Brest-Litovsk with Germany in March 1918. Following Germany's last push across the Western Front, the Allied forces fought back, bolstered by the arrival of over one million American troops. The war against the Ottoman Turks had also run its course. On 30 October Ottoman Turkey signed an Armistice, followed by Austria-Hungary on 3 November. Finally, on 11 November an armistice was agreed with Germany concluding what became known as the Great War (and subsequently as the First World War).

After the Armistice in November 1918 the Harwich Force gradually dispersed. 'We happy few, we band of brothers' went our several ways to the four corners of the earth, but for many years afterwards, until the death of our famous and beloved leader in 1951, an annual dinner was held in London over which Admiral Tyrwhitt presided and which those of us – who were able – attended. If by the 'Nelson touch' one means the capacity to inspire in his subordinates a passionate loyalty and devotion, then Com (T) possessed it in full measure.

We paid the *Torrid* off in Saltash Creek, Plymouth in February 1919. We were glad to get back to our home port but it was a sad day for all that. Most of us had been together for over three years and the comradeship founded on our common experiences during the war was something which meant a good deal to officers and men alike. Leave, however, is good in any circumstances and we all had a long spell to which we could look forward.

Between 1914 and 1918 – including the losses at Jutland – the Royal Navy lost two dreadnoughts, three battlecruisers, eleven battleships, twenty-five cruisers, fifty-four submarines, sixty-four destroyers and ten torpedo boats. Total naval casualties were 34,642 dead and 4,510 wounded. Worldwide casualties for the First World War are estimated at approximately forty million, those of the United Kingdom under one million.

We yield Thee praise and Thanksgiving for our deliverance.[9]

Chapter Four

HMS *Renown*

'Ich dien'[1]

1919

In February 1919 I was appointed watchkeeper to the battleship HMS *Marlborough*, then about to sail to the Mediterranean, but the influenza germ which ravaged Europe at the end of the Great War set at naught the Admiralty's plans for my future employment and I was still in bed when she sailed. After I had recovered, I received a new appointment directing me to proceed to Scapa Flow to join HMS *Renown* on 6 April. In the event it was a fortunate turn of fate. Although I served in her for less than a year, little did I know that those few months would be so interesting and exciting. HMS *Renown* and her sister ship, HMS *Repulse*, both launched in 1916, were a new design of fast, very lightly armoured battlecruiser designed for overtaking and overwhelming the German light cruisers. Their main armament was six 15-inch guns. The absence of side armour meant that every cabin had a scuttle, hence she was a very comfortable ship in which to live. The *Renown's* captain at this time was Ernest Taylor and he commanded a very happy and efficient ship.[2]

In early May we moved to Rosyth before sailing south to Portsmouth. On 6 June we welcomed on board His Excellency the President-Elect of Brazil, Epitácio Pessoa, in order to take him on the first leg of his homeward voyage as far as Lisbon. He had been on a state visit to Britain and several other European countries, having led the Brazilian delegation during the negotiations of the Treaty of Versailles. The president was accompanied by his wife, Maria da Conceição, and daughter, Laurita, and when they dined with us in the wardroom during the passage they entertained us with some delightful Brazilian folk songs. The president played the piano and his daughter the guitar. I still have the score of one of these songs which the president gave me, entitled *Luar do sertão* (Hinterlands Moonlight). When he bade us farewell on our arrival at Lisbon we did not know that, before the year was out, we would have the pleasure of visiting him in his own country.[3]

At the beginning of July we were at sea on patrol in the Atlantic during the epoch-making flight of airship R34 to New York and back. Having left Britain on 2 July, the airship arrived in Long Island four days later with hardly any fuel left. The airship returned to Britain on 10 July. It was the first transatlantic flight undertaken by an airship (following the first aeroplane flight on 14/15 June).

A Royal Tour

On our return to Portsmouth we were greeted with the exciting news that HMS *Renown* had been selected to convey HRH The Prince of Wales to Canada on the first of his memorable tours to countries of the Commonwealth. The date fixed for our departure was 5 August before which there was a lot to be done. The ship was docked, painted and polished. Cabins were prepared and specially furnished for the royal suite. Everyone had some leave and then at last the day came when we were berthed at South Railway jetty in the dockyard which had been the scene of so many royal occasions. HM King George V and Queen Mary accompanied by Princess Mary travelled from London in the royal train to see their eldest son depart on his travels. With his customary thoroughness the king inspected all the arrangements made and shook hands with all the officers. Queen Mary too expressed a wish to have the officers presented to her. After lunching on board, the royal party went ashore and stood on the jetty while tugs towed us out into the stream. The band played, the crowds, assembled along the Hard, cheered and the royal tour had begun.

In addition to my duties as officer of the Quarterdeck Division, I was detailed to assist the navigating officer, Commander James Campbell, so I spent a great deal of my time on the bridge. Campbell was an expert in his particular profession and his skill and experience were soon put to the test. In terms of entertainment, instead of the usual ship's band, the Band of the Plymouth Division of the Royal Marines had been embarked for the cruise. They were over forty strong, under the baton of Captain

Patrick (Paddy) O'Donnell, a member of a family of renowned military bandmasters and who had brought a large library of music suitable for all occasions. The first night at sea the prince sent for Paddy and enquired if he had the music of 'Buzz-Buzz', a show then running in London. Paddy had to admit that it was not amongst his band's repertoire. 'Well report to me tomorrow morning and I'll whistle it to you,' said the prince. The following morning Paddy reported to the prince, as directed, and faithfully recorded the royal interpretation. That night at dinner the string orchestra rendered the music Paddy had transcribed.

We called first at Conception Bay on the south-east coast of Newfoundland; from there we went to Halifax, Nova Scotia. Passing through the Gut of Canso, which divides the Nova Scotia Peninsula from Cape Breton Island, we entered the wide estuary of the St Lawrence River; almost immediately we ran into a dense fog. It was important to arrive at Quebec on time if the prince's schedule was not to be seriously upset. A few miles east of the city, the Isle of Orleans divides the river in two and the main channel on the south side, known as the Traverses, had only sufficient depth of water for us to pass through it at high tide. There was no radar in those days with which to see through the fog. All night long we groped our way up the narrowing estuary, our siren bellowing mournfully. We could only estimate our position by dead reckoning and by judging what allowance to make for the strong and uncertain tidal streams. When daylight came, pale and wan, the fog was as thick as ever and it was out of the question to attempt the passage of the Traverses until it lifted. Fortunately, we had an hour or two in hand and so Captain Taylor decided to anchor. Campbell estimated that we were opposite Murray Bay and so, sounding carefully, we edged towards the shore and let go. As we left the bridge he said to me: 'If it doesn't clear by noon the prince will be twenty-four hours late as it's sure to shut down again tonight.' At five minutes to twelve the fog rolled away, giving place to a gloriously sunny day!

When we fixed our position by the land we were within 300 yards of our estimated position. We quickly got under way and, with the aid of an extra knot or two, we arrived at our anchorage off Quebec at the exact minute given in our schedule on 21 August. The prince and his controller, Admiral Sir Lionel Halsey, were both delighted and Campbell was congratulated on a very fine piece of navigation. The responsibility lay, of course, with the captain who alone could decide whether to continue through the fog or not. 'The *Renown* must have looked fine steaming up the St Lawrence,' the prince wrote to his father, 'and', he continued, referring to the visit his father had made in 1908 to celebrate the tercentenary of Quebec's founding, 'it thrilled me to think that she was moored in the same billet opposite the citadel as that occupied by the *Indomitable* during your visit.' Describing the crowds in Quebec (and throughout Canada) as 'so volatile and vigorous as to constitute at times an almost terrifying phenomenon', the Prince then set out in a special train to tour the great Dominion. Everywhere he went it was the same story of tremendous personal success. He virtually took Canada by storm.[4]

Travelling through Canada by train to Toronto, Ottawa, Montreal, Winnipeg, Calgary and Vancouver, among the Prince of Wales's activities, he laid the foundation stone of the Peace Tower on Parliament Hill, opened the Canadian National Exhibition in Toronto and met members of the League of Canadian Indians at Sault Ste Marie. He also took a three-day canoe trip down the Nipigon River to fish and hunt with two Ojibwa guides. In Saskatchewan he renamed a branch library in Regina as the Prince of Wales Library. During his tour of Vancouver, he opened the New Westminster Exhibition. In Victoria he laid the foundation stone of a statue of Queen Victoria on the grounds of the province's parliament building.

We spent ten days in Quebec and during our stay, as previously mentioned, I was able to set at rest any fears which the parents of the sub lieutenant in the *Torrid* may have had about their son's bride. I also enjoyed some excellent trout fishing in the stream in the neighbourhood of Valcartier. It had been arranged that, during the prince's absence touring Canada, we should carry out a cruise to the West Indies and Rio de Janeiro. After a call at Halifax we steered south and were soon basking in hot tropical sunshine.

Our first stop was St Kitts which we reached on 9 September; we then proceeded to Barbados, the most southerly of the Windward chain of islands. A big programme of sporting events had been arranged which included a polo match. This was a rather formidable proposition as there were only two of us who had ever attempted the game, of which I was one. The challengers agreed that a match was out of the question and suggested that we should have a friendly game with two of them and two of us on each side, the balance being made up from midshipmen who could ride but had never played polo. At the appointed time we reached the ground, situated in the middle of the race course. One of our hosts approached me and said he would be glad to mount me on a chestnut pony which he had recently acquired. He admitted that he did not know much about him nor the pony about the game. 'So we're two of a kind,' I said as I mounted. A large crowd had turned out to see the fun, including the governor and his lady. As I manoeuvred my steed onto the ground, I soon realised that he had steam up in all boilers and was raring to go.

When the game started I had some difficulty in steering him in the right direction; however, the ball chanced past us in the way in which we were heading and we set off in pursuit. One of my messmates, who was playing on the opposite side, decided to try and head me off. We were on converging courses and both going full speed. Neither of us drew rein and the inevitable happened. We met with a resounding thud that nearly unseated us both. This was too much for my pony. Seizing the bit between his teeth he bolted, and, much to the amusement of the crowd, we left the ground and made two complete circuits of the race course before I could persuade him to reduce speed. By this time the chukka was over and I was thankful to be allowed to manoeuvre him back to the place where the grooms were waiting. As I dismounted a cheerful face looked up at me, grinning from ear to ear and said: 'Massa, you sho did make a race horse outta dat pony!!'

On another occasion I was invited to a decoy pigeon shooting party. The rendezvous was for 6.30am. Although it was a rather tame sport, our hosts were such charming company that the first two hours passed pleasantly enough. By 9am I was beginning to feel hungry but politeness forbade any enquiry regarding the possibility of breakfast. The time dragged on with leaden feet and conversation became more desultory until at last at 10.30 our host said genially: 'Well, I don't think we'll get any more [pigeons] and I daresay you could do with some breakfast.' I exchanged glances with my brother officers and, with difficulty supressing our real feelings, we replied that it sounded quite a good idea. Only when we reached the club did we understand the West Indian interpretation of 'breakfast' and any pangs of hunger were a small price to pay for such a sumptuous meal. Never have I eaten such a breakfast, not even in Australia where chops and steaks are normal fare, gin and fresh limes figuring prominently besides the customary eggs, bacon and pancakes.

After a brief visit to the delightful island of Granada, famous for its nutmegs and spice, we arrived off Port of Spain in Trinidad where we stopped for fuel. The voyage from Trinidad to Rio de Janeiro meant Crossing the Line, which provided the opportunity for a good day's sport on 27 September. There were many on board who had never crossed the line, myself included, so we were all subjected to the attentions of King Neptune's surgeon and barber before being tipped over backwards into the big canvas bath which had been rigged for the purpose. Esteemed as a 'Son o' Neptune', we were given a certificate signed by Neptune, Rex for 'having been duly presented to His Majesty King Neptune with the ceremony proper to the occasion'. Having researched the origin of this custom, there seems no doubt that it is an adaptation of the ancient rites connected with the propitiation of those gods who were believed to control the elements. To the ancients, the sea was a terrifying place peopled with monsters, dragons and giants lying in wait for the mariner. Islands and rocks were inhabited by beautiful sirens seeking to entice sailors to their doom. The only way to ensure a safe passage was to placate these deities with some sacrifice or other. There is nothing mystic or sinister about the present-day ceremony which affords an occasion for fun and a certain amount of horse-play and is generally enjoyed by everyone on board.[5]

The harbour of Rio de Janeiro, as seen in the early morning light when approaching from seaward, is surely one of the most beautiful sights in the world. The white buildings of the city stand out against a background of dark mountains and, as the windows of the houses and offices catch the first rays of the rising sun, the city appears to be on fire. The dark cone of Sugar Loaf mountain stands like a sentry guarding the left side of the entrance, while, on the right, and hardly less impressive, stands a large rock known as Pico. As we passed between these two sentinels the pear-shaped bay opened out before us and the lush vegetation of the numerous islands added to the beauty of the scene. High up on the port hand I watched the sun gilding the summit of the Corcovado (meaning 'hunchback') mountain on which a large white stone statue of Christ now stands with arms extended over the harbour. Far below, on the left, the warm waters of the South Atlantic surged and tumbled over the white coral sand of the famous Copacabana beach. Standing on the bridge and not being directly concerned with the navigation of the ship, I was able to enjoy this magnificent scene to the full.

While we were in Brazil, HE President Pessoa did everything to make our stay as enjoyable as possible. On 13 October he came on board and we fired a 21-gun salute in his honour. We also attended a reception at his palace. There was cricket and football, swimming and rowing and night life as exotic as anything Paris can offer. Another event of interest was going up country to see the big hydro-electric power station which supplied Rio with electricity. On another occasion I took a party of midshipmen shooting in the jungle about 100 miles up the Sao Paolo railway line. Although our bag was nil we saw a good deal of wildlife and particularly some of those beautiful large butterflies indigenous to South America. On the way back, while we were having dinner in the train's dining car, we roared over a bridge at high speed. As soon as we were on the other side, a stranger sitting opposite me heaved a sigh of relief. Noticing the enquiring look on my face he leaned over and said: 'I'm always thankful when we are safely across that bridge. Last year this same train left the rails and plunged into the gorge.'

During our stay there was much talk in the city about the impressive United States' squadron which had visited the port a short time previously and we were naturally anxious to wipe the eye of our rivals. It had been arranged that, on the evening of our big reception on board, we should give a firework display and illuminate the ship. Since the event had been advertised in the press, at the appointed time the harbour was thronged with thousands of spectators. The ship was darkened with not a light showing, a bugle sounded and suddenly she appeared outlined in green flares held by men stationed all along the side. Green is the national colour of Brazil and an audible 'Ah-h' rose from the crowd followed by ecstatic cheers as burst after burst of 250 rockets electrically fired from the fo'c'sle roared into the air. As the green flares died out the illuminating circuits were switched on and the ship became a blaze of light. From that time onwards we heard no more about the American squadron.

We left Rio de Janeiro on 14 October and headed north again for Port of Spain, Trinidad where we spent an enjoyable leave, swimming, playing cricket and partaking in some of the finest duck shooting which has ever come my way. With the onset of cold weather in North America the mallard and widgeon migrate in their thousands to the mangrove swamps to the south of Port of Spain. Although we had no dogs to retrieve the birds we shot we got some pretty good bags. During our stay I took a party consisting of the subaltern of the marines and some midshipmen in a whaler in search of alligators, which we had heard were to be found in these swamps. Unfortunately, I had neglected to consult the tide tables before we set out. There was a good breeze and we covered the six miles to the edge of the swamp in good time. We had not penetrated very far before one of our party sitting in the bows spotted an alligator and bagged it. With such encouragement, the excitement amongst the midshipmen was intense and, using the oars as poles, we punted further into the swamp. At 4pm I decided it was time to return. We had seen no more alligators, only flocks of parrots and egrets which screeched high overhead and the heat was oppressive. We were making slow progress when suddenly the boat struck an obstruction. Since we were returning by the same channel by which we had entered, I was momentarily puzzled until I realised that the level of the water had fallen about a foot which was just enough to prevent us clearing the fallen tree trunk on which we had grounded.

In an attempt to lighten the boat, we got out into the soft, oozy mud, but, like the Yorkshireman's pig, we could push and we could shove, but 'she was hanged if she'd be druv'. We were trapped until the tide rose again. With darkness came the mosquitoes and the alligator in the bottom of the boat began quite forcibly to remind us of its presence. At last the tide turned and at about midnight there was enough water to take us over the tree trunk. But when we reached open water our troubles were not over. The wind had dropped and a brilliant tropical moon shone over a glassy sea. There was nothing for it but to out oars and pull. By the time we reached the *Renown*, dawn was breaking. It was the longest six miles I have ever known!

From Trinidad we set course for New York. As we left the warm sunshine of the tropics in early November we ran into a full northerly gale, obliging us to reduce speed. On the second morning of bad weather the boatswain took a party of men onto the fo'c'sle to re-secure the cables, the lashings of which had parted during the night. I was in the chart house working on some charts when I felt the ship pitch heavily and I heard a rush of water as a big green sea swept over the fo'c'sle. A moment later I heard the cry of 'man overboard' and the clang of the telegraphs as the engines were stopped. I rushed to the bridge where, by this time, the captain and Commander Campbell had arrived. The port cutter, which was the only one turned out, had been manned by willing volunteers. While the ship was being allowed to make a lee it was lowered level with the gunwale. The life buoys had been let go, but, as we scanned the churning water, we could see no sign of our unfortunate shipmate. Suddenly a great wave rode down the ship's side and, lifting the half-lowered cutter as it passed, dropped it. Unfortunately, the safety pins of the dropping gear had been withdrawn and the boat fell into the trough left by the wave and, in so doing, turned completely over. We now had not one but sixteen men overboard, but fortunately the officers and men in the cutter had put on their lifebelts. The ship had to be turned before the starboard cutter could be lowered. Meanwhile hailstorms and squalls beat down on the unfortunate men bobbing up and down like corks in the tempestuous sea. Eventually all were recovered with the exception of the man originally washed overboard and one of the cutter's crew who had disappeared. The midshipman of the watch, who had been sent down to tell the boatswain to clear the fo'c'sle and who had arrived there as we shipped the green sea, was washed against a breakwater and seriously injured. It was an unlucky day.

After nearly three months in Canada the Prince of Wales went to Washington DC where he was present on Armistice Day. He then travelled to New York in order to rejoin HMS Renown *for the homeward journey.*

There is no city in the world with such a striking skyline as New York and seeing it for the first time on a cold, grey November morning as we steamed slowly up the Hudson River to our berth, I experienced a feeling of wonder and excitement which is always repeated whenever I return. Great preparations had been made for our reception. A team of glamorous chaufferettes in private cars had assembled to drive us about the city. We were made honorary members of numerous clubs, given free seats in the theatres and cinemas and free rides on the subway, our hosts sparing no effort to ensure that everyone from the captain to the youngest sailor had a good time. The problem of prohibition caused us some concern for the city was officially 'dry' and there were we, lying a few hundred yards off shore, with liquor – and good liquor at that – on call. When the sailors went ashore they were offered strange concoctions of bootleg liquor, often with disastrous results.

Soon after our arrival I heard that a gala performance was to be given for the Prince of Wales at the Metropolitan Opera House and that the great Enrico Caruso was to sing the part of Canio in Leoncavallo's opera, *Pagliacci*. The captain of the marines, another lieutenant and I, who were all very fond of opera, decided to seize this unique opportunity of hearing the world's greatest tenor, but, when we made enquiries about seats, we were told that they had all been sold long before the ship had arrived. The liaison officer promised to see what he could do, but when the day came and he told us he had had no success, we virtually abandoned hope. The captain of the marines had a long-standing invitation to dine with a colonel friend on the British Army staff in Washington who was visiting New York and so he rang him up. In the course of their conversation, he disclosed our plight. The colonel, a man of resource, said: 'Why not try bluff, old boy? It often works.' His suggestion was that we should all have dinner with him first.

We arrived at 7pm in full war paint, that is to say mess dress. Our host looked us up and down and said he had not the slightest doubt that such an abundance of gold lace would gain us admittance to Valhalla itself. By the time we had finished dinner we were ready for almost anything! We drew up at the brightly lit, red-carpeted entrance and stepped out of the taxi. In response to a request for tickets from a tuxedo–clad official, I explained who we were and said that we had dropped in on the off-chance that there might be some last-minute cancellations. The official hesitated, obviously taken aback by such a naïve suggestion and asked us politely if we would stand aside and wait. As we were waiting we watched a bevy of bejewelled ladies and their escorts entering. They eyed us with that curious look which an unfamiliar uniform invites and which always makes me feel self-conscious. After what seemed an interminable time another official arrived, looked us up and down and disappeared. Then, after a pause, another came and repeated the process. Just as we were about to accept defeat, the curtains at the back of the foyer parted and a man of medium build in full evening dress, with a red carnation in his button hole, advanced towards us. It was the great Mr Otto Kahn, the redoubtable president and chairman of the board of directors of the Metropolitan Opera, in person.[6] As he approached, we detected an understandable look of annoyance on his face, but it vanished in a flash as he came towards us. 'Gentlemen, it's a pleasure to have you with us. Come this way. I guess I can fix you up if you don't mind being separated.' We looked at each other hardly able to believe our good fortune. He led us up the stairs to the rear of the Grand Tier boxes, then, opening a door and taking me by the shoulder he propelled me into the semi-darkness within, saying 'Mrs Brown, I'd like to have you meet Lootenant—' and he paused. 'Schofield', I supplied. 'Lootenant Schofield of the Royal Navy', he repeated, 'would you mind letting him sit in your box?' Mrs Brown was delighted and so was Mr Brown and their two charming daughters. He disposed of my two companions with equal success.

I shall never forget that evening. When the Prince of Wales entered the royal box the whole audience rose to its feet. The augmented orchestra, which overflowed into the stage boxes, rolled out 'God Save the King' with pomp and majesty. Instead of resuming their seats people remained standing, looking up at the prince who stood there bowing and smiling and nervously fingering his tie. Then the lights went down and the performance began. Caruso gave of his best. As he poured forth the heart-rending words of *Vesti la giubba*, the tears rolled down his face and he made one feel what he was singing was his personal tragedy. Less than two years later this glorious voice, which had given so much pleasure to thousands of music lovers, was stilled for ever when he died, having fallen ill, aged only 48.[7] I count myself fortunate indeed to have heard him sing. There was no prohibition for us that night. Our hosts took us to a hotel where they regaled us with sandwiches and champagne. We returned to the ship in the small hours feeling incredibly pleased with life and ourselves in particular.

Hectic days followed for all of us from the prince downwards, the informal hospitality which was pressed upon him sometimes making it difficult to keep the exact schedules demanded of royalty. Once, after a strenuous day of official engagements he decided to have a game at the

Racquet club before returning to the ship. I was keeping the last dog watch from 6pm to 8pm and I knew that the prince was giving a large dinner party on board and that the guests would begin to arrive at about 7.45pm. As ordered, I had sent the barge in for him at 6.45pm and was walking up and down the quarterdeck when Admiral Halsey came on deck and enquired if the barge was inshore. On assuring him that it was, he started to walk up and down and invited me to accompany him. Every now and then he glanced anxiously at his watch and looked towards shore, but all that could be seen were the twinkling lights along Riverside Drive against the dark background of skyscrapers in which the office lights had been extinguished.

The picket boat came off shortly before 7.30pm with a load of officers and the midshipman reported to me that the barge was quite all right but that there had been no sign of the royal car with its police escort on motor cycles when he left. I conveyed this information to the admiral who received it with considerable concern. Then suddenly I caught sight of a tongue of flame and the steaming lights of a boat heading towards the ship. As she drew nearer I guessed it was the barge being driven at full speed. She had an oil-fired boiler which, when forced, was apt to belch flame like a volcano. As she breasted the gangway the prince leapt out. Running up the ladder two steps at a time he waved his racquet to the astonished but relieved admiral, saying: 'Don't worry – I'll make it' – and he did!

Before we sailed from New York, by His Majesty's command, the prince held an investiture on board. There were many British and American subjects who had received honours and decorations for their services during the Great War on whom the insignia had not actually been bestowed. Among those who were knighted was Ashley Sparks, who, as head of the New York office of the Cunard Steamship Company, had rendered great service in the organisation of the American end of our life-line across the Atlantic. He received the insignia of a Knight Commander of the British Empire. Little did I know, as I marshalled the assembled company on the quarterdeck, that twenty years later he and I would be sitting in his office in New York discussing how to maintain that lifeline against another attempt by Germany to sever it.[8]

On our way back we stopped at Halifax where the prince took formal leave of his Canadian hosts and, after an uneventful crossing, we reached

Portsmouth on 1 December 1919. Before he left the ship the prince announced that he would be setting out on a voyage to Australia and New Zealand the following spring and he told the captain that he hoped as many of the officers and ship's company as possible would remain in the ship for the next trip. I had already applied for a specialist course in navigation and received an appointment to attend the Royal Naval College at Greenwich in January 1920. I knew I could withdraw my application if I wished and I was very tempted to do so but Captain Taylor advised me to think of my future career and forego the pleasures of another royal tour. I did not regret taking his advice.

Chapter Five

'A most reliable Navigator'

At midnight in his guarded tent
The Turk was dreaming of the hour
When Greece, her knee in suppliance bent
Should tremble at his power.[1]

1920–24

January is not the best month in which to make a first acquaintance with those venerable buildings beside the River Thames, which Sir Christopher Wren designed, Charles II caused to be built, William III appointed as an asylum for disabled seamen and of which, since 1873, the greater part has been in use as a college for the further training of officers of the Royal Navy. The batch of lieutenants (of which I was one) who had been selected to specialise in navigation and who, because of the war, had missed their sub lieutenant's courses, were first sent to Greenwich for a two-month refresher course in astronomical navigation, after which we would commence the specialist course proper at the Navigation School in Portsmouth.

I am sure it was a sound idea, but, coming fresh from a ship such as HMS *Renown*, it seemed like a sentence of confinement in a dank, cold and inhospitable vault. We climbed many flights of well-worn stone stairs to our cabins beneath the eaves and we dined in a subterranean dungeon beneath the famous Painted Hall, with its ceiling decorations by the British artist, Sir James Thornhill, which, in those days, was still a museum. When a cold, yellow fog rolled up the river and enveloped us in its clammy embrace we groped our way about the buildings like lost souls. There was one redeeming feature and that was our proximity to London and its compensatory advantages which have been the solace of many a young officer appointed for a period of study within those gloomy portals. We took our departure from Greenwich at the end of the Easter term 1920 and went to Portsmouth. It was fourteen years before I again took up residence in the college by the river.

Lieutenant (N)

HMS *Dryad*, which is the ship's name by which the Navigation School is known, was a small building inside Portsmouth's dockyard walls; its motto was *Nobis Tutus Ibis* (with us you go in safety). Built nearly 200 years ago, the amenities of the building, although adequate, were dreary. Over the course of the next twenty years many improvements were carried out so that, by the beginning of the Second World War, it had become a comfortable establishment within the limits imposed by its location and the lack of room for expansion.

Books have been written about the romance of navigation and certainly the early navigators with their crude instruments and imperfect charts had every reason to be proud of their achievements. Even today – in the 1950s – with all the scientific aids which are at the service of the modern navigator, there is great satisfaction to be obtained from making a good landfall after a long ocean passage or piloting a ship safely through some difficult channels. At the time of which I am writing the only piece of electrical apparatus about which we had to learn was the gyro compass and for this we spent a fortnight at the Admiralty Compass establishment at Ditton Park, near Slough. At Portsmouth, besides astronomical navigation, we learnt about pilotage, meteorology, ship-handling, tides, fleet manoeuvres and surveying, all subjects of absorbing interest.

Two officers of the Royal Hellenic Navy were attending the course and, when we reached the final stages, they announced that they would like to present the mess with a suitable memento in appreciation of the kindness which they had received. The executive officer, the president of the mess, accepted their offer and we all imagined that they would produce a piece of silverware, as is customary on such occasions. At the final guest night when the president took his seat he found himself confronting a beautiful reproduction in ivory of the statue of Venus de Milo standing on a suitably inscribed pedestal! Having satisfactorily passed our final examinations in August 1920 we were allowed to call ourselves lieutenants (N) and were deemed to have joined the ranks of those who dare to style themselves 'the salt of the earth'.

My first appointment, which I took up in September, was on board HMS *Shakespeare*, the half flotilla leader, attached to the Home Fleet flotillas. I was glad to be back in destroyers again – at sea off Invergordon, and Port Edgar – but after I had been there six months the Admiralty decided to reduce the size of the flotillas to one leader and eight destroyers instead of the two leaders and sixteen destroyers which they had been during the war. As a result, the *Shakespeare* was paid off into reserve.[2]

Fisheries

In May 1921 I received an appointment to the sloop, HMS *Godetia*, which, at that time was part of the Royal Navy Fisheries Protection Squadron under the command of Acting Captain Clarence Trelawny DSO RN, the Local Fishery Naval Officer (LFNO), to give him his full title.[3] Trelawny was a destroyer man but he had taken a nasty knock at Jutland commanding HMS *Spitfire* when his ship collided with the German ship *Nassau*. Although both ships survived, for a period Trelawny had been knocked unconscious and the doctors had recommended that he have a quiet job for a year or two to recover: the Fishery Protection appointment was all that could be desired. For my part I found the work extremely interesting and agreeable. I learnt a great deal about pilotage in tidal waters and gained a useful knowledge of fish and their habits. Our base was Lowestoft and our beat extended from the latitude of the Farne Islands, off the coast of Northumberland, south through the Strait of Dover to the longitude of the ancient Cinque port of Rye in East Sussex. In the past there were fights between the fishermen of the various nations who set out to gather the silver harvest of the sea and it was agreed that the countries concerned should provide armed fishery patrol vessels to act as policemen and keep the peace.

We arranged our own programme and while the seasonal migration of fish, such as the herring, influenced our movements, we managed to find occasion to visit Scarborough when a county cricket match was in progress, and perhaps Grimsby or Hull for the Doncaster races. The herring fishing season, which begins in May off the Shetland Islands and ends in November off the Essex coast, kept us busy. As soon as the big fleets of drifters came into our area we started to pay them visits. We used to thread our way out between the drifters just before dusk and, as they were shooting their nets, then we stopped our engines and drifted with them all night. As dawn broke and the men in the drifters started to haul their nets, away went our dinghy and soon it would return loaded down to the gunwale with gleaming fish. Fresh cooked out of the sea, whether grilled whole or split and fried after being rolled in oatmeal in the Norfolk fashion, a herring would tickle the palate of the most jaded epicure. A kippered herring fresh from the curing hooks and not over-smoked, as they often are, is something to remember. The men in the drifters used to cook them in salt water and bite out the fleshy parts of the back, throwing the rest overboard for the gulls. At Great Yarmouth, which has always been closely associated with the herring industry, I learnt of a curious custom. Once a year the town had to deliver 100 herrings baked in twenty-four pasties to the Sheriffs of Norwich. These were then sent to the Lord of the Manor at East Carlton as fief or due for the land on which the town of Great Yarmouth stands.

One of our duties was to visit the various fish markets and obtain information about the state of the industry. At the Lowestoft market there was a champion skate cutter whose operations never ceased to fascinate me. He stood in front of a wooden block and, in his right hand, he held a large knife of razor-like sharpness, while, on his left hand, he wore a thick fearnought glove with which to grasp the slippery fish which lay in a barrel beside him. In front of the block stood three empty barrels. When all was ready he began and no machine-driven knife worked faster than his. On the down stroke he severed the right wing, with a flick of his wrist on the up-stroke he shot it into the right barrel, then the process was repeated with the left wing and the body of the fish shot into the centre barrel. The slightest error in the fall of the fast-moving knife would at least have cost him the fingers of his left hand, but I never once saw him so much as touch the seam of his glove.

It was usual for the LFNO North Sea to pay a visit during the summer months to some of the fishing ports on the continental coast of our patrol area, Ostend, Calais, Dieppe but, owing to the coal strike which had occurred earlier in the year, our foreign cruise was cancelled, much to everyone's disappointment. However, we received a visit from the Belgian fishery patrol ship and we were glad of the opportunity of entertaining them.

When I had completed a year's service in the *Godetia* the captain of the Navigation School wrote and told me that he intended nominating me for the flotilla leader, the 1,530 ton destroyer, HMS *Montrose*, attached to the Mediterranean Fleet. Launched in 1918 she had been completed too late to take an active role in the last war. I was sorry to leave HMS *Godetia* at the end of April, but it was a good appointment and the prospect of going abroad again appealed.

In Turkish Waters

When I joined HMS *Montrose* at Malta on 15 July 1922 she was still a half leader, as the Mediterranean flotillas had not yet been reorganised on the lines of those in the Home Fleet. The bulk of the Mediterranean Fleet, under the command of Vice Admiral Sir Osmond Brock, was concentrated in Turkish waters on account of the Greco–Turkish war which had resulted from the refusal of the Turks to accept the terms of the Treaty of Sèvres by which they had lost control over Armenia, Thrace, Syria, Mesopotamia and Palestine in 1920.[4]

On 18 August, having spent the past weeks ammunitioning and preparing the ship for sea, we sailed to join the rest of the fleet in the Bosphorous. I was greatly impressed with the beauty of the waterway which divides Europe from Asia. During the hot summer weather the flotilla was based at Büyükdere Bay in the northern part of the straits. We steamed past the Golden Horn and on past the city of Constantinople with its many mosques and minarets, its palaces and embassies, its tall cypress trees and picturesque gardens and threaded our way through the narrow defile between the fortresses of Rumeli Hisari and Anadolu Hisari, sometimes known as the Devil's Gap, through which the current flows with great strength. Next we passed the pretty suburb of Therapia (Tarabya) where the summer residences of the various embassies are situated, all glistening white against the dark green background. On the opposite side in the Bay of Beikos the fleet flagship, HMS *Iron Duke*, lay at anchor, her upperworks hidden beneath a canopy of white canvas awnings. Then, rounding a bend we came up on the rest of our flotilla lying head on to the cool north-easterly breeze which blows down from the Black Sea. A detachment of one of the Lancer regiments was stationed ashore at Büyükdere and we lost no time in making their acquaintance and borrowing their horses, which they were only too pleased to lend us.

As the situation seemed to be fairly quiescent, at the beginning of September the *Montrose,* accompanied by several other destroyers, set out on a cruise which took us first to the Romanian port of Constanta; there we encountered some ex-German naval officers who, because of the recent redrawing of the frontiers at the peace treaty, suddenly found themselves to be Romanians! Our destination was the historic town of Galati in eastern Romania, lying about 120 miles up the River Danube; when we reached the mouth we embarked a pilot who was relieved by another one at Sulina, lying just inside the bar. Towards evening we reached Galati safely. I was the duty officer the day after our arrival so I was looking forward to a run ashore the following day, but the next morning we received a signal directing us to return to Constantinople with all despatch. By the time we had explained to the local authorities the reason for our hurried departure, and embarked the river pilot, stopping at Braila, it was nearly midday. As the bar at the river entrance was poorly lit and not very well buoyed it was imperative that we should be clear of the river before dark.

Disregarding the pilot's protests, we set off at a fair speed. I doubt whether the inhabitants of the farms and villages which we passed had ever seen anything like the sight presented by eight destroyers racing down river with enormous stern waves due to the shallow water and making a wash which rolled over the low-lying country like a tidal wave! We reached Sulina just as it was getting dark and stopped to allow the river pilot to disembark and another pilot acquainted with the entrance channel to take over. The river pilot, however, turned a deaf ear to the captain's requests to leave the ship, instead entering into a long and exciting conversation with his relief, which presumably concerned the nerve-wracking experience to which he had been subjected. In desperation, the captain took me aside and asked me if I was prepared to lead the division out without the pilot's assistance. I said I would have a shot at it. Pushing the two gesticulating men aside, the captain gave the order to go ahead and signalled to the remainder to follow closely in our wake. Fate was kind and we all got safely out to the utter astonishment of the two pilots who were so engrossed in their conversation that they were unaware of what had happened until it was all over!

When we reached Constantinople we heard of the defeat of the Greek Army and the Turkish capture of Smyrna (Izmir) on 9 September. The rout of the Greek forces brought the Turkish forces led by Mustafa Kemal face to face with our own troops stationed at Chanak in the neutral zone and so we were ordered to the Dardanelles to support the flanks of our army.

For a time it seemed as if hostilities might break out at any moment, but at last Kemal agreed to negotiate with General Sir Charles Harington, the Allied Commander-in-Chief. Known as 'Tim', he was a veteran soldier whose service in the British Army dated from the Boer War. In response to his request for a despatch vessel to convey him to Mudanya, on the southern coast of the sea of Marmara, where the talks were to take place, HMS *Montrose* was placed at his disposal. This was a welcome assignment since the view of even such an historic site as that of ancient Troy (Hsarlik – the place of fortresses) before which we had been anchored for over three weeks, can lose its attraction![5]

On the night of our arrival, the captain and I and two other officers dined with General and Lady Harington. I was greatly impressed by his calm and confident manner. He did not give the impression of a man charged with a most delicate mission which was to rank as one of the most successful in the annals of British diplomacy. He laughed and joked, talked about cricket of which he was very fond and we ended the evening sliding down the banisters of the elegant staircase! Ismet Pasha, the Turkish chief negotiator (and a future President of the Republic of Turkey), was difficult to deal with, feigning deafness whenever it suited him. As General Harington later told us, he let it be known that he carried an ultimatum in his pocket and whenever Ismet became obstinate he would move his hand very slowly towards his pocket and it always had the desired effect![6]

While the negotiations with the Turks were taking place we made several trips to Mudanya, known for its olive oil and silk exports. Once the Armistice of Mudanya was signed on 11 October 1922 – my twenty-seventh birthday – between Turkey on the one hand and Britain, France and Italy, the general expressed a wish to visit the work of the Imperial War Graves Commission on the Gallipoli Peninsula and we were again placed at his disposal. He very kindly invited another officer and me to accompany him on the trip around the battlefields. I was glad to have the opportunity of seeing the territory over which such heavy fighting had taken place and to visit the fort at Cape Helles which we had shelled in the *Indomitable*. If we had known as much about the technique of combined operations in the First World War as we did in the Second, the Dardanelles campaign might well have been a resounding success instead of a dismal failure.

We spent Christmas 1922 at anchor off Constantinople; the *Montrose* was now under the command of Captain the Hon Edward Bingham, who had been awarded the VC for his 'dauntless courage' in command of HMS *Nestor* at Jutland. Lucky to have survived when the *Nestor* was sunk, he was picked up and remained as a prisoner-of-war until the end of the war.[7] As a great sportsman, he never missed an opportunity of getting ashore with a gun or astride a horse. The city was flooded with White Russian émigrés, mostly from the Crimea, and many of noble birth, who had settled down to earn their living as best they could. They had opened several restaurants such as the *Rose Noire* and the *Muscovite,* where one could dine extremely well and enjoy a good display of Russian dancing.

There was a large dance hall called the *Petitchamps* which employed a number of Russian girls as dancing partners and many of these supplemented their incomes from tribute paid by the votaries of Venus. With the presence of such a large international force in and around the city, these establishments flourished, but after the withdrawal they must have fallen on hard times. Tiring of borsch and piroshki, the traditional Russian buns stuffed with a variety of fillings, I went in search of different fare and discovered a little restaurant where, for a modest sum, one could enjoy a bowl of black caviar with crisp French bread and butter, which went extremely well with a glass of black Munich beer. If one wished for something sweet, with which to finish, one could enjoy a succulent *mille feuille* over which honey was poured.

The main form of transport in the city was by means of two-horse *droshkies*; the drivers carried long and savage looking coach whips which they cracked with a loud report when plying for a fare or as a warning on their approach to a blind corner. One evening at about 7pm I was returning to the ship along the road which skirts the waterfront in the vicinity of the Dolmabahçe Mosque, when I heard one of these *droshkies* approaching. As it came in sight, I was surprised to see a French sailor running along the pavement beside it. The street was badly lit but, as the man came closer, I could see that the driver was cutting at him with the long heavy lash of his whip and that the sailor was doing his best to shield his head with his arms as he ran. I yelled to the driver to stop and, as soon as he saw me, he wheeled his horses around and set off at a gallop in the direction from whence he had come. The sailor almost fell into my arms and I saw that he had a terrible cut across the face which fortunately had missed his eye by a fraction. We were not far from the landing stage where my boat was waiting, so I took him on board and our doctor soon stitched up his wound. The Frenchman explained to me that the trouble had begun when he refused to pay the fare demanded by the driver which he had considered excessive.

There was much to see and do in this fascinating, cosmopolitan city. I found the exterior of the famous mosque of San Sofia disappointing, but the magnificence of the marbles and patterns of the mosaics inside and out exceeded anything I could possibly have imagined. In contemplating such splendour, I am always lost in admiration for the designers and craftsmen whose minds and whose skill could produce such a wonderful result. In the bazaar across the Galata bridge in the old city of Stambul, carpets, embroidery, swords, daggers, jewellery and oriental perfumes like musk and attar of roses could all be bought. In the sweetmeat shops the famous *rahat lokum*, or Turkish delight, could be purchased in a variety of flavours and of a quality far surpassing that generally found in Britain and it provided very acceptable presents for friends and relations at home. Interest was added to our shopping expeditions by the abdication of the Sultan, Mehmed VI, which had taken place in November. As a result a number of choice items from his palace found their way into the bazaar. A friend of mine secured a beautiful set of crystal and silver ice cream or sherbert bowls for what would nowadays be considered a mere song and which came from the royal household.[8]

We spent the next nine months in Turkish waters with intermittent breaks in Malta. In early January 1923 we were at Mudros (Moudros) in the northern Aegean, before moving again to the Dardanelles.

During periods of leave and while the terms of the Treaty of Lausanne were being hammered out, we shot red-legged partridges on the Gallipoli Peninsula as well as pheasants and pigeons. The treaty's signature on

24 July 1923 signalled international recognition of the newly formed Republic of Turkey (officially proclaimed on 29 October) in succession to the old Ottoman Empire, whereby Turkey recovered sovereignty over its territory and all foreign zones of influence established after the war were abolished. No reparations were to be exacted. By now HMS *Montrose* had risen to the status of a flotilla leader. In the summer I spent some time making a sextant survey of Gallipoli with the assistance of a friend, another navigating officer, Frank Slocum, our objective being to correct some of the more prominent errors on the chart.[9] The *Montrose* also took a turn of duty as guardship of the *Goeben* (renamed *Yavuz*) which was anchored in the Sea of Marmara. The ship, which had eluded our pursuit in 1914, was now a sorry sight. She had a large hole aft where she had struck a mine returning from one of her infrequent sorties after coming under Turkish control and so guarding her was a merely formality.

By the beginning of October the last of the Allied troops were embarked and the allied occupation of Constantinople came to an end. We formed an arch of searchlights for General Harington as the trooper in which he was embarked passed through the fleet. We then set course for Malta. There were great rejoicings among the Maltese as the Grand Harbour once more filled with ships and long lines of destroyers took up their moorings. Soon the dances and parties, for which the winter season on the island is famous, were in full swing. Many wives who had remained in England came out to join their husbands and life resumed the same pattern as that which I had known when serving in the *Indomitable* before the war.

After exercising with the Home Fleet off the Balearic Islands, on 19 March 1924 I was relieved and returned to the Navigation School at Portsmouth to undergo the course and examination which would qualify me to navigate First Class Ships; in his report of my service Captain Bingham described me as 'conscientious, painstaking and careful to a degree' and that I was 'a most reliable Navigator'.[10]

HMS Montrose *remained with the Mediterranean Fleet until 1929; her service during the Second World War included assisting with the evacuation of troops from Dunkirk and acting as an escort for the Arctic convoys. She was sold for scrap in 1946.*

Chapter Six

Of Languages

Yet He that is but able to express
No Sense at all in Severall Languages
Will pass for learneder then Hee that's known
To Speake the Strongest reason in but one.[1]

1924–26

On 4 July 1924 I passed my examination in navigation and pilotage for First Class Ships. I then spent a year on the junior staff of the Navigation School, taking successive classes of sub lieutenants through their pilotage courses. One of my pupils was His Royal Highness Prince George, the Duke of Kent, the king's fourth son, who, like his older brothers, Edward and Albert, had joined the Royal Navy, following in their footsteps at Osborne and Dartmouth. He had a most engaging and attractive personality and his untimely death, aged 39, in an air crash in August 1942 during the Second World War must have been a great blow to the royal family; he was certainly a great loss to the nation.

Towards the end of my year at the Navigation School, having been promoted lieutenant commander on 15 June 1925, I applied for permission to go abroad to study for the Interpretership examinations. I was fortunate in having been brought up to speak French at an early age, my parents travelling frequently to the Continent, and during my time on the staff I learnt enough Italian to pass the preliminary tests in both languages. The time allowed for the study of each language was four months but the dates for the exams were fixed by the Civil Service Commissioners and, when approval for my application came through, I found that I should have to fit my studies into six months, spending only three months in France and three months in Italy.

Paris

My instructress in French was Madame Callède, who had been recommended by the Admiralty, having had a large number of successes to her credit. Normally resident in Paris, she had a cottage at Saint-Aubin-sur-Mer, between Dieppe and Fécamp on the Normandy coast, where she spent the summer. Since she would be there for the first month of my stay she kindly engaged me a room in a small nearby pension. In early August 1925 I crossed to Dieppe where I was met by an elderly man called Verdot with a motor car looking as old as himself. He took my two suitcases, fastened the handles together with a piece of string from his pocket and slung them across the bonnet, since the car had no luggage rack. After embarking a couple more passengers we set off. I discovered that this was the only taxi at Saint-Aubin on which everyone was dependent for communication with the outside world! We reached our destination safely with my suitcases warm and dusty but otherwise intact.

The pension was a modest wooden house on the main road leading through the village to the beach. It knew neither bathroom nor indoor sanitation and the floorboards of the upper storey served as the ceiling for the downstairs rooms so that every word uttered upstairs could be plainly heard by anyone sitting below. This would not have mattered too much had a young French couple with a tiny baby not taken up residence soon after I arrived. She was an attractive young woman with dark hair fastened into a bun and a complexion of peaches and cream. Her husband worked in a bank in Paris and came down for the weekends. The baby was well-behaved and interfered little with my studies but, at midday on Saturday, the moment 'Papa' entered the house peace was at an end. He embraced his wife, kissed the baby, greeted the proprietress, saluted me and kept up a running stream of conversation about his journey, the weather and anything that came into his head. Then, like a hound at bay, he would pause for an instant and sniff the air, trying to catch a whiff from the kitchen. Having done so he would continue in full cry: *Que cela sent bon! Ah, que j'ai faim! On fait bien la cuisine ici, n'est-ce pas?* and then to his wife: *As-tu allaité le petit chéri?* A faint blush suffused the young woman's cheeks as she nodded in answer to such a very personal question. Then the proprietress would appear with a tureen of steaming soup and we would sit down to lunch. Tucking his napkin into the top of his waistcoat, the banker monopolised the conversation throughout the meal, after which he retired to his room to change his clothes and I betook myself with my books to the garden.

Staying in the village was a retired British naval officer, Admiral Philip Dumas. He was, I believe, descended from the famous French novelist, Alexandre Dumas, and one of his close relations was an admiral in the French Navy. The French side of the family with whom the admiral and his wife were staying were all of the Protestant faith and there were so many of them that on Sundays they held their own service in the drawing room of a big house belonging to one of the families. The admiral asked me if I would like to attend this service and I gladly accepted the invitation. The pastor, who took the service, was a Dumas and his sermons were of a most personal nature. Beginning with the children who occupied the first three rows, he mentioned by name all those who, during the week, had been guilty of some transgression. He then moved on to the adults, to whom he handed out similar treatment. At first it was strange to hear the familiar prayers and hymns in a foreign tongue but I soon got used to it and I was agreeably surprised to discover how well the beautiful prose of our English Bible sounded when rendered into French.[2]

Madame Callède was a formidable lady of some forty-five to fifty summers, but she was an excellent tutor and her daughter, Simone, had given her the nickname *L'Amiral* on account of her prodigious knowledge of nautical terms. She could describe the mechanism of a gun turret as well as any gunnery officer and she had collaborated in the publication of a dictionary of naval terms in French and English. Simone had been assigned the task of giving the students dictation. She was engaged to be married to a young man of her parents' choosing and who worked in Paris, a fact which madame made a point of announcing to all new arrivals. There were several other naval officers besides myself studying French under her guidance, but we were purposely scattered over the countryside and so rarely met, which was just as madame wished. One Saturday evening, on the strict understanding that only French would be spoken, she allowed me to invite one of my brother officers to dinner at the pension where I was staying and I asked if Simone could come along as well. On being informed of her guests, the proprietress said she would prepare something special for the occasion and so it was in anticipation of a good dinner that we all foregathered in the sitting room.

The banker was in great form and insisted on replacing the *vin ordinaire* with a wine of greater distinction. He also produced a bottle of Calvados, a powerful liqueur of local origin. The evening appeared to be a great success. The *plat special* turned out to be a timbale of fish of various kinds over which a delicious cheese and tomato sauce had been poured. It tasted very rich and so I only had a small portion, but all the others enjoyed a second helping. The following morning I received a note from Madame Callède informing me that Simone was seriously ill and asking what we had had for dinner. When I learnt from the proprietress that the timbale contained oysters, mussels, crab and lobster besides a variety of white fish, I understood why all the guests (except myself) had been affected in some way, Simone being the worst. I felt wretched at having been the indirect cause of such a misfortune. A few days later Madame Callède announced that she would hasten her return to Paris so that Simone could have the attentions of the family doctor.

I joined them in Paris soon afterwards. With madame's help I found lodgings on the left bank with the widow of a French army doctor who had died as a result of gas poisoning received during the First World War, leaving her with a teenage son and daughter to educate. Her mother, who was proud of her Corsican lineage, lived with her. They were a charming and happy family and I shall always remember the two months I spent in their *apartement* in the Rue Rosa Bonheur in Paris's *15ième arrondissement* near the Boulevard Garibaldi and the Place de Breteuil. It was through them that I learned to know and love the enchanting city of Paris.

As I soon discovered, they were very poor and only ate meat twice a week. This caused me some embarrassment because every evening I would find a piece of steak in front of me, while the rest of the family sat down to soup or potato soufflé and cheese. My protests at such disparity were ignored. 'The English always eat meat, for us it is different,' said my hostess. One day I had gone into the kitchen for a glass of water and caught sight of her mother near the larder. When I saw her at the cupboard I turned back. She bade me return. '*Tiens*,' she said, holding up a small piece of gruyère cheese and a biscuit, 'when one is old one needs to eat little and often.' I smiled. '*Pas un mot*,' she went on, putting her finger to her lips. '*Bien sûr,*' I answered. One day she told me the amount of her daughter's pension – I forget the exact figure – but it was very small. 'That is why we are obliged to let a room,' she said. 'But we would not let to anybody. After all one has one's pride. But you are a fighting man. I salute you.' There our conversation ended, the spirit of Napoleon shining through her dark brown eyes.

Florence

After returning to London to sit my examination in October, I set out for Florence which I had decided to make my headquarters for my three months' Italian study. I took up residence in a small pension at 14 Piazza Indipendenza, north of Florence's historic buildings, which was excellently run by an Italian signorina of great charm. There were several other English and American guests staying there and so it was virtually impossible to adhere to the rule of not speaking my own language which I had tried to follow in France. I arranged to take lessons from a *Nobile Professore* who normally earned his living by giving lessons to the children of distinguished Florentine families. He did not speak a word of English so at first communication was difficult. Moreover, he knew nothing about naval terms and so, had I not been fortunate enough to meet an English lady, the sister of a British admiral whose daughter had married an Italian naval officer who was a member of a very old Florentine family, I should have been in a fix! I shall always be most grateful to this officer for his help, as without him I could never have passed my exams.

My professor was a small man with fair hair and the well-modelled features of a Tuscan. He lived in lodgings near the Ponte Vecchio and I arranged to have my lessons at 8.30am in order not to interfere with his other commitments. When I first arrived the weather was warm and pleasant but at the beginning of November it turned cold and my daily lesson became a matter of physical endurance since my professor could not afford a fire in his room and we were obliged to sit huddled up in our overcoats. Sometimes my hands were so cold I could hardly write my notes. But that was a small price to pay to find myself living in a city with such a wealth of art and history. I devoted part of each day to visits to the galleries, churches and places of historic interest. The more I saw and learnt, the more astonished I became at the fertility of mind and the industry of those painters, sculptors and architects who have left to posterity such a priceless heritage.

The signorina at whose pension I was staying was frequently visited by a courtly old gentleman, a former postmaster general of the city. He had retired with the title of *Commendatore* and, although he had been widowed some years previously, he still dressed completely in black even to his gloves. He sometimes arrived just as we were about to sit down to lunch. Standing at the head of the table beside the signorina's chair, he would wish us all *buon appetito* but could never be persuaded to stay and have lunch with us. He had a fund of risqué stories which he told with delightful unconcern, much to the signorina's embarrassment, especially when some of the young American girls were present. Happily, their Italian vocabulary was not equal to the *Commendatore*'s wit.

One day the signorina invited us all to meet her in the drawing room at noon. When we saw Brunetta, the maid, carrying in a tray full of glasses we knew something unusual was afoot. Soon the *Commendatore* appeared, wearing a white carnation in the button hole of his black suit. In a short but witty speech, he announced that the signorina had consented to marry him. It was a touching scene for we had become fond of both of them and we drank their health and wished them many years of happiness together. The *Commendatore* beamed and, by way of saying thank you, told us one of his famous stories.

We were a strangely assorted but extremely companionable party in the pension over Christmas 1925. In addition to two young American girls and their mother, there was a young British Army officer and an English school teacher. These two set out one day to visit the town of San Gimignano in Tuscany, famous for its walls and ancient towers. Due to some misunderstanding they missed the last bus and had to spend the night there, thus providing excellent food for the *Commendatore*'s romantic mind. It took a long time for them to live down their adventure.

There was a very respectable dance hall in Florence called Raiolla's, where for 1s 6d one could spend the evening dancing with the company of one's choice and, if so disposed, drinking asti spumante at 3s 6d a bottle. On occasion I used to go there with some American friends. The party often included a Life Guards officer from Sweden who was studying music and one or two scions of aristocratic Florentine families. We generally went on afterwards to one of the many *bucas* or restaurants where we devoured huge plates of spaghetti while listening to music played by a party of itinerant musicians who were prepared to carry on singing all night if anyone would pay them. A favourite forenoon rendezvous was a café called Donni's in the Via de' Tornabuoni, near the Ponte Santa Trinita, where most delicious hot cheese biscuits were served with the aperitif. And there was always the opera of which music-loving people never tire.

It was a sad day when the time came for me to return to London to take my examination. To have had the privilege twice daily for three months of being able to pause and admire Benvenuto Cellini's 'Perseus with the head of Medusa' in the Loggia dei Lanzi, the bronze doors of the Baptistry and the intricate work of Giotto's famous Campanile on my way to and from my lessons was something not to be relinquished without regret. It was a chapter of my life which I could never forget and on which it has been a pleasure to reflect throughout the years which have since passed.

Chapter Seven

East of Suez in the *Enterprise*

Ship me somewhere East of Suez, where the best is like the worst.[1]

1926–28

In January 1926 I received an appointment as navigating officer and acting interpreter in French of a new light cruiser, the 7,100-ton HMS *Enterprise*, then completing at Devonport. I have called her a new cruiser because, although she had been laid down in 1918, she had only just been commissioned eight years later. Instead of the two single 6-inch gun mountings forward, for which she had been designed, a 6-inch twin mounting, a prototype of that to be fitted in the new Nelson-class battleships *Nelson* and *Rodney*, had been installed. In consequence, before proceeding to the East Indies Station, for which we were destined, we were ordered to carry out extensive gunnery trials in Scottish waters. We reached Invergordon at the end of April and were getting on well with our programme until the General Strike started on 3 May and we were ordered to Hull to guard the docks. The inhabitants were surprised at seeing a long, white ship with yellow funnels steaming up the Humber and they had every reason to be because HM ships in tropical guise are not often seen in home waters.

Soon after our arrival, parties of undergraduates from both Oxford and Cambridge began to appear to tackle the job of unloading some of the ships. Our chaplain, the Reverend Harry Goulding BA, was recently down from Oxford and knew some of the men; when someone suggested that it would be rather fun to stage an Oxford and Cambridge boat race in the King George V dock, they readily agreed to organise it. It was proposed that the race should be rowed in the ship's two whalers and, as we assured the two crews that there was very little to choose between them, they left it to us to make the allocation.

On the appointed day at 11.30am the dockside was thronged by the ship's company and a crowd of undergraduates from both universities out to see the fun. We were interested to see what sort of a show these freshwater boatmen would put up in our heavy service boats. As soon as the order 'Get ready' was given by the starter, both crews leaned forward, poised ready for the strike. Bang! went the gun. The Cambridge boat shot ahead and the crew settled down to a steady pull, but there was something seriously the matter with Oxford. Despite the herculean efforts of the crew, the boat moved in fits and starts as if it were being propelled through a sea of treacle. When Cambridge reached the finishing line, Oxford were only halfway down the course. 'There you are, Padre! I told you Oxford were no good,' said a red-faced lieutenant grinning at the disconsolate priest. 'There's been some skulduggery somewhere,' replied the chaplain; and he was right. Since joining the ship, the padre had talked a great deal about Oxford, so much so that certain members of the mess saw in the proposed race a heaven-sent opportunity of getting their own back. To the keel of the Oxford boat a washdeck bucket had been so lashed as to form a drogue, which could not be seen when the boat was in the water. It took quite of lot of beer to soothe the ruffled feelings of the Oxford crew!

East Indies Station

By the time we had completed our delayed gun trials and had some leave, it was mid-August before we left home waters. We had both a change of captain and chaplain: Captain Herbert Fitzherbert was relieved by Captain Stephen St Leger Moore while the Reverend Goulding's successor was the Reverend Harold Stephens. Our responsibilities in the East Indies Squadron extended from the Red Sea to the Persian Gulf and across the Indian Ocean south to Ceylon (Sri Lanka).[2] After an uneventful passage, stopping at Aden and Bombay (Mumbai), we reached Colombo on 17 September, moving onwards to Trincomalee (or 'Trinco' as the base was affectionately called) in early October. Our first cruise began in November when we sailed for Karachi, a port we came to know well.

With the first wave of callers to the ship came a one-armed colonel who, we learnt, was a very fine game shot despite his disability. After the usual courtesies he casually remarked that if any of us cared for some good duck shooting he knew where we could get it. What was more, he was willing to make all the arrangements. As the gunner's store was almost bursting at the seams with the number of boxes of sporting cartridges it contained, and which belonged to various members of the mess, his offer was accepted with the alacrity of a bookmaker's clerk accepting a bet ten seconds before the 'off'. 'I shan't be able to come myself,' the colonel continued 'but my *shikari* [hunter], Khandu, will take good care of you. By the way, do any of you speak Hindustani?' We shook our heads. 'Pity,' he murmured, 'because Khandu doesn't speak a word of English and of course none of the beaters do – anyhow the boys at the station rest house where you'll be staying, can interpret for you.'

Two days later, in company with three of my brother officers, I boarded the Lahore night mail for the 60-mile journey to the little village of Jungshahi on the edge of the Sindh desert which was to be our headquarters for the shoot. We were met by a white-coated red-turbaned young boy who conducted us to our rooms in the upper storey of the station buildings. Khandu was waiting to meet the sahibs entrusted to his care in the lounge. A lean, wiry-looking man with dark piercing eyes shining out of a face of polished mahogany, he looked every inch a hunter. With the young boy interpreting, a zero hour of 4.30am was fixed for the start of the day's shooting. As we had dined on the train we wasted no time in turning in so as to be ready for our pre-dawn rendezvous with the duck.

In what seemed like the middle of the night we were called and breakfasted by the rest-house staff and sallied forth into the cold air to find a strange conglomeration of figures standing like ghosts awaiting us. Crouched on the ground were a number of camels and Khandu, with business-like efficiency, assisted each of us in turn to mount. I was the last to do so and, although I had ridden around the pyramids on one of these ungainly creatures, I was ill-prepared for the sudden manner in which it rose to its feet and had it not been for Khandu who leapt on behind me, I feel sure I should have come off. After an hour's endurance of this uncomfortable mode of travel we reached the *jheels* or ponds frequented by the duck and the *shikari* busied himself posting us in favourable positions.

The first flight of birds was soon on the wing and although in numbers less than there had been in the swamps of Trinidad, it was capital sport. All too soon, it seemed the sun came up over the rim of the horizon in a great ball of orange and gold, causing us to discard the thick sweaters we were wearing. As we could not converse with Khandu we had to follow blindly the directions he gave us. It was now the turn of the painted sand grouse which come down to quench their thirst at the water vacated by the duck. They gave us some difficult shots and by the time we had finished with them we were getting rather thirsty ourselves. But Khandu was inexhaustible. The camels re-appeared and he indicated us to mount, and we set off again into the unknown. While we were going along a big bustard took the air and after an exciting chase he was brought down. At last we reached the spot where Khandu was aiming and he came out with what was probably his only word of English 'snipe'. But by this time we were too exhausted to continue the chase without a stand-easy and replied with one of the few Hindustani words we knew: 'tiffin'. After a welcome bottle of beer and the adequate lunch which the rest house boys had packed for us, we went off again and succeeded in bagging quite a few of these fleet-winged little birds. We returned to the rest house just before dark, tired but well content with the day's sport. The following two days we repeated the performance with equal success. Our total bag was: 54 duck, 115 sandgrouse, 147 snipe, 1 francolin and 1 bustard. An eventful year was to elapse before we once again saw the sunrise over the rim of the Sindh desert and heard the duck calling to one another across the *jheels*.

On leaving Karachi we went to Bombay to carry out combined exercises with some army units and students from Quetta. We were in the middle of an exercise when we suddenly received orders to proceed to Hong Kong and place ourselves under the orders of the commander-in-chief of the China Station, who, since November 1926, was my former Harwich Force Commander, Com (T), now Vice Admiral Sir Reginald Tyrwhitt.

Revolutionary China

The death of Sun Yat-Sen, the first president and founder of the Republic of China, in March 1925 had once again thrown China into turmoil with a power struggle developing among his followers. In March the following year a Nationalist army under the command of Chiang Kai-shek had secured ascendancy over the communists in Canton (Guangzhou). His army then marched northwards, reaching Hangkow (Hankou) – a major centre of foreign trade on the Yangtze River some 600 miles upriver from Shanghai – by the end of November. A great deal of anti-foreign propaganda had prepared the way for the advance of Chiang's army which was now in a position to attack the foreign concessions in Hangkow and possibly Shanghai.[3]

The China Squadron, which consisted of four light cruisers and a few destroyers and submarines, was not large enough to meet all the commitments with which it was now confronted, so both we and our sister ship, HMS *Emerald*, had been ordered to reinforce it. By the time we reached Hong Kong on 18 December 1926, Hangkow had already fallen to Chiang Kai-shek's army, but, much to our surprise we were told we could remain at Hong Kong over Christmas. There was plenty to do and see in this hospitable beehive. The weather was crisp and cold and very enjoyable after the tropics. We played golf at Fanling, football in Happy Valley, climbed the Peak and spent our money in the fascinating Chinese shops.

Four days after Christmas we were ordered to take over guardship duties at Shanghai and on New Year's Day we steamed up the Huangpu River and made fast to the flagship's buoy off the Bund. We learned from the consul general that there was a good deal of anxiety amongst the 50,000 inhabitants of the foreign concessions, some 7,000 of whom were British. The news received two days later, of Chiang Kai-shek's plan for his forces to seize the British concession at Hangkow, increased their concern. No one had any faith in the ability of the opposing General Sun Chuanfang, whose forces had taken up a position astride the Shanghai–Hangkow railway, to defend the city and the force of local volunteers which had been raised was quite inadequate to defend the perimeter of the concessions.[4]

There were one French and two Japanese cruisers in harbour besides ourselves, but of course there was not much we could do except raise morale by our presence. Help, however, was at hand. On 24 January 1927 the Shanghai Defence Force, under the command of Major General John Duncan – who had fought at Gallipoli during the First World War – arrived and troops were disposed for the protection of the foreign concessions. While the arrival of these troops gave great comfort to the concessionaires, it caused the Chinese nationalists, with whom we had been trying to come to some sort of terms, to break off negotiations and for a time the situation looked grave.[5]

Life in the cosmopolitan city of Shanghai with its magnificent, modern buildings, banks, hotels and shops went on much as usual. The barbed wire and machine-gun posts enfilading the street crossings lent a military aspect to the scene but did little to interfere with the night life which ranked amongst the gayest of any city in the east. I played a good deal of golf and managed to get some riding on Mongol ponies hired from a Russian émigré colonel who ran a riding school at the top of the Bubbling Well Road, named after a spring near the Jing'an Temple. They were sure-footed animals which was just as well, as the country over which we rode was interspersed with deep ditches which could only be crossed by bridges one plank in width. At first I used to dismount and lead my pony across, but later on I entrusted myself to its care.

On 19 February 1927 agreement was reached between the representative of the British Government and the Nationalists, (known as the Chen–O'Malley agreement) handing back the British concession in Hangkow to China.[6] This was the signal for dissenting Chinese in the city to try and bring about a general strike. The Chinese military authorities, however, rounded up some of the ringleaders and executed them. The heads of the victims were then suspended in bamboo cages at the street corners as a warning to others, in accordance with the usual Chinese practice. Shortly after this, Chuanfang withdrew his army into the city and I shall never forget the sight of his troops, many of whom were mere lads, disembarking from sampans and junks in the Soochow creek. Their uniforms were notable for their lack of uniformity. A few staggered beneath the weight of a rifle of Boer War vintage and for the rest they appeared to be armed with spears or bamboo poles supplemented in many cases by umbrellas. There was nothing now to stop the advance of Chiang Kai-Shek's troops. In late March they entered Shanghai. But unlike Nanking, where there was considerable trouble, initially the presence of the Shanghai Defence Force had a sobering effect on the conquerors and the city changed hands practically without bloodshed. Two weeks later a violent purge of communists was carried out, which ushered in a decade of civil war.

HMS *Enterprise*, meanwhile, had moved down river and anchored so that we could cover the forts at Woosung (Wusong) in case these tried to interfere with British ships leaving Shanghai. Having received orders to leave for Hong Kong and Singapore, we sailed southward and entered the harbour of Colombo on 4 April. Contrary to expectations, our stay was brief. HMS *Yarmouth*, an old cruiser carrying reliefs out to the China Station, had broken down between Aden and Colombo. She had managed to make the latter port on one engine but was unable to go further until repairs had been carried out. We were therefore told to embark her passengers and return with them to Hong Kong and Shanghai. We sailed three days later on this 6,000 mile run!

By the time we reached Hong Kong on 17 April the good weather, which is characteristic of the north-east monsoon on the China coast and which had favoured us on our previous trip, was beginning to break up. The cold air had been replaced by a hot, steamy dampness which brought with it what, in pre-radar days, was the navigator's greatest menace – fog. When we left Hong Kong two days later we literally had to grope our way out through the narrow Lei Yue Mun, the main channel into the harbour, and I just caught a glimpse of Tathong lighthouse at its seaward end before the fog shut down around us like pea-soup. Dante's verses in *Il Purgatorio* might well have been written to describe our present circumstances:

> *Hell's dunnest gloom or night unlustrous, dark,*
> *Of every planet 'reft, and pall'd in clouds,*
> *Did never spread before the sight a veil*
> *In thickness like that fog.*[7]

Our course up through the Formosa Strait to Shanghai was clear of navigational hazards so Captain Moore decided to carry on at a speed of eight knots. Presently we heard the sound of a siren on the starboard bow, so we stopped and navigated with caution. Then the mournful notes of two or three other sirens could be faintly heard. We knew that the 1st Cruiser Squadron, on loan from the Home Fleet, had been out exercising but we were not aware of its position nor course. Soon the presence of four ships was confirmed as we heard them sounding their fleet numbers.

We kept just enough way on to give us steerage whilst all of us on the bridge peered through the grey swirling fog trying to catch a glimpse of ships whose siren notes were getting louder and louder. They appeared to be crossing ahead but sound in a fog is notoriously deceptive. Suddenly the lookout stationed in the eyes of the ship reported: 'Ship on the port bow, sir.' All eyes turned in that direction. Dimly we caught sight of the stern of a cruiser which was disappearing into the mist. But was it the last ship? That thought flashed through the captain's mind as it did through mine. The wail of a siren then came moaning through the fog and this time it appeared to be coming from the starboard beam. It was a perilous position. 'Full speed ahead,' ordered the captain. The ship shook as she gathered way, then faintly, like a phantom, we caught sight of the outline of a cruiser passing under our stern. It was a close shave. We had passed between two cruisers in line ahead! All that night and all the next day the fog persisted. The hundreds of junks scattered over the China Sea and the Chinese belief, that the closer a sailor can cut across the bows of a man of war, the greater will be the number of devils prevented from following him, make navigation of those waters tricky even in clear weather, but in that fog it was a nightmare.

We were approaching a group of islands known as the Side Saddle Islands, which lie some 60 miles south-east of the entrance to the Yangtze River and Shanghai. The tidal streams amongst these islands are notoriously strong and the channel through them, though deep, is narrow and rocky, making it out of the question to try to pass through it in the prevailing visibility. It was just after midnight and we had groped our way through a fleet of junks when I heard, faintly at first, a strange noise coming from somewhere ahead. As it grew louder it took on the sound of an express train rushing towards us. I had never heard anything like it at sea before. Then suddenly it struck us that it was a mighty wind of gale force. In literally the twinkling of an eye, the visibility changed from perhaps half a mile to extreme. Lights bobbed up all along the horizon and in no time at all I had the ship's position accurately fixed and we were able to increase speed to 20 knots. It was the most dramatic meteorological phenomenon I have ever encountered.

Outwardly we found Shanghai little changed from our last visit. The longest bar in the world in the Shanghai Club was still well patronised, but the turning point in the city's greatness had been reached. From then onwards the fortunes of the western traders began to decline, culminating in their final expulsion by the communist regime of Mao Tse-tung in 1950.

We encountered a good deal of fog on the return journey to Hong Kong but nothing like that we had met with on the way north to Shanghai. After stopping at Singapore, we were back in Colombo on 11 May 1927 and were recompensed by a long spell (three months!) in the up country naval camp at Diyatalawa in Ceylon's central highlands. In late August, our leave over, we spent a week in Trincomalee, before weighing anchor and making for Bombay and Karachi.

The Persian Gulf

With the exception of a return visit to Karachi in October, we spent the next few months in late 1927 mainly cruising in the Persian Gulf. This was an interesting experience, for it was a part of the world in which time has virtually stood still. To the north was the vast land of Persia, with its seaports of Bushire and Bandar Abbas on the Strait of Hormuz. In the north-west corner of the Gulf was the Sheikhdom of Kuwait, which had been a British protectorate since 1899. Along the southern coastline, known as 'the trucial coast' were autonomous sheikhdoms, of which Abu Dhabi (meaning 'father of the gazelle') and Dubai were important staging posts for British ships. In the previous century Great Britain had formed truces with these sheikhdoms to protect the trade routes to India from attacks by pirates, which had given the coast its name.

The first port we visited was Sohar where the local sheikh entertained the officers to tea. We then steamed up the Gulf of Oman to Dhibar (Dibba) at the head of a large bay; although we were anchored three miles inland, we still had eight fathoms of water under the keel. When we moored in the tiny harbour of Muscat, it was such a tight fit that we had to tow the ship's stern around with our motor boat to keep it clear of the rocks when unmooring. During one of our visits we ran into a *shamal*, that hot sand-laden wind which is worse than a fog. It covers the ship with a fine powdering of dust which gets into every nook and cranny and chokes the fan inlets. But all this was as nothing compared with the receptions accorded to us by the local sheikhs on whom we called. After the usual exchange of courtesies, the shekih would invite the captain and some of the officers to dine with him. Sometimes we would walk to his palace, at others we would be sent camels or ponies. When we visited Sur, about sixty miles south of Muscat, a troop of horsemen dashed out when we least expected from behind some rocks and fired their rifles in the air in a friendly but frightening gesture of welcome.

The palaces or forts in which the sheikhs lived and which we visited, though built of mud, were comfortably furnished with modern sofas and cushions and equipped with electric light, gramophones and sewing machines. The dinner was generally served on the flat roof which was covered with carpets on which we were bidden to squat. I shall never forget the first of these repasts. A large mountain of rice was brought in on top of which reposed a whole roast sheep or kid. Several small dishes, containing delicacies and piles of Arab pancakes, were dotted around. We were then bidden to fall to. If you are unaccustomed to eating with your hands it requires almost as much courage to begin as it does to get under a cold shower. We all held back and watched our host deftly seize a handful of rice, roll it into a ball and pop it into his mouth. Some of the attendants, noting our timidity, leaned over and, tearing pieces of meat off the carcass with their hands, handed them to us to eat. Captain Moore fared a little better as, sitting on the right of the sheikh, he was plied with titbits which his host selected from some of the small side dishes, but the signal honour of the sheep's eye was one I did not envy him! We made little impression on the mass of food, but it was never wasted; the moment we had finished, the sheikh's entourage set to and polished off the lot. I am afraid I never learnt to appreciate Arab food as did the narrator that of Mahbub Ali in Kipling's *The Ballad of The King's Jest*.

> *So we plunged the hand to the mid-wrist deep*
> *In a cinnamon stew of the fat-tailed sheep*
> *And he who hath never tasted the food*
> *By Allah! he knoweth not bad from good.*[8]

A thrilling sight while anchored off Bushire (Bushehr), Persia's main seaport on its south-western coast, was witnessing the arrival on 12 November of the Far East Flight of Southampton flying boats, which had come from Plymouth and were en route to Singapore via Karachi (later flying on to Australia and Hong Kong). The following day we sailed for the island of Henjam, which was the flight's next landing. At the time of which I am writing Henjam, in the southern part of the Gulf, was leased from the Persian government and used as a fuelling and stores base by the British squadron of sloops which patrolled these waters. It is a small, rather desolate island containing one village of about 200 inhabitants at that time ruled by Sheikh Ahmed Obaid bin Juma, whose residence was at the opposite end of the island.[9]

Our next port of call was Basra. We were the longest ship (at 570ft) to make the eighty-mile passage up the Shatt al-Arab River, which we accomplished without a pilot. Although turning in the river off Basra presented something of a problem as the duration of slack water is very short, we managed it successfully thanks to having plenty of reserve power. We found the town of Basra to be a mixture of decaying east and utilitarian west and which still bore traces of the Mesopotamian campaign of the First World War. Through the kindness of one of the local residents I was able to visit the walled-in town of Zubair (Zubayr) about eight miles out in the desert. Here one stepped back to the time of Haroun al-Rashid, the fifth Abbasid Caliph who lived in the eighth century AD, and one encountered the real Bedouin who plugs his nostrils to keep out the smell of the defiling townsmen.

Coppersmiths, silversmiths, cobblers, bakers and confectioners plied their crafts and trades in ways that can have changed little with the centuries. We purchased bright coloured hand-woven rugs made by the Bedouin which were on sale in the bazaar and took our time over the bargaining, as is the custom, drinking innumerable cups of strong, black coffee. I dined with a man who supervised a date farm outside Basra and we sat in a kind of meat-safe he had built on his verandah whilst myriads of insects of every size, sort and description buzzed outside. Each guest was supplied with a spray gun to deal with those which managed to enter when a servant brought in the food. His wife, who was English and who I discovered had been at school with my younger sister, told me that it took her a long time to get used to the life there and I could well believe it. Flies would seem to be the curse of Arabia. They swarm over the food displayed in the open market and are responsible for many of the diseases from which the Arabs suffer.

Our first visit to Abadan, renowned for its abundance of oil, lying twenty miles down river from Basra, coincided with the celebration of St Andrew's Day on 30 November. Since a large number of the employees of the Anglo-Persian Oil Company (the future BP) were exiles from their native Scotland, the festivities went on into the 'wee sma' hours. On our subsequent visits, mindful of the hospitable instincts of our hosts, we chose a time when there would be no additional incentive for celebration! From Abadan we returned homewards, reaching Karachi on 9 December, Trincomalee on the 18th and finally Calcutta.

Christmas in Calcutta

To spend Christmas at Calcutta was the ambition of every ship on the East Indies Station. Due to the troubles in China we had not been able to do so in 1926. We were therefore delighted when the Admiral, Sir Bertram Thesiger, in command of the East Indies Station since 1927, detailed us to accompany his flagship there for our second Christmas.[10] After three months in the Persian Gulf and the long voyage around India, stopping again at Karachi, Colombo and Trincomalee, the impact with civilisation seemed all the greater. In order to reach the great city of Calcutta, ships have to pass a certain distance up the Hooghly River, which has several awkward bends and where two ships cannot pass safely. The sand banks are continually shifting so that only someone with up to the minute knowledge knows where the channel lies. In making the journey, I was very glad to have the assistance of an expert Hooghly pilot whose training in understanding the river would have taken many years. By the time we reached our moorings off Prinsep Ghat it was getting dark and our first impression of the second city of India was that of a blaze of lights.

Add to this an overwhelming hospitality and there were all the ingredients for an unforgettable visit. We were made honorary members of the stately Bengal Club and the sprightly Saturday Club. We dined at Firpo's restaurant – established by an Italian, Angelo Firpo, after the First World War – and played golf at the Tollygunge Club. His Excellency the Governor of Bengal, the Right Honourable Sir Stanley – a renowned cricketer – and Lady Jackson gave a state ball at Government House. I am glad I witnessed the pageantry displayed on such occasions. Once the glittering assembly of guests had collected around the sides of the ballroom, the doors at the far end were opened and their Excellencies entered in stately procession, followed by a selected number of high-ranking guests. When all were in position, the band began to play and no one else was allowed to take the floor. It was a most dignified and pleasing spectacle against a background of brilliant uniforms and lovely dresses.[11]

Another event was the governor's arrival – with his bodyguard of Lancers – at the Calcutta Turf Club on Viceroy's Cup day. The great mass of Indians in robes of every hue and colour formed a bright kaleidoscopic background for this simple but dignified ceremony on which the sun shone out of a cloudless sky. For a few days I was fortunate in being the guest of Mr and Mrs Burns of the Calcutta Port Commission (the Kolkata Port Trust). For the first (and last) time in my life I knew what it was to be waited on literally hand and foot. I was not even allowed to dress myself; when I emerged from the bath, there stood a bearer ready to hand me each garment, to fasten my braces, put on my socks and shoes and fill my cigarette case. The diligence of the servants and the kindness of my hosts was something I shall never forget.

On 11 January 1928 we left Calcutta, our departure requiring us to back down river before we could turn the ship. We made our progress across the Indian Ocean by first going to Akyab, capital of Arakan district on the Burmese coast. During our stay, the Akyab Club arranged for the performance of a Burmese historic play, known as *Anyan-Pwe,* which lasts all night, both audience and actors periodically going away to refresh themselves. From Akyab we returned across the Indian Ocean to Madras. In order to check our position, I had counted on sighting the powerful light from the big lighthouse which stands at the back of the harbour. When it did not show up I thought that some strange and unpredictable current had swept us off our course, but when daylight came there was the lighthouse very nearly on the bearing on which I was expecting to see it. I discovered on calling on the harbour master that, for the first time in ten years, the mechanism of the light had failed!

As the site of the first British fortified settlement in India, Madras had much to interest me. Besides Fort St George, the construction of which was completed in 1644, there was St Mary's, the oldest Anglican church in India, which was designed by a master gunner and opened in 1680. Robert Clive was married in this church and something of the spirit of the man who fought to establish British supremacy in India still lingered there. In the present day we were convincingly reminded of the difficulties which faced the government by the proclamation of a *hartal* or general strike, which coincided with our arrival, but which was called as a protest to the landing of the Simon Commission sent from London to study the constitutional question. In a country such as India, composed of a heterogeneous mass of nations with different faiths, languages and customs, and containing religious, social and racial minorities, I doubt if any other nation in the world would have gone to such lengths to attempt to solve the well nigh unsolvable as we did. But that is now past history, the great subcontinent of South Asia gaining its independence in 1947, and I am not qualified to comment on such a vast subject, about which many books have been written. The strike caused a cancellation of some of the entertainments which had been planned in our honour. Two of my messmates had an unpleasant experience when the car in which they were travelling was surrounded and stoned by a seemingly angry mob. Just when things looked their worst, a company of the West Kent Regiment drove up in a truck. The sergeant blew a whistle and the soldiers, armed only with swagger canes, jumped out and threatened the rioters who dispersed as rapidly as chaff before a breeze.

The Governor of the Madras Presidency at the time of our visit was the Rt. Hon. Viscount Goschen, whose father had served as Chancellor of the Exchequer under the Marquess of Salisbury from 1887–1892.[12] One morning one of his ADCs appeared on board to say that a French minister, who did not speak a word of English, was dining at Government House that night and that the governor would be glad if anyone who spoke French would come to dinner. As I was the only French interpreter on board I was glad to comply with the governor's request. The minister, in his mid-forties, was charming and we got on very well. He told me that, on behalf of the French government, he was making a tour of the French possessions in India – which included Pondicherry on the Coromandel coast, Mahé on the Malabar coast and Chandernagore in Bengal (transferred to the Republic of India in 1954). After dinner there was a dance to which some of my brother officers had been invited but the minister said he did not dance and so Lord Goschen suggested that I take him out onto the veranda where there was a cool breeze.

We settled comfortably into cane chairs and the minister, who was a very good conversationalist, fell to discussing a number of interesting topics. An attentive servant kept us well supplied with iced whisky and soda and the time passed pleasantly. At about 11pm the minister looked at his watch and said gravely: *Il faut que je m'en aille*, but when he got to his feet I realised, to my horror, that the whisky had gone to his legs. To reach the main door we had to traverse the length of the ballroom which was flanked on both sides by tall pillars. Supporting him as best I could, we slowly walked down the side of the ballroom from pillar to pillar. I was in fear and trepidation lest the music should stop, since, with the floor cleared, we would have been in full view of the other guests. We managed to gain the main entrance without mishap and, with a tactful ADC supporting him on the other side, the minister made his adieu to the governor in the manner of a beer-laden sailor passing the officer of the watch on his return from a run ashore. It was certainly *un mauvais quart d'heure* as far as I was concerned!

By the beginning of February we were back in Trincomalee. Soon after our arrival the German cruiser, *Berlin*, put in, and gave a 21-gun salute which we returned, our respective captains exchanging visits. The *Berlin* was a pre-war built ship and the German officers made no secret that they were rather ashamed of her age. For most of us, the encounter was our first contact with our late enemies, but any feeling of restraint either of us felt soon dissipated. I was impressed with the fine physique of the eighty cadets which she carried and by the strict discipline with which they were treated. The two wardrooms entertained each other to dinner and the toast on each occasion was 'to our future allies'. Alas we reckoned without the mad house painter and doubtless many of those fine young men were sacrificed on the altar of his insensate ambition.[13] The Germans had an excellent band and during dinner it played a programme of music, which included ten items, the initial letters of which spelt out our ship's name. In the intervals they played stirring fanfares on silver trumpets. It is interesting to note how the national characteristics of both the German and the Japanese each contain opposing elements. The German's love of music contrasts with a sometimes ruthless nature, as does the Japanese love of beauty with the potential for cruelty.

Back to the Gulf

In late March we began our second cruise up the Gulf. Our first port of call was Kuwait. The Sheikh of Kuwait, Ahmad Al-Jaber Al-Sabah, had received news of an impending attack from neighbouring Nejd (part of modern Saudi Arabia) and asked for help. As was evident, in the aftermath of the dismantling of the Ottoman Empire, the emergent nations had their own rivalries. Although, in 1922, the British Government had tried to diffuse tensions between Kuwait and Nejd by imposing the Uqair Protocol, defining (and reducing) Kuwait's borders, it had remained subject to a continuing economic blockade from its more powerful neighbour as well as intermittent raids.[14]

On 2 April we put a landing party ashore and the RAF sent an armoured car unit from Basra. In preparation, it was decided to carry out a dummy run to test the organisation. As it was intended to use live ammunition in the automatic weapons, the sheikh was requested to give instructions to the shepherds, who normally grazed their sheep in the vicinity of the palace walls, to keep well clear between the hours chosen for the exercise. Zero hour was 0530. Just as the deep indigo of the night began to pale, a bugle call rang out. In an instant the stillness was broken by the jangle of harnesses as horsemen leapt into the saddle, the low rumble of the engines of the armoured cars and the shouts of the soldiers as they ran to their stations on the walls. At a given signal the great doors at the entrance to the fort were thrown open and the armoured cars, their machine guns blazing, roared into the desert, closely followed by a company of Arab horsemen who added to the din by a discharge of their rifles. The 2-pounder 'pom-pom' anti-aircraft gun which we had landed from the ship joined the noise, which alone was enough to frighten any would-be attackers. After a few minutes the notes of the 'ceasefire' sounded, but it was several minutes before all firing ceased. Too late, it was discovered that the shepherds had taken no notice of the sheikh's warning and there was mutton for everyone. Happily, no shepherds were included in the bag!

Since oil had not yet been located on the Arabian side of the Gulf, we found Kuwait much as it would have been in Biblical or Quranic times, a busy entrepôt for goods destined for the interior of Arabia and the headquarters of the famous pearl fishing fleet. Famed for its boat building, along the harbour front I saw dhows in all stages of construction; although the tools employed would be described as primitive, the work of these shipbuilders would compare favourably with that of similar craftsmen anywhere in the world. No iron nails were used in the building of these craft, all the planks being pegged with wood. The completed hulls were coated with fish glue which has one of the most nauseating smells I have ever encountered. The big lateen sails with which the dhows are rigged are all handmade and it was interesting to see forty or fifty men squatting on the ground, stitching away with palm and needle at a sail, the roping of which has been stretched to the required shape around pegs driven into the ground.

After a few days the sheikh announced that he no longer feared attack and so we re-embarked our landing party and sailed to Abadan. Due to 'political differences' with the Persian government, we were not permitted a berth and so went up the Shatt-al Arab to Basra where we were greeted by our friends from the previous cruise. Once permission was granted to berth at Abadan we returned downriver. With a temperature of 107 degrees Fahrenheit (41 degrees Celsius), we only stayed for a day. Back at Kuwait a plague of locusts descended upon us, making it impossible to walk about the deck without treading on them. They provided, however, a welcome change of diet for the ship's pet monkey which sat on top of the standard compass, heading and tailing them like prawns.

Our experiences 'up the Gulf', as we called it, were varied. From Kuwait we stopped off at the island of Farur, inhabited by a variety of gazelle, which afforded good sport to those who are minded to chase after these nimble creatures. Only one was bagged. By early May we were back in Henjam. There had never been any trouble between the naval authorities and the sheikh, but on this occasion we had received a message from the British Political Resident in Bushire, to the effect that the Persian government, under the rule of Reza Shah Pahlavi, was accusing the sheikh of having abducted a young lady to whom he had taken a fancy from the Persian mainland. Since this was common practice in this part of the world it would have been a matter of small importance had not the Persian government indicated that they were intending to send a punitive expedition against the sheikh. As we were responsible for maintaining law and order on the island, this raised a delicate problem. Having gone at once to see Sheikh Ahmed, our Arab interpreter reported that he had no intention of returning the 'stolen goods', nor did the lady herself appear to be particularly anxious to return to her native village.

The captain decided that the best way of dissuading the Persians from carrying out their threat was by a show of force, and so, at 6.10am on 10 May a Royal Marine platoon, about eighty strong, was landed on the only available pier. The Persians were embarked in a gunboat, *Pahlava*, while a launch was towing two dhows full of soldiers. We estimated there were about 200 of them all told. As their vessels nosed their way alongside the pier, the Persian officer in command stepped out and climbed up the steps. On reaching the top he was received by the Captain of the Marines and the guard drawn up right across the pier presented arms. The officer eyed with obvious disfavour the machine-gun detachment at the seaward end of the pier covering the steps. On being informed that he would not be allowed to land his men, he turned about muttering something about having to report the matter to his superiors and returned with his troops to Bandar Abbas.

While we were congratulating ourselves on the success of our action, the Persian Ambassador in London was about to sign an agreement with our government concerning the air route to India passing over Persian territory. Having received an urgent message from Tehran giving a highly coloured account of the way in which Persian honour had been affronted, he is reported to have laid down his pen in high dudgeon and called for his car. A terse message from the Admiralty that same evening enquiring what we thought we were doing by offending Persian susceptibilities at such a critical moment was the first we knew of the repercussions of our action. We had, of course, a very good answer which apparently satisfied their Lordships for we heard no more of the affair.

In early 1927 an air route, operated by Imperial Airways, was opened between Cairo and Basra; it was expected that the Basra–Karachi route would be opened by April. But the negotiations had stalled. The link between the Middle East and India was eventually completed in 1929.[15]

Our first cruise had revealed a major laundry problem and so, for this second one, we had engaged four Ceylonese youths who undertook to do all the officers' laundry for an agreed sum. The scheme had worked well. Early one Sunday morning we all donned clean, white uniforms for Sunday divisions and were waiting on the quarterdeck for the bugler to sound off when the principal medical officer came aft looking very glum.

'What's the matter PMO?' chirped half a dozen voices, 'not another acute appendix?'

'Much worse than that,' came the lugubrious reply, 'the Ceylonese dhobi boys have got smallpox.' The PMO's announcement was at first regarded as one of the leg-pulls for which he was well-known but when he assured us it was the solemn truth we looked at one another in consternation and almost instinctively started to scratch. The clean clothes we had so cheerfully put on that morning had probably been handled and washed by the afflicted boys. With a ship's company of over 600 cooped up on board in hot weather there seemed every possibility of an epidemic. A message was sent to Bombay asking for sufficient vaccine to re-vaccinate everyone on board to be placed on the first fast mail steamer sailing for the Gulf.

The stricken boys were secluded in a camp outside the naval base and arrangements were made with an Indian doctor to look after them. As soon as the vaccine arrived we moved to a remote anchorage and, during a prescribed period in quarantine, we all went fishing. The waters of the Persian Gulf are more densely populated with fish than any others I have visited and we made some big catches in the ship's seine net. We also captured a couple of turtles which the ship's butcher carved up into suitable joints and they made very good eating. We filled the rest of our quarantine period by returning to Ceylon at the very economical speed of ten knots and miraculously no more cases occurred. Happily, the Ceylonese boys recovered.

By the end of May we were back in Colombo, returning again to the camp at Diyatalawa, where I was appointed camp commandant. The sailors were organised into ten platoons, including seamen, stokers, the band, the guard and finally the marines. In the coming weeks, a series of inter-platoon competitions was held; the sports included soccer, cricket, hockey, netball, tug of war, relays and even billiards! Although the ship was not due to return home to re-commission until the end of the year, in August 1928 I was relieved and returned home by the P&O liner, SS *Rajputana*, to take up another appointment for which I was required at the holding barracks at Portsmouth. For two years and four months in the *Enterprise*, I had steamed just under 48,000 miles, or just over twice around the world, which meant that I had added considerably to my experience as a navigating officer.

The Enterprise's *commission with the East Indies Station ended in December 1928; she was ordered home via East Africa, reaching Mombasa shortly before the Prince of Wales and the Duke of Gloucester arrived on a semi-official visit. Once the royal party had gone upcountry to Nairobi, the* Enterprise's *rugby team left for a two-week tour of Kenya and Uganda. At the end of the tour, on behalf of the ship's company, the tour manager, the Reverend Stevens, offered a silver trophy to the Rugby Football Union of Kenya (RFUK) to be awarded annually to the winners of an inter-district championship. Since rugby union was only an amateur sport, the offer was refused. The* Enterprise *then left Mombasa and sailed to Zanzibar, Dar es Salaam and Tanganyika (Tanzania) playing more matches and completing the first rugby tour by a Royal Navy ship of all three African Great Lakes nations. By late November HMS* Enterprise *had reached Aden but was recalled in order to pick up the Prince of Wales from Dar es Salaam and take him to Brindisi since King George V was seriously ill. He boarded the* Enterprise *on 2 December and reached Brindisi eight days later.*

Meanwhile a parcel had arrived at the RFUK's headquarters containing a silver goblet. It transpired that the officers and men of the Enterprise *had benefited from their return to Africa to have inscribed a trophy to be sent to Nairobi; having gained approval from the RFU in London, the RFUK accepted it. Ever since, with a gap in 1940–46 and in 1987 when an international rugby competition was held on the RFU East Africa ground as part of the All Africa Games, the* Enterprise's *silver trophy has been awarded annually.*

During the Second World War, HMS Enterprise *received the battle honours of the Atlantic, Norway, Biscay and Normandy; she was scrapped in 1946.*[16]

Chapter Eight

'The good ship *Malaya*'

Tigers have courage, and the rugged bear
But man alone can, whom he conquers, spare.[1]

1928–31

I joined HMS *Malaya* at Portsmouth as navigator (N) and acting interpreter in French and Italian in November 1928. A battleship of the Queen Elizabeth-class, she had been named in honour of the Federated Malay States in British Malaya. During the Battle of Jutland in 1916 she had been hit numerous times, the crew suffering heavy casualties. Having been in dockyard hands for over two years, she was completing a very extensive refit. To say that she was dirty would be a masterpiece of understatement. Any ship which has been without a crew for so long cannot be otherwise. The new crew joined from Devonport at the beginning of February 1929 and, as a ship's company, I have met their equal but never their superior. Everything seemed to go right from the start, for which the credit must go to Captain Nicholas Archdale and Commander G.C. Crookshank.[2] We settled down to what was to prove a very happy and successful commission. On completion of machinery and other trials we sailed for Malta via Gibraltar to join the Mediterranean Fleet.

With the Mediterranean Fleet

We reached Malta on 11 April 1929; our days fully occupied with gunnery and torpedo practice. In early June Captain Archdale went over to call on Vice Admiral Sir Howard Kelly, second-in-command of the Mediterranean Fleet and commander of the 1st Battle Squadron, on board his flagship. He had recently relieved his brother, Vice Admiral Sir John Kelly (both of whom, as captains of their respective ships, the *Gloucester* and the *Dublin,* had been involved in the chase of the *Goeben* and *Breslau* in 1914 when I was a midshipman in the *Indomitable).* Captain Archdale returned with the disconcerting news that the admiral, who had responsibility for administering the battleships, intended to visit the ship the following Sunday. Although we had worked very hard since commissioning we all knew that we were a long way short of the standard required.[3] The day came and the admiral walked around the ship hardly uttering a word, even when an unerring instinct meant he uncovered some 'glory hole' which we had hoped he would miss. He inspected the ship's company, commented on a few men who needed the barber's attention, then, telling his flag lieutenant to get his barge alongside, strode to the top of the gangway. When the notes of the bugle and the shrill call of the bo's'n's pipes had died away, he turned to the captain and, in a voice which could be heard the length of the quarterdeck, he said: 'When I next visit your ship, Captain, I do not want to see an improvement – I want a revolution. Good morning!' Whereupon he descended the ladder.

Many a lesser man might have taken offence at the admiral's remarks but the captain calmly ordered the commander to 'clear lower deck' and when the ship's company were fallen in aft, he told them what the admiral had said and cheerfully invited them not just to give what had been asked of them, but to make the ship so clean that the admiral, in his turn, would be surprised.

The sunshine and fine weather of a Mediterranean spring are certainly encouragements to clean ship, but we had other things to think of as well. Besides gunnery practices and exercises, the most keenly contested sporting event of the year, the Fleet Regatta, was due to take place on 15 August. I took on the job of regatta officer and soon discovered that we had the makings of some very good crews. As we had so recently commissioned, none of the other big ships took very much notice of us, it being generally accepted that only a ship in the second year of her commission had any hope of winning the coveted silver cock, which is awarded to the ship scoring the greatest number of points. We practised hard whenever we were in harbour and, when the whole fleet assembled for the event in Argostoli harbour, one of the Ionian Islands, we were hopeful of picking up a few of the plums.

As is usual, the flagship ran a small totalisator which gave a fair indication of what the rest of the fleet thought of the crews. Nobody seemed to be prepared to risk any money on ours except our own ship's company. As the day progressed and *Malaya's* boats consistently appeared amongst the first three in every race, surprise turned to incredulity. When the racing ended we were second, being only two-and-a-half points behind the winning ship, the C-in-C's flagship, HMS *Queen Elizabeth*. Although we had not won, we had every reason to be pleased with the result and returned with renewed vigour to the task of preparing for the admiral's inspection, which we expected to take place during the second half of the summer cruise.

After stopping at Malta to take in stores and provisions, we sailed in company with the vice admiral's flagship, for the first port on our programme, Venice. I was greatly looking forward to renewing my acquaintance with the city of lagoons and was much relieved when news came from the flagship that the inspection would not take place until we reached our next port of call which was Brioni in the northern Adriatic. We were too big to enter the harbour of Venice and so we anchored outside. As this meant over an hour's trip in the picket boat to reach St Mark's quay, the torpedo officer and I asked for – and obtained – forty-eight hours' leave, every waking minute of which we spent exploring the treasures of this beautiful and remarkable city.

An admiral's inspection is a very thorough affair and usually lasts two days, the first of which is devoted to inspecting the ship and the ship's company, and the second to exercising the officers and men at various drills and evolutions. We were fully prepared for the most rigorous scrutiny but the unexpected is always around the corner and no admiral does exactly what he is expected to do. On 24 September Vice Admiral Kelly arrived on board. He studied each man individually, the length of his hair, the cut of his uniform and the shine of his boots. He fired questions at the officers about their men. He peered into every nook and cranny, ran his finger along the top edges of high beams and stooped to peep under kit lockers. He descended to storerooms and magazines and climbed up into turrets. He deviated from the chosen route and, in so doing, ran straight into a sailor in an overall suit who had been excused muster so that he could clear up any last-minute untidiness. Despite this unscheduled encounter, when we talked over the day's happenings in the wardroom that evening, we decided that so far nothing disastrous had happened and prayed that our luck would hold when he returned for our second day's inspection.

At precisely 0905 on 30 September, under a blue and hot Mediterranean sun, all hands fell in for drill. 'Everybody forward' – 'Prepare to tow aft' – 'Everybody aft' – 'Let go a bower anchor' (one of two main anchors carried attached to cables on either side of the ship's bow, hence 'bower anchor'). We scampered to and fro, and, passing Admiral Kelly in his immaculate white uniform, as he stood there watching every movement, we sought to learn from a look or a word how we were doing. Three hours later the inspection was complete; we crowded on to the quarterdeck and everyone stood tense and expectant as the admiral climbed on to the after capstan and, telling the captain to stand us at ease, he started to address us. 'Three months ago,' he began, 'I told your Captain that on my next visit to your ship I wished to see a revolution – my wishes have been carried out in a most satisfactory manner.' A sigh of relief went around the 800 officers and men who formed his audience. He continued for some minutes to express his approval of our efforts and especially of our performance in the regatta. He ended by granting us a 'make and mend' i.e. the afternoon off, and, as he got down from the capstan, he told the captain that he would look for him on the first tee of the golf course at 2 o'clock that afternoon! From that moment we never looked back and it is not too much to say that we were the happiest ship on the station.

The island of Brioni, off which the above events took place, was then a playground for the rich. The hotel, which consisted of several buildings grouped around a small bay, had everything which the most sophisticated seeker after pleasure could desire: swimming, golf, tennis or polo, or one could simply content oneself by wandering gently along the island's shady paths. There was an attractive bar on the quayside where it was pleasant to sit in the cool of the evening. After dinner there was dancing in the 'bull ring', as the open-air dance floor was called, and after midnight in the intimate atmosphere of the night club, a Viennese orchestra played dreamy waltzes and wild gipsy music. Since there was not much ashore for the men of the ship's company, our visit was short and we moved down the Dalmatian coast to the ancient Yugoslav town of Split. I managed to spend a couple of days' trout fishing at Plitvice, north towards Zagreb. The sport was poor but the scenery splendid and the local wine very potable.

After leaving Split we steamed southward across the Mediterranean, reaching Alexandria in early October; on arrival we fired a royal salute in honour of the accession of His Majesty King Fuad I, who, having been Sultan of Egypt since 1917, had been crowned king in 1922. A big programme of entertainment had been arranged in our honour which included a lunch party hosted by the king at his palace at Ras El Tin for the admiral and the officers, which I attended. The king had a peculiar cough which sounded rather like the bark of a dog and which, I was told, was the result of a throat injury incurred during a quarrel with his brother over a lady.[4]

During our stay parties of officers and men went to Cairo to visit the sphinx and the pyramids but, since I had seen both these as a midshipman, I welcomed the commander's suggestion that we should pay a flying visit to Luxor, site of the ancient Egyptian city of Thebes. In order to have a full day's sightseeing, we travelled by train at night both ways. We felt sure it would be worth it and we were not disappointed. It is impossible not to be excited by the ruins of a civilisation which, in sheer magnificence, must have excelled that of either Greece or Rome. The temple of Karnak and Luxor, the temple at Thebes of Queen Hatshepsut who had reigned in 1478BC, and the tombs of the Valley of the Kings, all of which we visited, gave me an understanding of the splendour of this kingdom of the Pharaohs which no pictures could ever have done. Looking on the lovely features of Queen Nefertiti, as depicted by her statue (and by her golden mask in the Cairo museum), I was aware that here was no female of a barbarian race but a refined and beautiful woman, the equal of any now gracing this earth thirty-five centuries later. On our way back we stopped at Cairo and visited the museum, where the treasures removed by the archaeologist, Howard Carter, from the tomb of Tutankhamun and of others were displayed. As we sat that evening in the train which was carrying us back to Alexandria it was hard to believe that we had seen so much in so little time.

Proceeding via Haifa, Jaffa and Corfu, HMS *Malaya* returned to Malta at the beginning of November. Much to our surprise, we heard that we and the other battleships of the Queen Elizabeth-class, except the *Queen Elizabeth* herself, were to return to England to join the Home Fleet. On 12 November we sailed for our home port, Devonport and, after a period of Christmas leave, joined the rest of the Home Fleet assembling at Portland Harbour for the spring cruise 1930.

With the Home Fleet

It was customary for the Home Fleet to go to Gibraltar in January, returning at the end of March and it was a cruise to which I always looked forward, if, for no other reason, than that it took us out of England for the worst two months of the year. It is true that we generally came in for a good dusting on the way out, but, once we reached our destination, the weather, if not always fine, was at least warm and pleasant. Gibraltar itself is very attractive in the early spring. The Rock is covered with masses of sweet scented jonquils and in Spain the orange trees are heavy with their load of golden fruit. Our engineer commander had brought his car with him in the ship and when he suggested that I should accompany him on a trip to Spain I readily accepted. We decided that the famous sherry town of Jerez de la Frontera would be a good place to make for, and so, armed with an introduction to Mr Williams of Messrs Humbert and Williams, we set off through the bare Andalusian countryside.[5] We had been advised to stay at the Hotel Atlantico in Cadiz in preference to Jerez itself and, since it was only 30 miles from Cadiz to Jerez, by making an early start we reached Mr Williams's office well before the sun was over the yard arm and he very kindly arranged for us to make a complete tour of his bodegas.

There is something very attractive about all wine-growing districts. The people who make wine seem to absorb something of the soil of their vineyards and, like the wine they produce, they mellow with age. The story of the growing and making of sherry is one of enterprise and endeavour. It is the life history of such families as Domecq, Garvez, Gonzales Byass, Humbert and Williams and many others. These men are justly proud of their bodegas and of the carefully nurtured traditions which go to the making of this unique and delectable wine. I say 'unique' advisedly, because, for all their excellence no wine of a similar type grown in any other part of the world can truly claim the title of sherry unless made from grapes grown in the district around Jerez de la Frontera. We saw dry sherry maturing and how much sugar is added to amontillados and sweet sherry for export, as the Spanish themselves prefer the dry. (Alas! A crippling import duty has now placed this wine in the luxury class in Britain and it no longer stands on the sideboard of the average home so that the chance guest might be entertained with a glass of sherry and a biscuit.) On leaving Jerez the boot of the car was well-stocked with 'finos' and 'amontillados' which our hosts insisted we take away as a memento of our visit.

Soon after this excursion, at the end of February the *Malaya* stopped at Malaga. The high mountains of the Sierra Bermeja which eventually join those of the Sierra Nevada further to the eastward, form a massive background which dwarfs the town nestling on the coast below. The mountain peaks were capped with snow in strange contrast to the warm sunshine in which the town was basking and for which it is renowned. Our visit coincided with the great festival of *Mi-Carême* which is celebrated in Roman Catholic countries in the middle of Lent and we found the whole town *en fête*. A dance was given in our honour which went on into the small hours and our hosts plied us lavishly with local wine, a proof of the excellence of which was a total absence of a hangover. After a period of exercises with the Mediterranean Fleet we returned to Devonport for the Easter leave period.

In early May the Home Fleet gathered at Invergordon for gunnery practice. We immediately started practising for the regatta which was to take place at Scapa Flow at the beginning of June. After the tideless waters of the Mediterranean, pulling in the Moray Firth was a much more strenuous exercise and called for great co-operation between the crews to ensure adherence to the timetable. After the showing we had made the previous year, our spirits were high and everyone was out to win the Home Fleet cock, the most highly prized of trophies and the reward of considerable training and joint effort. We knew we had some tough opposition in the Fleet flagship, HMS *Nelson*, the present holder of the trophy, and then there was HMS *Hood*, flagship of the Home Fleet Battle Cruiser Squadron and something of a dark horse. I bought a small cine-camera and took pictures of the crews during their practices and by this means I brought home to them their mistakes, the novelty of seeing themselves on the screen adding considerably to their interest. We also heeded the advice of Captain Rory O'Conor, one of the Royal Navy's best executive officers, in his admirable book, *Running a Big Ship on 'Ten Commandments'*: 'There is only one way to win a service pulling regatta and that is for your crews to pull harder than the rest.' We therefore tried not merely to have one or two star turn crews but to get every single crew member up to the best possible standard.[6]

After just over five weeks' intensive training the fleet moved up to the deserted anchorage of Scapa and moored in two long lines in preparation for the great event. A chilling Scotch mist covered the low hills surrounding the anchorage. It was a very different setting from that of the previous year but we had the same crews and the same boats. Our training paid off handsomely. We certainly hoped to win but we never dreamt of the overwhelming victory which was ours. By the end of the day we had won the cock and four of the principal trophies with a score of 683½, the highest total ever recorded in a Fleet Regatta at that time. By comparison, HMS *Hood*'s sweeping victory five years later was obtained with a score of 503 points. That evening a giant Malayan tiger – the ship's badge – made of wood and canvas paraded around the fleet with a realistic and gory-looking cock in its mouth![7]

After the Regatta the Home Fleet dispersed to visit various ports to show the flag, which is always part of the summer cruise. Our programme took us first to the Norwegian port of Trondheim, then to Stonehaven, Scarborough and finally to Margate and Eastbourne. At each port we were open to visitors and were entertained by the local authorities. In the autumn we were at Invergordon, where we were able to play golf at the weekends. After calling in at the Firth of Forth and sampling the delights of Edinburgh, we steamed south to Portland and then Devonport where we remained until after Christmas. It was a routine which I was to get to know well over the next few years.

At the beginning of 1931 we set sail for Gibraltar. En route we spent a week in Lisbon where we undertook the customary exercises including tactical, submarine, manoeuvres and night action, which, as usual necessitated darkening the ship. Once back in Gibraltar, during a period of shore leave and again accompanied by the engineer commander, I repeated my visit to Jerez with equal pleasure and success. In March the *Malaya* visited the enchanting island of Madeira which, if it possessed a really sheltered harbour, would be a delightful place for ships regularly to visit. Unfortunately, the anchorage is very exposed and, with little or no warning, a big swell can get up, making boat work very difficult and sometimes impossible. In consequence, one may land quite happily over a smooth sea and find, a few hours later, that it is not possible to return to the ship. This happened to me and some of my brother officers who went to a dance at Reids Hotel in Funchal. After spending an uncomfortable night in the lounge, we were eventually able to persuade the pilot boat to take us out and we arrived alongside at about 9am, just as the men were falling in for divisions and prayers. There was too big a sea still running for a gangway to be lowered and the sailors were entertained by the sight of a bunch of their officers climbing up over the stern boom, clad in full evening dress! Nevertheless, I have the happiest recollections of this flower-decked island and its hospitable inhabitants. Old Boal Madeira, a rare specimen of the local wine, is worthy of the most discriminating palate.

It was my last cruise in the ship. In April 1931 I was relieved. When I asked the captain of the Navigation School what my next appointment was likely to be, I was told to go on leave and await publication of the June promotion list. I am glad to say that when it came out my name was on it confirming my promotion to commander. For that I have to thank all those who served with me in the good ship *Malaya*.

In September 1931 HMS Malaya *was one of several ships involved in what became known as the Invergordon Mutiny, which took place after the government of Ramsay MacDonald annnounced an emergency budget, introducing means tests, cuts in employment benefit and a reduction of public sector pay. A well co-ordinated strike was called by the sailors in the ships gathered in Cromarty Firth, which had the effect of precipitating a fall in the markets. Within days Britain was forced off the gold standard. Officially described as 'unrest' the episode was hushed up; there were no court martials and no commission of enquiry.*[8]

During the Second World War HMS Malaya *served in the Mediterranean. She was damaged by German torpedoes in 1941. In the summer of 1943 she escorted convoys to Malta and Capetown and at the end of the year was placed in reserve. Withdrawn from service in 1944, she was scrapped in 1948. The ship's bell is preserved in the East India Club, London.*

Chapter Nine

'The bands of Orion'

Can'st thou bind the sweet influence of Pleiades,
Or loose the bands of Orion?[1]

1931–37

After a course at the Tactical School at Portsmouth in the autumn of 1931, I returned to my alma mater, the Navigation School as executive officer, an appointment which included the command of one of the two sea-going tenders attached to the establishment. Located in the dockyard (as the school was), we were at a considerable disadvantage compared with the Gunnery and Torpedo Schools which, having more space, enjoyed far better amenities. Although improvements had been made since I first went there in 1920, one objective had so far eluded our grasp and that was the building of a squash racquets court. One morning I was standing in the billiard room, on the high walls of which were hung the photographs of the officers who had passed through the establishment during the previous fifty years. Suddenly the idea came to me that, by sacrificing one of the three billiard tables and turning the other two around, it might be possible to construct a squash court within what was left of the room. A few measurements confirmed its potential. I then submitted my suggestions to the captain who approved it. In due course we had a full-sized squash court. Since we had only had to build two new walls it had cost far less than any of the previous estimates.

My duties as executive officer were to supervise the instruction and see that the sub lieutenants undertaking courses behaved themselves. In those days it was possible to obtain a motor car of sorts for quite a small sum and thus most of the young officers possessed one. Some of these cars were hardly worthy of the name and I gave orders that only ones of a respectable appearance should be allowed to park in front of the building. One day I saw a wreck of a car, literally held together with string and with one side almost completely missing, parked outside. I sent for the owner and enquired how he had come by such a perilous and disreputable-looking vehicle. 'Oh, I swopped it for an old raincoat,' came the reply! Each summer I took the class of lieutenants who were undergoing the long navigation course for a fortnight's cruise and this formed a very pleasant break in my shore service.

After completing two years at the Navigation School, in early 1934 I was destined to spend the remainder of the year ashore since I had been selected to undergo a staff course at the Royal Naval College, Greenwich. Although fourteen years had passed since I first attended this venerable seat of learning, my impressions remained the same, but the work of the course was so interesting and absorbing that it more than compensated for the lack of amenities. Besides we could go away for the weekends as well as being able to visit London and the time passed quickly. Uppermost in my memory was a visit to the Guards Depot at Caterham in Surrey, where we were shown how the finest soldiers in the world are made. Also memorable was a visit, sponsored by the Port of London Authority, to the London Docks, where we saw proof – if any were needed – of how dependent we are in this island on our imports of food and raw materials.

HMS Orion

After completing the course at Greenwich, I received an appointment to HMS *Orion*, a Leander-class 7,070-ton light cruiser which had recently commissioned. My instructions were 'to repair on board that ship at Chatham on 13 December 1934' to take up the dual position of squadron navigating officer and staff officer (operations) to the rear admiral commanding the 2nd Cruiser Squadron in the Home Fleet.[2] As a measure of economy, it had been decided to combine the two appointments and so I was relieving two officers. It fell to me to prove whether or not it was possible for one man to do what had formerly been two men's work. Had it not been my great good fortune to have as my admiral, Rear Admiral Sir Sidney Meyrick, I am quite sure I should not have made a success of it. By his patience and understanding he made things easy for me. *Orion*'s captain was Edward de Faye Renouf with whom I had served in the *Enterprise*.[3]

We joined the Home Fleet at Sheerness on 10 January 1935. Contrary to custom, instead of sailing for Gibraltar, we headed south for the West Indies where the fleet was to carry out the first gun trials ever held against a pilotless aircraft. We exercised continuously, night and day, except on Sundays, so that, after nearly two weeks at sea, any cobwebs collected ashore had been blown away. On reaching the islands, the fleet dispersed to various ports, our first call being at the harbour of St John in Antigua. All the West Indian islands have their charm, but, for naval officers, Antigua has a special attraction in English Harbour, which is a unique and picturesque monument to a glorious period in our naval history. Admirals Rodney, Hood and Jervis all used it; as captain of HMS *Boreas* and senior naval officer of the Leeward Islands, Lord Nelson was there from 1784 to 1787. The house in which he lived, known as Admiral's House, and from which he wrote letters to his wife-to-be, the young widow, Mrs Nisbet still stands at the head of the bay. On the opposite side is Clarence House, now the governor's summer residence which was built for the Duke of Clarence and St Andrews, who served in the Navy until 1790, later ascending the throne as King William IV.

At the time of which I am writing the rapacious tropical vegetation and successive hurricanes were steadily obliterating the remains of this fascinating old dockyard but, thanks to the enterprise of the then Governor, Sir Kenneth Blackburne, the Society of the Friends of English Harbour was founded in 1950. Funds were raised enabling repairs to be carried out and the disintegration was stopped, thus ensuring that this interesting link with the past would be preserved for many years to come.[4]

From Antigua we moved to Kingstown, the main port of the island of Saint Vincent which is dominated by the great volcano of La Soufrière, happily in a quiescent state since the great eruption of May 1902.[5] I remember this visit particularly because of a conversation I had with the governor about the dreadful poverty which was so apparent in most of the islands. He told me that if only Great Britain would pay a penny a pound for sugar from our own islands instead of buying it from Cuba at a half-penny a pound, it would spell the difference between abject misery and a reasonable standard of living. Twenty years have passed since then but only recently has an attempt been made to give these patient and loyal people a fair deal.[6]

The war had destroyed the European beet-sugar industry and so, along with the US, the United Kingdom had become dependent on Cuba for its sugar. In 1956 the Sugar Act was passed establishing a free market in sugar.

After a brief visit to Port of Spain, Trinidad, allowing me no time to revisit the mangrove swamps, the fleet reassembled in the big bay – Basse Terre – of Saint Kitts before starting back across the Atlantic to Gibraltar which we reached in mid–March. We carried out a very extensive exercise with the Mediterranean Fleet to the west of Gibraltar in which we were technically sunk by the *Queen Elizabeth* during a night action! Both fleets foregathered at Gibraltar so that there could be a discussion about the exercise, after which we returned to our home ports for Easter leave, remaining in Chatham throughout April.

The main feature of the 1935 summer cruise was the Jubilee Review Day of the Home and Mediterranean Fleets at Spithead by His Majesty King George V in celebration of his Silver Jubilee on 16 July. As I recorded in the ship's log: '1425. Fired Royal Salute of 21 guns on occasion of H.M. Yacht joining the Fleet...cheered ship as H.M. the King passed down the lines.' That evening the ship was illuminated and there was a rocket and flare display.

Despite the strain which the Jubilee celebrations had necessarily imposed on him, the king was in his customary jovial mood on board the royal yacht with his admirals and captains. There is a delightful story told how, after dinner one evening, when he was going around having a few words with each of his guests, as he always did, he stopped before a junior captain. Looking him up and down he called out: 'Here, Admiral, we have an officer improperly dressed!' It so happened that the officer concerned had been at some pains to have his uniform checked over by his tailor to conform with what he believed were the regulations; standing opposite the king, he noticed that George V had two more buttons than he had on his mess jacket. Believing some explanation was necessary, he said deferentially: 'But, Sire, my tailor assured me that my uniform was in accordance with the regulations.'

'Regulations!' repeated the king with a chuckle, 'I am the regulations.' As the officer in question said afterwards: 'There was no answer to that!' It was the last time His Majesty went afloat among his sailors.

Once the summer leave period was over, we normally went to Invergordon but in 1935 we returned to Portland together with the Battle Cruiser Squadron. Having received orders to raise steam for full speed with all despatch, on the evening of 14 September, in company with the *Hood* and *Renown* and a flotilla of destroyers, we slipped out of Portland and headed for Gibraltar. There were unpleasant rumblings in Mussolini's Italy and information indicated that he was planning to attack Abyssinia (Ethiopia) with whom he was obviously trying to pick a quarrel. Disregarding the principles of the League of Nations, Mussolini used a clash between Italian and Abyssinian troops on the borders of Somaliland as a pretext: on 2 October 1935 he set in motion the invasion of Abyssinia. Resolute intervention by the League could have nipped Il Duce's plans in the bud but instead the first chapter of the dismal period which ended in Munich in 1938 was written. Powerful British naval forces were assembled at Gibraltar and Alexandria ready to strike but the order to do so never came.

Instead we had remained at Gibraltar undertaking exercises which, in December, included visits to Tangier and the white-walled town of Casablanca, a fine example of French colonial development with its wide boulevards, handsome buildings and good hotels. Little did I know that my next visit to Casablanca in 1943 would be in the distinguished company of the world's leaders. Our return to Sheerness in early 1936 alas coincided with King George's death on 20 January. The following day at 0900 we carried out a seventy minute gun salute to the late king and the day after that we fired a royal salute of twenty-one guns to mark the accession of King Edward VIII. Back in Gibraltar, we continued to undertake exercises, paying another short visit to Tangier in early May. I shall never forget the fields of wild flowers which carpet the surrounding countryside at that time of year.

In late May the deposed ruler of Abyssinia, Emperor Haile Selassie, arrived in one of our cruisers, HMS *Capetown*, in order to take passage onward to England. Before departing he was invited to lunch by the Commander-in-Chief, Admiral Lord Cork, on board his flagship, HMS *Nelson*. As the emperor spoke French but no English, I was requested to act as interpreter. During the lunch the conversation was confined to generalities but afterwards, when I was showing him around the ship and pointed out to him the *Nelson*'s big 16-inch guns, he remarked rather ruefully that it was a pity they had not been used in the cause of liberty and justice. I was unable to reply to this comment which was undoubtedly true although it ignored the diplomatic complications surrounding such action. On completion of our tour I returned the emperor to the admiral's cabin and took leave of this sad-looking ex-monarch.[7]

Haile Selassie's exile was spent in England. Following the outbreak of the Second World War and Italy's entry into the war on the side of Germany, British and Allied forces together with Abyssinian irregulars fought against the Italians, enabling Haile Selassie to regain his throne in April 1941; he was overthrown in a military coup in 1974.

Although we could not go far into Spain, our periods in harbour at Gibraltar were always enjoyable. We made many friends among the soldiers stationed there and I also made the acquaintance of a couple who owned a motor yacht. They were en route to the south of France but, because of the deteriorating international situation, they had stopped at Gibraltar. Together with some of my brother officers, they often took me out in their yacht. Finding a suitable anchorage off the Spanish coast, we would swim, surf-board and water ski to our hearts' content. In the warm evenings after dark we would lie out on deck listening to gramophone records of classical music of which they had a large library on board. One hot summer's evening we were anchored just south of Algeciras. There was not a breath of wind and the lights of the town were reflected in the mirror-like surface of the water. Having had plenty of exercise, a delicious dinner and good wine, we were in a mellow mood, listening to the magic notes of Mendelssohn's Violin Concerto, when we heard the rhythmic sounds of rowlocks responding to the movement of oars. Looking over the side of the yacht, the shape of a rowing boat could be seen approaching. As the boat breasted the gangway, a young girl, who had been sitting in the stern sheets, jumped out and ran up the steps of the gangway to the yacht. As she gained the light, we recognised her as the daughter of a wealthy Spanish landowner. We rose to greet her but, ignoring our salutations, she began: 'There's going to be a war in Spain,' she said, 'and it will be terrible.' This was the first indication we had of the Spanish Civil War which was to take such a heavy toll on life, destroy much property and arouse bitterness and hatred throughout the length and breadth of the land. We sat around until the small hours discussing the future.

The Spanish Civil War, which began in July 1936, was fought between Republicans, loyal to the left-wing Second Spanish Republic (and supported by the Soviet Union and Mexico) and the Nationalists led by General Francisco Franco (and supported by Italy, Portugal and Germany). The war, which was noted for its atrocities, with casualties estimated at between 250,000 and one million, ended with a Nationalist victory in July 1939; Franco ruled as a dictator until his death in 1975.

In early June 1936 the Home Fleet returned to home ports for the summer leave period, after which we followed our usual practice and sailed for Invergordon in late September. We carried out gunnery practices in the Moray Firth and enjoyed playing golf at the weekends on one of the many attractive courses in Scotland. In November 1936 the fleet returned to Portland where we were honoured by a visit from His Majesty King Edward VIII who arrived on board HM Royal Yacht *Victoria and Albert*. It was wet and blustery weather which did not make the task of visiting and inspecting ships any too easy. Writing in later life the king remembered the two 'blowy' days which he spent with the Home Fleet 'moored in its snug anchorage' as 'good days. Engrossed in inspecting ships, talking to sailors and reminiscing with old shipmates, I was able to put off for a few hours the burning issue which was pressing for a decision,' by which he meant of course his impending abdication. For my part, I was glad to have the opportunity of talking over with His Majesty our times together at Osborne and Dartmouth and in the *Renown* in 1919.[8]

On the night of His Majesty Edward VIII's abdication – 10 December 1936 – I was attending one of the Harwich Force dinners in London. As usual our beloved chief, Com (T), now Admiral of the Fleet Sir Reginald Tyrwhitt, was presiding; but, despite the pleasure of reunion, we were all conscious of the momentous event which was about to take place. The port was passed, the loyal toast drunk and Com (T) rapped on the table. 'Gentlemen', he said. 'There is a broadcast about to take place which some of you may wish to hear.' Many of us went out in to the lobby and listened to the king's farewell speech, but Com (T) remained at the table, his head bowed. Two days later the proclamation of His Majesty King George VI's accession was read to the ship's company.

We spent the Christmas leave period at Chatham. Having completed his two years in command of the squadron, Vice Admiral Meyrick had hauled down his flag. His successor was Rear Admiral Tom Calvert.[9] I had also been in the ship for two years but the 'bands of Orion' were to hold me for another cruise.

In January 1937 we sailed once more for Gibraltar. On arrival we took over the naval patrols from the Mediterranean Fleet. These had been established as part of the Non-Intervention Agreement which, together with the French, the government of Prime Minister Neville Chamberlain had sponsored, but to which neither Germany, under the leadership of Adolf Hitler and his National Socialist (Nazi) party, nor Italy – although both signatories – would adhere.[10] There had been quite a number of incidents at sea between opposing factions of the Spanish Navy and, as each side was trying to prevent the other from obtaining sea-borne supplies, it was our business to see that legitimate British trade was not interfered with by either party. We called first at Palma, Majorca, where our consul, a former British naval officer, put us in the picture regarding the local situation.

After a few days we went out on patrol and anchored off the port of Valencia, which is a busy place in the orange season. While we were there we heard that Barcelona had been heavily bombarded the previous night by unknown warships, so the admiral decided to investigate. The information that we had been given indicated that whatever ships had done the bombarding they were certainly not Spanish, since neither side possessed any ships mounting guns of heavy calibre. We also heard of the curious behaviour of a German destroyer which had entered the port in the late afternoon of the day of the bombardment and hurriedly left again, taking up a berth in the anchorage reserved for neutral shipping. She was still there so the admiral sent a note across to her commanding officer asking him if he had any prior knowledge of the attack. Back came a most diplomatic answer: 'I suggest you ask the Italian admiral.'

We returned to Palma to find the German battleship *Deutschland* in the harbour flying the flag of Rear Admiral Hermann von Fischel as well as an Italian destroyer leader flying the flag of Rear Admiral Angelo Iachino, whom I had met when he was Italian Naval Attaché in China between 1923 and 1928.[11] Since he was the senior of the three admirals, it was Admiral Calvert's place to call on him first and I accompanied him. We had only been on board the Italian flagship a few minutes when Admiral von Fischel arrived. He and Calvert had met before and they greeted each other warmly, much to Iachino's annoyance. Fischel was a typical hearty sailor with an honest open face and very different from his Axis colleague. The greeting over, Admiral Calvert placed himself between the two men. Taking each by an arm he started to walk aft with them saying: 'This is indeed fortunate. Now we can try and get to the bottom of this bombardment of Barcelona. I am anxious to find out who did it.' Iachino perceptibly blanched and looked anxiously across at Fischel. 'Don't ask me,' said the latter laughing, 'I know nothing about it.' 'Nor do I,' said Iachino. But his looks and guilty manner belied him.

Towards the end of the cruise Rear Admiral Calvert sent for me and asked if I had heard of my next appointment. I said that I had not. I was very pleasantly surprised when, a few days later, he again sent for me to inform me that, on our return to England, I was to take up the post of staff officer (operations) on the staff of the Commander-in-Chief, Home Fleet, Admiral Sir Roger Backhouse, one of the Navy's great 'brains' and, as I was to discover, a tiger for work.[12]

The bombardment of Barcelona took place on 13 February 1937 when shells were fired at an arms factory from an Italian cruiser. They missed their target but killed eighteen people. This was the prelude to an estimated 200 air raids on the city, culminating in the fall of Barcelona to Franco's forces on 26 January 1939.

After serving with the North America and West Indies Station in 1939, in June 1940 HMS Orion *was transferred to the Mediterranean Fleet as Admiral Sir John Tovey's flagship. During the Second World War the ship received thirteen battle honours: a record exceeded only by HMS* Warspite *and matched by two other ships (HMS* Nubian *and HMS* Jervis*). She was sold for scrap in 1949.*

Chapter Ten

Staff Officer on board the *Nelson*

Such is the power of order and arrangement.[1]

1937–39

I joined Admiral Backhouse's staff on board his flagship, HMS *Nelson*, at Portsmouth on 15 April 1937.[2] As I, and my fellow staff officers were to learn, the commander-in-chief, Home Fleet, never spared himself and he expected the same of his staff. His chief of staff was Commodore Henry Moore, and under him we all worked happily together.[3] One of our responsibilities was attempting to stop certain ship owners who – contrary to terms of the Non-Intervention Agreement – were trying to supply the so-called Spanish 'Reds' with materials through some of the northern ports like Bilbao, to which end we had established a destroyer patrol along the coast. Every incident was reported to the admiral who had to decide on the action to be taken. Another undertaking was preparing for the review of the fleet by His Majesty King George VI (following his coronation at Westminster Abbey on 12 May) when the Home Fleet would assemble at Spithead. Later Admiral Backhouse was scheduled to visit various Scandinavian ports. Orders for all these events had to be drafted, approved and issued.

In my new position as a staff officer (operations), I experienced a strange sensation of having nothing whatsoever to do with the navigation of the ship. One staff officer took turns in keeping watch on the admiral's bridge in order to keep the admiral and the chief of staff informed of what was going on if they were in their sea-cabins. On the bridge below Captain Alan Ramsay Dewar – one of four brothers who were all naval officers – controlled the flagship's movements.[4] There was one officer, however, who doubled both as a ship's and a staff officer and that was the Master of the Fleet, who was responsible for the navigation of the flagship and, under the admiral's direction, that of the whole fleet.

The Royal Review

HMS *Nelson* was at Southend on Coronation Day and the ship was dressed in King George VI's honour. The review of the fleet at Spithead over a week later was to be the final coronation event of 1937. A naval review calls for considerable organisation and no matter how one may try to condense the orders, they inevitably run into several pages; but, coming so soon after King George V's Jubilee Review, my task of drafting the orders was comparatively easy. In the days preceding the appointed day – 20 May – foreign warships began taking up their berths. The long lines of battleships, battlecruisers, aircraft carriers, cruisers and destroyers, besides submarines and a host of smaller vessels, made a brave show in their coats of glistening paint. Once the king had duly reviewed the fleet from the Royal Yacht, *Victoria and Albert,* there was a fly past by squadrons of the Fleet Air Arm. That night the ships were illuminated and there was a combined searchlight and firework display. The next day, all the captains of HM ships assembled came on board the *Nelson* to receive King George who arrived on board accompanied by his brother, the Duke of Kent.

Among the seventeen foreign warships present were the USS New York, the French battleship, Dunkerque, Germany's heavily armed cruiser, the Admiral Graf Spee, and Japan's heavy cruiser, Ashigara. Over 100 surface warships (including for the first time four aircraft carriers), twenty-two submarines, and eleven auxiliaries from the Home, Mediterranean and Reserve Fleets were assembled, making it the largest gathering of warships since George V's coronation review in 1911. Representing the Commonwealth and British Empire were two warships from Canada, one each from New Zealand and India; there was also a large contingent of British merchant ships.

The summer of 1937 was to be the last occasion on which a fleet of big ships, such as I had grown up with, assembled at Spithead. The emphasis now, and rightly so, is on anti-submarine vessels but they do not give the same sense of might as a line of battleships.

Brian Betham Schofield as a naval cadet, Hawke Term, Osborne, 1908. *'The cadets were organised into six terms based on the date of entry into the college.'* Schofield is sitting on the tutor's left.

Bill of uniform from Gieve Matthews & Seagrove Ltd. *'The most expensive item was the sea chest.'*

LONDON, PORTSMOUTH, DEVONPORT, CHATHAM, WEYMOUTH, SHEERNESS.

Head Offices
109 High Street, Portsmouth   September 1908

Naval Cadet B.B.Scholfield,

(T.D. Scholfield Esq,)

7184

D*to Gieve, Matthews & Seagrove Ltd.

					GOODS.			CREDITS.
1908								
Sept, G.		108A	1 Sea Chest		5	10	0	
			2 Counterpanes			13	0	
			6 Sheets		1	2	6	
			3 Pillow Cases			3	0	
			4 Bath Towels			9	0	
			1 Soiled Linen Bag			1	9	
			1 Key Ring & Name			1	6	
			1 Super Uniform Jacket)					
			1 " " Vest)		3	15	0	
			1 Pr " " Trousers)					
			1 Winter Working Jacket)					
			1 " " " Vest)		3	3	0	
			1 Pr " " Trousers)					
			1 Summer Working Jacket)					
			1 " " " Vest)		2	15	0	
			1 Pr " " Trousers)					
			1 Pair Extra Ditto			16	6	
			1 Flannel Lined Waistcoat			17	6	
			1 Osborne Overcoat					

Above: HMS *Indomitable*: 'I was pleased at being appointed to serve in a ship which already had a distinguished record: in 1908, when Quebec celebrated the 300th anniversary of its founding, she had carried the then Prince of Wales – the future King George V – across the Atlantic.'

Below: Extract from 'Journal for the use of Midshipmen', 5 August 1914. '*At 1.20 am a signal was received "War is declared. Commence Hostilities against Germany at once".*'

H.M.S.	*Indomitable*	At *War Bizerta*	
DATE.	*August 1914*		
Wednesday	Belgium to give her free access for movement of her Troops in Belgian territory.		
Wednesday 5ᵗʰ	At 1.20 am a signal was received "War is declared Commence Hostilities against Germany at once" At 10. am arrived off Cape Bon nothing having been seen during the night Flagship & Chatham & Dublin also joined & several destroyers The Chatham having held up two German steamers one the Hawah of 2000 tons a Hamburg ship. no news having been received of the Goeben & Breslau. Fleet then proceeded for Bizerta where we are detailed to coal. Italy intends to maintain her neutrality & we are not at war with Austria. Arrived off Bizerta at 6·opm, Inflexible fired a salute & then with Indefatigable proceeded out to sea. We entered the harbour amidst prolonged cheers from all the French ships & inhabitants		

HMS *Indomitable*'s Q turret's crew. '*Action sounded (0845) grab everything, including notebook and pencil and up on deck and into my turret,*' Schofield wrote home, describing the action at Dogger Bank, January 1915.

Sub Lieutenant Schofield.
'*In September 1915 I got my first gold stripe as an acting sub lieutenant.*'

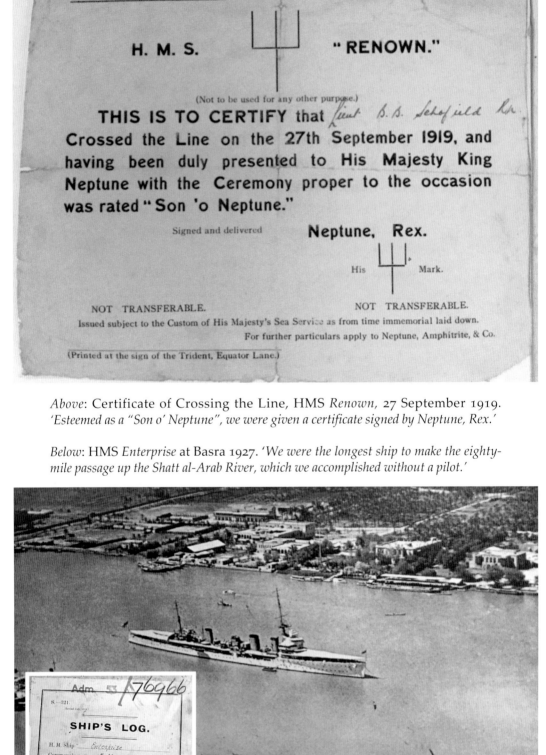

H. M. S.   **"RENOWN."**

(Not to be used for any other purpose.)

THIS IS TO CERTIFY that *Lieut. B. B. Schofield RN.*
Crossed the Line on the 27th September 1919, and
having been duly presented to His Majesty King
Neptune with the Ceremony proper to the occasion
was rated "Son 'o Neptune."

Signed and delivered   **Neptune, Rex.**

His   Mark.

NOT TRANSFERABLE.   **NOT TRANSFERABLE.**

Issued subject to the Custom of His Majesty's Sea Service as from time immemorial laid down.

For further particulars apply to Neptune, Amphitrite, & Co.

(Printed at the sign of the Trident, Equator Lane.)

Above: Certificate of Crossing the Line, HMS *Renown*, 27 September 1919.
'Esteemed as a "Son o' Neptune", we were given a certificate signed by Neptune, Rex.'

Below: HMS *Enterprise* at Basra 1927. 'We were the longest ship to make the eighty-mile passage up the Shatt al-Arab River, which we accomplished without a pilot.'

SHIP'S LOG.

H. M. Ship: *Enterprise*
Commencing: 1st May 1927
Ending: 30th April 1928

Above: The Mediterranean Fleet at Gibraltar, 1929. *'Gibraltar itself is very attractive in the early spring. The Rock is covered with masses of sweet scented jonquils and in Spain the orange trees are heavy with their load of golden fruit.'*

Below: Winning cutter's crew, HMS *Malaya* Mediterranean Fleet, 1929. The Regatta Officer, Lieutenant Commander Schofield, is seated second from the right. In the background is the ship's bell, now in the East India Club, London.

Left: The ship's badge of HMS *Malaya* was a tiger: *Tigers have courage, and the rugged bear / But man alone whom he conquers can spare. (Edmund Waller)*

Below: Home Fleet Regatta 1930: the silver 'cock' won by HMS *Malaya*: '*There is only one way to win a service pulling regatta and that is for your crews to pull harder than the rest,*' wrote Captain Rory O'Conor.

Commander Schofield, by Amies Milner, 1933.
'For my promotion, I have to thank all those who served with me in the good ship Malaya.*'*

Captain Schofield in full dress as Naval Attaché, the Hague, 1940.
'I donned my full dress uniform for the last time when I accompanied Sir Nevile Bland to the opening of the Dutch Parliament by Her Majesty Queen Wilhelmina.'

Above: Painting of HMS *Galatea*. Schofield was Captain of the *Galatea* from 1940-41; after he was relieved the ship was sunk off Alexandria in December 1941.

Below: Church Service on board HMS *Prince of Wales*, Placentia Bay, August 1941. *'As the combined chorus of British and American voices echoed across the still waters of the bay, it was impossible not to feel deeply moved and spiritually uplifted.'*

President Franklin D. Roosevelt and Prime Minister Winston Churchill talking after the service on board HMS *Prince of Wales*, Placentia Bay, August 1941: Schofield is in the third row, 5th from left. *'It was a great hour to live,'* Churchill later wrote. *'Nearly half of those who sang were soon to die.'* The ship was sunk off Singapore in December 1941.

Prime Minister Winston Churchill on board HMS *Prince of Wales*, Placentia Bay, August 1941. *'The words of William Blake came readily to mind: "I will not cease from mental fight/ Nor shall my sword sleep in my hand."'*

Above: The Trade Division: 'Convoy Brains Trust has the answer to the U-Boats', *The Daily Sketch*, 9 June 1942. Standing on the left is Captain Peter Morey, seated in the middle is Rear Admiral Edward King. Captain Schofield is seated on the right.

Below: HM King George VI being received by Captain B.B. Schofield and piped aboard HMS *Duke of York*, 12 August 1943.

King George VI on board HMS *Duke of York* accompanied by Admiral Sir Bruce Fraser. *'When Admiral Fraser told the king that I had only just assumed command of the ship and had not yet taken her to sea, the king laughed and asked me if I was nervous. I answered, of course, that I was not!'*

HMS *Duke of York* in rough seas off Scapa Flow. *'The day was wet and stormy but the king, quite undaunted, carried out a full programme of visits to other ships.'*

Above: Fuelling at Sea, August 1945. USS *Missouri* in the background with HMS *King George V* in the foreground with a US tanker in between the two flagships.

Below: The Japanese surrender. *Certifying the presence of Captain B.B. Schofield CBE RN at the formal surrender of the Japanese Forces to the Allied Powers, USS* Missouri, *2nd September 1945.*

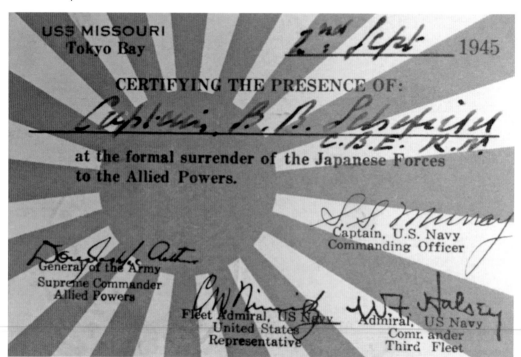

Vice Admiral Sir Bernard Rawlings KCB KBE, Flag Captain, Officers & Ship's Company of HMS *King George V*, Sydney, October 1945. *'We were immensely proud to have had the honour of being in his flagship and of serving under his command.'*

Officers of HMS *King George V*, Sydney, October 1945. Vice Admiral Rawlings is seated centre front with Captain Schofield on his left.

Above: HMS *King George V* coming alongside Princes Pier, Melbourne, October 1945. 'Tooronga *took the bow hawser, belching smoke and threshing water as she endeavoured to overcome the seeming irresistible force of the battleship.*'

Below: Farewell to Hobart, Tasmania, January 1946. Captain Schofield on the bridge. '*With perfect weather our sixteen-day voyage across the Indian ocean was a veritable yachting trip!*'

HMS *King George V* off Torquay, 1946: '*I had obtained special permission from the Admiralty to have the ship illuminated, requiring over two miles of wire and 5,000 lamps for a ship of her size.*'

Admiralty House,
PORTSMOUTH.

9th July, 1947.

My Dear Schofield,

I was delighted to see that my old Flag Captain had been promoted and heartily congratulate you.

With all best wishes,

Yours ever,

Fraser

Rear-Admiral B. Schofield, C.B.E.,

Letter from Admiral Sir Bruce Fraser: '*I was delighted to see that my old Flag Captain [of HMS* Duke of York] *had been promoted and heartily congratulate you.*' 9 July 1947.

Wood carving of the ship's badge of HMS *Duke of York*.

Wood carving of the ship's badge of HMS *King George V.* 'During the long hours a Captain has to spend alone, both at sea and in harbour, I occupied my spare time in wood carving, for which I appeared to have some aptitude.'

One of the many foreign admirals who called on the commander-in-chief was Admiral V.M. Orlov of the Russian Navy, the Soviet battleship *Marat* being one of the foreign warships present. When Admiral Backhouse returned his call at 3 o'clock one afternoon, he found, to his astonishment, an enormous repast awaiting him, to which, despite having had lunch, he felt he must do justice. Orlov seemed a convivial officer and we were sorry to learn that, shortly after his return to the Soviet Union, he had been liquidated by Stalin during what was commonly called the Great Purge.[5] Once the celebrations were over and the berths at Spithead vacated, HMS *Nelson* returned to Portland.

Scandinavian Waters: HMS Rodney

On 17 June Admiral Backhouse's flag was transferred to the battleship, HMS *Rodney*, which meant that his staff went with him. The following day the ship prepared for sea and we set course for Oslo, escorted by two destroyers. We were favoured with good weather on our passage up through the long fjord at the head of which the city lies against a beautiful background of pine trees which descend right to the water's edge. During our week's stay we were received with great kindness and friendliness by everyone from King Haakon and Queen Maud downwards and we appreciated the general air of informality. We gave a large ball on board to which the king and queen and members of their entourage were invited as well as a few hundred guests. Queen Maud – King Edward VII and Queen Alexandra's youngest daughter, now in her late sixties – loved dancing and so the best dancers in the ship were lined up to obey the royal command. While she was being well taken care of, the king, who did not dance, sat on a dais and talked to various officers who were presented to him. I was talking to one of his ADCs when the king looked up and beckoned to him. He returned a few minutes later and told me that His Majesty would like a game of bridge. I hurriedly selected three good players and presented them to the king, who spent the rest of the visit quite happily in the admiral's cabin.[6]

A few evenings later the commander-in-chief, chief of staff, flag captain, captain of the fleet and some other officers, of which I was one, were invited to dine informally with the king and queen at Bigdo (Bygdøy) Royal Manor, on a peninsula a little way outside the city. As soon as dinner was over Queen Maud proposed that we roll up the drawing room carpet and dance, for which purpose she sent her lady-in-waiting in search of gramophone records. It so happened, unknown to us, that the queen's lady-in-waiting had a tryst with an officer from one of the destroyers, which had accompanied us. When she saw that the evening was likely to be prolonged her face fell, so much so that I believe the queen guessed her secret and released her as soon as she returned with the records, much to our loss but to the destroyer officer's gain as I understand they later married.

At the mention of the word 'dance', the king had taken the commander-in-chief, the British minister and his brother (who happened to be staying with him) to his private study where they spent the rest of the evening playing bridge. Queen Maud, like her father, was so full of life and it came as a great shock to us all to learn of her sudden death only sixteen months later; suffering from abdominal pain during a visit to England in October 1938, she died after being operated on, shortly before her sixty-ninth birthday.

Leaving Oslo with many regrets, we crossed the Skagerrak, which runs between the south-east coast of Norway, the south-west coast of Sweden and the Jutland peninsula. We headed down the Kattegat for the Danish port of Aarhus, the reputed scene of Matthew Arnold's poem 'The Forsaken Merman'.[7] Although we were anchored some distance off the shore many pseudo mermen and mermaids swam to the ship and it became quite common to find a golden-haired damsel resting at the bottom of the gangway after her long swim!

Soon after our arrival on 1 July His Majesty King Christian X of Denmark on board the royal yacht dropped anchor and the commander-in-chief went at once to pay his respects.[8] It was expected that the king would return the call after the usual interval of fifteen or twenty minutes but, to everyone's surprise, hardly had Admiral Backhouse set foot on the quarterdeck when the royal yacht was seen to be approaching. I have never shifted into a frock coat and epaulettes so quickly as I did then and I remember the last staff officer rushing up the ladder onto the quarterdeck just as the king stepped on the gangway, only to find he had forgotten to change his sword belt to the gold-embroidered full dress one! A tall, dignified figure,

King Christian will always be remembered for his courage in standing up to the German occupation of his country during the Second World War, especially his action in helping to finance the escape of Danish Jews to Sweden.

While in Danish waters, the officers of a troop of Danish cavalry stationed in the town invited the ship's officers to a riding picnic and they indicated that they could mount as many men as we cared to send. About thirty of us landed one beautiful sunny morning to find a whole cavalcade awaiting us. There were also a number of ladies and for each horse there was a mounted horse-holder, who disappeared as soon as we were in the saddle. It was one of the most delightful rides I have ever had. Our hosts took us through shady woods to a lovely old farmhouse in the heart of a forest where lunch had been laid out on trestle tables in the courtyard. The horse-holders re-appeared as if by magic and took our mounts. We then sat down to feast on smorgasbord and schnapps, which had been so well-iced that we did not at first realise its potency; only when I began to feel something rather like liquid fire trickling down my throat did I realise that caution was necessary. After the loyal toasts to the kings of both our countries had been drunk, our hosts proposed innumerable other toasts, ending with each horse individually and by name. I looked anxiously at some of the midshipmen to see how they were faring in this trial of strength and was glad to see that they were holding their own.

Once lunch was over the horse-holders returned with our steeds and we remounted, blissfully unaware of the further test to which we were to be subjected. Telling us that we were returning by another route, we were led through the forest to some open ground on which some jumps and obstacles had been erected. We soon realised that this was the place where new riders were trained and with which the horses were well-acquainted! No sooner did one of the Danish officers lead off around the course than the whole cavalcade made to follow and, as in John Gilpin's famous ride: 'The trot became a gallop soon/ In spite of curb and rein'![9] The Danish officers and their ladies thought it great fun and looked around expectantly to see how many of us had come off, but I think we can claim that, with only two casualties, we acquitted ourselves quite well. Throughout our stay the weather was glorious and, when we had no other commitments, we joined the Danish sunbathers on the golden sands which surround the bay.

After the summer leave period at Devonport the Home Fleet, with Admiral Backhouse's flag still on board HMS *Rodney*, went north again to Invergordon for exercises. Scotland is very beautiful in the autumn and we were favoured with good weather. As we prepared to return south, I remember standing on the admiral's bridge admiring the scene. The blue sky was cloudless and there was no wind, the great bulk of Ben Nevis and the surrounding mountains standing out clearly. It was breathtakingly beautiful. My reverie was interrupted by the deep voice of Admiral Backhouse: 'Schofield,' he said. 'What do you mean by dragging me away from this heavenly spot?' We made our return via Edinburgh, which I am always glad to revisit since I consider it one of the most pleasing cities in the whole of the British Isles. By late October we were back in Portland, the admiral transferring his flag once more to the *Nelson* at Portsmouth on 15 November, Captain Bill Makeig-Jones taking command of the ship in December.[10]

Combined Exercises

It was the custom for the commanders-in-chief of the Home and Mediterranean Fleets to arrange between them the programme of exercises to be carried out when the two fleets met off Gibraltar. As staff officer (operations), it was my duty to take out a draft of the programme to Malta and obtain the views of the commander-in-chief, Mediterranean Fleet, Admiral Sir Dudley Pound, who had commanded the battleship *Colossus* with distinction at Jutland.[11] My instructions were to travel overland across France and Italy and onwards to Malta. Having crossed the Channel, I caught the Paris–Rome express which brought me to the Italian capital at about 6pm the following evening. My train which would take me to Syracuse in Sicily did not leave until 8pm and so I thought I would have time for dinner in the restaurant which adjoins the station, as I knew there would be no restaurant car on the train; but I had reckoned without the fact that Italy had become a Fascist dictatorship under Benito Mussolini and certain regulations were applicable.

'The Signor will visit the synthetic wool exhibition near the Coliseum and get his ticket stamped there before continuing his journey,' said the inspector. It was useless for me to protest since I could not continue my journey without the necessary stamp on my ticket. I took a taxi to the wool exhibition and made straight for the exit. The attendant, seeing that I had just arrived, waved me back, but when I explained that I was in a hurry and thrust a note into his hand, he stamped my ticket and allowed me to depart onwards.

On arrival in Malta I was met by my opposite number on Admiral Pound's staff, Commander Guy Grantham who looked after me very well. Having accomplished my mission, on my return to Rome a week later I had to visit another exhibition, but I was not so pressed for time and it was more interesting than synthetic wool.[12] It was early morning when I arrived back in Paris. Since I had over three hours to wait for my train to Calais I put my suitcase in the *consigne*. Clutching my despatch case (which I had had great difficulty in getting through the Italian customs despite my *laissez-passer*), I sallied forth to renew my acquaintance with the city, albeit the weather was cold and dull. Entering the first attractive café which I came to, I sat down on a high stool at the counter on which stood a basket of freshly made croissants. A stout woman on the other side of the counter set a steaming mug of *café au lait*, a plate and a generous portion of butter before me. I think it was the most delicious breakfast I have ever enjoyed. The café was full of young men and women all breaking their fast before going to work and I reflected that if they had been Britons the men would all have been reading the morning papers and the women mostly silent. But here there was a buzz of conversation and hardly a newspaper to be seen, presenting an unforgettable portrait of pre-war Parisian life. By the following morning I was back in London; on re-joining the flagship I handed over the comments on the draft programme of exercises.

On our way out to Gibraltar in early 1938 the commander-in-chief paid a visit to Lisbon which provided the opportunity of seeing something of this picturesque city. We were very hospitably entertained by our Portuguese hosts who arranged visits to Sintra, in the foothills of the Sintra mountains, and Estoril, on the Portuguese Riviera, as well as golf and football matches. During our visit President Óscar Carmona gave a reception for us in his historic palace at Belém. One recollection, among many, was the impressive appearance of the statuesque halberdiers who lined the magnificent stairway leading up to the president's room.[13] After calling at Gibraltar, we carried on to Malta so that the two commanders-in-chief could discuss any issues not connected with the exercises, which would fully occupy their time once they met again at Gibraltar.

The exercises took place as arranged to the west of Gibraltar. Everyone looked forward to this reunion of the Home and Mediterranean Fleets, with some of the most powerful ships in the Royal Navy packed into Gibraltar harbour. There was a good deal of entertaining and the opportunity to meet old friends and shipmates. One senior visitor, known to some of us, was the First Sea Lord – Admiral of the Fleet Lord Chatfield – who arrived on 12 March to observe the exercises. It was his ship, HMS *Lion*, which the *Indomitable* had towed back to port after the Dogger Bank action in 1915.

While the manoeuvres were taking place we staff officers were kept extremely busy. We had to analyse all the exercises and prepare large diagrams showing what had taken place and why. Any discrepancies in the movements of ships had to be sorted out and briefs had to be prepared for the various flag officers taking part in the discussions. As soon as all was ready the flag officers, captains and officers of the two fleets gathered in one of the local coal sheds on the south mole, which had been converted into a lecture room with the aid of canvas side screens and flags. The post mortem on the exercises would then begin. There was often a great deal of humour expressed by the rival commanders. On one occasion Vice Admiral Andrew Cunningham, second-in-command, Mediterranean Fleet, and in command of the Battle Cruiser Squadron, claimed that if a certain exercise had been real war, he would have rammed and sunk the flagship of the Rear Admiral (Destroyers) – Rear Admiral John Tovey – in HMS *Galatea*. The latter replied that the admiral commanding the Battle Cruisers might be the eel-spearing champion for Scotland but that gave him no title to claim similar marksmanship with his flagship, HMS *Hood*, even if her power and size had given her the nickname, the 'Mighty Hood'.[14]

We returned to Portsmouth at the end of March; on 12 April Admiral Sir Roger Backhouse hauled down his flag to become First Sea Lord in succession to Lord Chatfield. His successor was Admiral Sir Charles Forbes, who had had the distinction of being present at the surrender of the German fleet in 1918. Henry Moore, who had been promoted rear admiral, left to take up an appointment as chief of staff to the commander-in-chief, Portsmouth. He was succeeded by Commodore Edward King, who had been Director of the Plans Division at the Admiralty in the mid-30s and with whom I was later to work when I was assigned to the Admiralty.[15]

War Clouds

The overrunning of Austria by Germany, which had taken place on 12 March 1938, quickened the thoughts of everyone in the services regarding the possibility of another war. The draft plan for this eventuality had been in the hands of the commander-in-chief, Home Fleet, for some time and Admiral Backhouse had gone to the Admiralty greatly impressed by our acute shortage of anti-submarine vessels. He made it one of his first tasks to press on with the building of what became known as the Hunt-class destroyers which, being much smaller and less complicated than the type of vessel then being laid down in the normal destroyers' programme, could be completed more quickly and in larger numbers. I remember the pleasure with which he announced the stepping up of this programme when I went to see him one day in his office in the Admiralty. Unfortunately, he was not to live to see the results of his foresight; in July 1939 he died suddenly of a brain tumour aged 60. His successor was Admiral Sir Dudley Pound, who was succeeded by Admiral Cunningham as C-in-C, Mediterranean Fleet.

There was one main point in the Admiralty's plan in the event of war with Germany with which, as C-in-C, Home Fleet, Admiral Forbes did not agree – and that was the proposal that the Firth of Forth should be the Home Fleet's main base. He considered that Scapa Flow, where the Grand Fleet had its anchorage during the First World War, was preferable and he lost no time in letting his opinion be known at the Admiralty. The Naval staff were not entirely convinced by his argument and there the matter rested until it was brought to a head by the Munich crisis in September 1938.

Meanwhile, after the customary period in Portsmouth and Portland, the Home Fleet had embarked on the summer cruise, which included a visit to the Clyde and Greenock in late June at the invitation of the Lord Provost of Glasgow in connection with the Empire Exhibition, which had recently opened in May at Bellahouston Park. During our stay, the end of June promotions were published and I was fortunate to find my name amongst those promoted to captain. Normally I should have left to take up another appointment when my relief arrived, but, as the international barometer was falling steadily under Hitler's baneful influence, Admiral Forbes requested that I remain on his staff in the new post of staff officer (plans). My duties were to draft for his approval the plans to be put into action by the Home Fleet in the event of war. I was in the middle of my work when, not content with the *Anschluss* with Austria, Hitler had begun demanding the cession of the German-speaking regions of Czechoslovakia. Before returning south we visited Kristiansand in southern Norway; from Greenock we sailed to Portrush, County Antrim, Oban and back to Portsmouth.

Due to the deteriorating situation in Europe, and in view of Admiral Forbes's belief in the importance of Scapa Flow, after the routine exercises at Invergordon in September, we sailed to the Orkneys. On arrival I accompanied the commander-in-chief on a tour of inspection of the defences. A party of Royal Marines had just finished demolishing the last of the First World War coastal batteries and the anchorage was as devoid of protection as a man caught in a storm without a coat or an umbrella. The boom across the main entrance was in the process of being laid but there were three other entrances to be blocked. We bought a concrete barge for £100 from a canny Orcadian (he had, I believe, paid £5 for it after the First World War) and this was sunk in one of the Holm Sound channels lying off mainland Orkney. For the others, all that could be done was to represent to the Admiralty our utter nakedness!

While, in the months to come, steps were taken to strengthen the defences, it was not until after the sinking of HMS *Royal Oak* at anchor in the Flow by Korvettenkapitän Günther Prien in U-47 on 14 October 1939, that these were brought up to the standard requested by Admiral Forbes a year previously.[16] Returning to Invergordon we carried out more exercises before stopping at Rosyth and then back to Portsmouth.

There was a temporary lull in tension after the Munich Agreement, signed by Hitler on 30 September 1938, whereby Great Britain and France sanctioned Germany's annexation of the Sudetenland; so, in January the following year, the Home Fleet sailed on the usual spring cruise to the Mediterranean. It was the last time that Gibraltar was to see the great display of sea-power exemplified by the combined pre-war Home and Mediterranean Fleets. By the time we returned to Portsmouth towards the end of March, I had virtually completed my task and Admiral Forbes kindly consented to release me to take up the post of assistant to the naval attaché in Paris, where new challenges awaited.

Chapter Eleven

Diplomacy before War

Ask who is wise? – You'll find the self-same man
A sage in France, a madman in Japan.[1]

1939

The Royal Navy has often been called upon to act in circumstances in which a knowledge of the political background has proved invaluable to a senior officer faced with a difficult decision. It is true that the Foreign Office and the Admiralty do not usually employ the same means to achieve their ends. The weapons of the former are the pen and polished phrase, while those of the latter are generally of a more explosive nature, but it is as well for each to know the other's rules. I therefore welcomed the opportunity of seeing the Diplomatic Corps at work. I soon discovered that, whereas in the Service the prefix 'Most Immediate' implies instant action, to the diplomat such an address is regarded as being more applicable to the messenger than the message. Again, for all Their Lordships' impersonality, they would hardly agree to being addressed as a 'Dear Department' by someone who signs himself, anonymously, 'Chancery', and while a naval officer is undoubtedly the Admiralty's 'most obedient servant', he does not admit to saying so 'with truth and respect'!

Paris

I arrived in Paris on a beautiful April morning, having taken the night train from London. The naval attaché, whose assistant I was to be, was Captain Cedric Holland, and I could not have had a better tutor than 'Hookey', as he was affectionately known to his friends. He and his wife, Barbara, were both very popular in diplomatic circles and they entertained at their house in the historic Rue de la Faisanderie in the *16ème arrondissment* with that easy grace and friendliness which rightly endeared them to all who enjoyed their hospitality.[2] The orbit of the Naval Attaché in Paris included Holland, Belgium and Spain. As the German threat grew and it became necessary to discuss with our French allies the steps to be taken in the event of war, it became more and more difficult for Hookey to leave Paris and so it was decided that, in due course, I should relieve him of responsibility for Holland and Belgium. Meanwhile I started to read myself in, which meant studying the diplomatic telegrams from our representatives all over Europe. It was fascinating to see with what Machiavellian subtlety Hitler pursued his plans, using first one pretext and then another as an excuse for a further act of territorial violation.

Our ambassador was Sir Eric Phipps who had spent 1933–37 as British ambassador to Germany; in July he was succeeded by the outstanding diplomat, Sir Ronald Hugh Campbell, (formerly British Envoy Extraordinary and Minister Plenipotentiary in Yugoslavia). The doyen of the embassy staff was the press attaché, Sir Charles Mendl. Probably no living Englishman knew more about the ramifications of French politics than him. His daily summary of the French press for the ambassador was a masterpiece of factual information and dry humour. He was a great connoisseur of wine and we had not long been acquainted before he took me along to introduce me to his wine merchant in his office just behind the Madeleine: a typical Frenchman with a large bushy beard and a reputation for being able to produce the perfect wine for every course. Sir Charles's own cellar was reported to be one of the best in the city. (I later heard that, when the Germans took Paris in 1940 Reichsmarschall Hermann Göring went straight to it.)[3] Lady Mendl, better known as Elsie de Wolfe, was a famous Parisian hostess, and one could meet all the prominent people of the stage and diplomatic world at her house in Versailles. One Sunday afternoon I was having a swim in their pool when the famous stage and film actress, Jacqueline Delubac, wife of the actor and director, Sacha Guitry, was brought along to be introduced. It is difficult to feel at ease dripping wet, clad only in a pair of swimming trunks, when confronted with a glamorous and beautiful actress, who is herself exquisitely dressed and *soignée* to the last degree, but Mademoiselle Delubac instantly dispelled my uneasiness and I passed a very pleasant half an hour in her company on the edge of the pool.[4]

Having made friends with a number of French naval officers in the *Ministère de la Marine*, I saw a side of Parisian life which the tourist cannot see. They took me to their favourite bistros, where we drank Neuilly cassis and, on high days and holidays, champagne! We went to cafés where *diseuses* or female artists sang topical French songs which meant nothing unless one had a good knowledge of the language. One of my first glimpses of the unreality of the situation came when I found myself sitting next to the wife of the Polish military attaché at dinner one night. In the course of conversation, I mentioned that the German Army was reported to have a large number of tanks. 'Nonsense!' said the charming lady. 'You have not seen our cavalry. They will make mincemeat of those German tanks.' I was so astonished by this remark that, after the ladies had retired, I sought confirmation from her husband. To my surprise he supported her opinion.

One day Admiral François Darlan, Commander-in-Chief of the French Navy, asked Hookey and myself to lunch. He was an excellent host but his jealousy of the position held by the Royal Navy throughout the world was only too apparent. Pointing with pride to the *Dunkerque* and the *Strasbourg* – the most heavily armoured ships afloat – and the flotilla of fast and heavily-armed destroyer leaders which accompanied them, he asked: 'Have the British anything as good as this?' Little did we know that, just over a year later, following the fall of France, Holland, as an accomplished French speaker, would be involved in the critical negotiations to save those same ships when their fate hung in the balance at Mers el Kebir.[5]

Although Europe may have been hovering on the brink of an abyss, life in the city seemed to pursue its normal course. The social life continued unabated, the chestnut trees in the Bois de Boulogne attracted the usual crowds and 'Jacques Bonhomme' took his wife and family for their customary visit to the *Jardin d'Acclimatation* to see the animals disport themselves in the warm spring sunshine.[6]

On one occasion I was taken to a party in a riding school to see a Russian colonel demonstrate how his horse had an unusual ear for music. There were lots of smartly dressed men and women who looked strangely out of place in the bare wooden gallery from where we were to watch the show. The colonel mounted his horse, a handsome white, high-spirited animal, and an assistant handed him a saxophone on which he played a variety of dance tunes, to which the horse responded with remarkable precision. The saxophone was then replaced by a clarinet and later a French horn and the terpsichorean performance continued. Meanwhile, champagne corks were popping below where we were sitting and soon a steady flow of glasses appeared, followed by the bottles themselves so that the applause which had hitherto been perfunctory and polite, became noisier and more pronounced. Towards the end of the performance a member of a well-known French aristocratic family suggested that we pass the rest of the evening at his flat over a game of cards. I felt my toe being heavily trodden on by the friend who had brought me and so I pleaded a previous engagement. When we had taken our leave, my friend told me that I had escaped from one of the most unscrupulous gamblers in Paris, who was always on the lookout for a 'pigeon' to pluck.

Despite the social pleasures, our lives were busy. There was a constant coming and going of VIPs who had to be met at the station, escorted to their destination and, if not otherwise engaged, wined, dined and taken to a show. I think I saw the current spectacle at the well-known cabaret, Moulin Rouge, no less than six times so that even the shapely blonde who realistically interpreted the part of Eve in the Garden of Eden left me as cold as she must always have felt. Underneath the apparent veneer of insouciance, I detected a hidden fear clutching at everybody's heart. While I was in Paris Virginia Cowles, the noted American journalist – who later married the British politician Aiden Crawley – came to stay with the assistant military attaché and his wife and they kindly invited me to lunch. As she was fresh from a visit to Poland and Germany, which included interviewing Hitler, we were all anxious to hear what she had to say. She confirmed our opinion that a clash over Poland was inevitable if Hitler continued his agitation over the Danzig corridor.[7]

Known also as the Polish corridor, the territory had been awarded to Poland after the First World War to provide the newly created republic with access to the Baltic sea. It meant that Germany was separated from the province of East Prussia. In March 1939 Hitler demanded that road access should be provided across the corridor from Germany to East Prussia; he also demanded the cession of Danzig, which had been established as a 'free city', separate from both Poland and Germany.

The Hague

At the beginning of May 1939 I boarded the *Etoile du Nord* train which took me to The Hague. I was met at the station by my military counterpart, Lieutenant Colonel William Gibson, who had taken up his post as military attaché a short time previously. The Envoy Extraordinary and Minister Plenipotentiary, Sir Nevile Bland, greeted me warmly. I soon realised how fortunate I was to have been appointed to his staff. Throughout my period of service at the legation he and his wife, Portia, showed me the greatest possible kindness and I welcome this opportunity of thanking them for the many pleasant hours passed under their hospitable roof.[8] The atmosphere in Holland was totally different from that of Paris. There was a much keener perception of the dangers. The Dutch had enjoyed an unbroken peace for over 100 years and, despite their martial history, they hoped and prayed that, if the cataclysm did occur, it would pass them by, as it had done in the First World War. But, as events during that summer of 1939 marched on towards their awful climax, they began to realise that neutrality as a cloak offered poor protection against the gathering storm.

Lieutenant Colonel Gibson and I were both starting from scratch as far as office accommodation was concerned. There was no room for us at the legation and so we rented an office in the Plaats area in the centre of town. It was on the first floor above an Italian bookshop, the proprietors of which were of Fascist persuasion and many were the hostile looks we received on entering and leaving our office. But we soon made friends with a number of Dutch people and before long felt quite at home.

When I first arrived in The Hague there were only two other naval attachés, those attached to the United States and Japanese Legations. The American naval attaché, Captain Munro Kelly USN, had a fund of rich humour, inherited no doubt from his Irish ancestors. He helped me in every possible way and we became good friends. He still owes me many hours of sleep lost while sitting up yarning in his flat and listening to the short-wave bulletins from the United States which, of course, could only be received in the small hours. We both liked Commander Shutei Tonaki, who had arrived in The Hague in 1938 as Japan's first full-time naval attaché to the Japanese Legation. There was a standing joke whenever Kelly and Tonaki met at a party: Tonaki would advance bowing and smiling and then, when he was within speaking distance, he would draw his breath in through his teeth and say: 'What for you fortify Guam?' whereupon Kelly would answer with a smile: 'To keep you from pinching it,' which always brought a broad grin to Tonaki's face. His pretty wife always appeared in a most decorative kimono, of which she seemed to have an inexhaustible supply. One result of her indigenous attire was to disguise the fact that another little Tonaki was on the way and the first the Diplomatic Corps knew was when we received an invitation to attend a party at Commander Tonaki's house to celebrate the birth of a son. During the course of one conversation, Tonaki told me that his great ambition was to be the gunnery officer of a battleship and fire the big guns at an 'enemy'. I often wonder what became of him in the war of opposing sides we were soon to be engaged upon. We had formed a good friendship and had many games of golf on the Haagsche Club course.

During my posting to The Hague, I was able to visit Amsterdam and the famous Rijksmuseum which houses, among many masterpieces, Rembrandt's 'The Night Watch'. I do not know of any better way to recapture the spirit of sixteenth and seventeenth century Holland than to browse amongst the pictures of her people, which the great artists of that time created for posterity's enjoyment and instruction. Of particular interest to me were the sea-scapes, for no more romantic figures ever sailed the sea than the Dutch naval officers, Admirals Maarten Tromp, his son Cornelis Tromp and Michiel de Ruyter who figure prominently in Anglo-Dutch maritime history.[9] I was glad to have been advised to visit the Dutch Historical Navigation Museum, where there was a magnificent collection of model ships including one of the *Hollandia* of 1665, in which two of these great admirals hoisted their flags. There was much of interest by way of pictures of naval battles, old charts and maps as well as the instruments with which the art of navigation was practised in those early days when conquest of the seas could literally open up a new world. As I was to find during my stay in Holland, everywhere I went there was a reminder of the close connection which the Dutch have always had with the sea. They have sailed upon it, fought upon it and wrested hundreds of acres from its grasp, waging relentless war against any encroachment. It is little wonder that they say the salt is in their blood.

The German naval attaché, Käpitan Kurt Besthorn, took up his post in early July 1939. I found him to be a classic example of the insidious working of the Nazi ideology. Short, thick-set with a square head and a smile ornamented by a number of gold-filled teeth, he was a former officer in the Imperial German Navy who had settled in Java, in the Dutch East Indies after the First World War, becoming manager of a coffee plantation. One night, so he told me, he heard the voice of the Führer over the radio, whereupon he decided to give up his job and return to the fatherland. After a course of indoctrination, he arrived in The Hague, where he set himself diligently to the undoing of the very people whose hospitality he had enjoyed for twenty years. We exchanged the usual formal calls, but, as the Polish situation began to build up to crisis proportions, I considered it appropriate to talk frankly with him. I had another purpose in mind in calling on him: I had heard that he had rented a large detached house, much more pretentious than his station required and that the top floor was being equipped as a wireless transmitting and receiving station.

Arriving punctually at his home, I was met by his secretary who apologised for the fact that he had been detained at the legation. 'Would I like coffee?' she asked. 'Or a cigarette, or perhaps an English newspaper?' Describing the English as *gemütlich* [pleasant], she expressed her admiration for my kinsmen. Perhaps I did not respond properly to her small talk, because after a short time she excused herself and left me alone. When Käpitan Besthorn arrived he was full of apologies. I began our conversation by admiring his commodious residence, expressing surprise that he should require so many rooms. 'They will be useful when my family comes from Berlin,' he responded airily, by which he meant a strange collection of 'relatives' who later took up residence. I then turned the conversation to the political situation, asking him whether, if the Poles refused Hitler's demands, he thought there would be a war. He assured me most emphatically that Germany did not want war.

'The Poles will fight,' I preferred, 'and I do not see how a clash can be avoided, if Germany persists with its demands.'

'I don't know, but the Führer, <u>he</u> knows,' he replied, pointing to a photograph of Hitler in a large silver frame on his desk.

'Herr Käpitan,' I said. 'In 1914 you Germans made the mistake of thinking that the Kaiser was the Almighty. Now you accord to that man the attributes of God. I can assure you that he is no better than you or me.' With that I began to make my exit. He did not respond but accompanied me to the door. As we shook hands he said, almost paternally: 'Don't worry, there will be no war.'

The French Admiralty had also recently appointed a naval attaché, Capitaine de Corvette Baron Louis Guichard. Tall, dark and slim with finely chiselled features, he was a charming and entertaining companion. He paid me the compliment of inviting me to become a member of the small mess which he established for his staff, a privilege which I much appreciated. One day we were in his chauffeur driven car when two Dutch girls on bicycles accidentally rode straight into the car at an intersection and fell head over heels over the bonnet. We jumped out to help the unfortunate young ladies to their feet. Luckily, they were unhurt, but to hear Guichard address them, you would have thought they had done him an honour by scratching the paintwork of his handsome Renault. 'You know,' he said, in his accented English. 'In France we talk about young ladies throwing their bonnets over the windmill, but this is the first time I see them throw themselves over the bonnet!'[10]

At the beginning of August I returned to Paris to take over the office for a fortnight while Hookey Holland took some well-earned leave. It was hot and sultry in the city with big grey clouds and thunderstorms. The busy days of spring had given way to a listless sort of inactivity. Everyone seemed to be going about their work, heavy in mind and body; a sense of impending tragedy was in the air. There was only routine correspondence to be attended to at the office and so I spent my free time visiting scenes and places which brought back memories of my student days when we thought the spectre of war had been banished for ever. When the time came for me to return to The Hague, I said goodbye to my friends on the embassy staff. None of us had an inkling in what dramatic circumstances we should meet again. I was glad to get back to The Hague and drive down to the seaside suburb of Scheveningen on the coast and fill my lungs with good, deep draughts of fresh air.

On 31 August 1939 Her Majesty Queen Wilhelmina celebrated her fifty-ninth birthday, the day traditionally celebrated as a national holiday. The usual orange decorations were set up and the trees transformed into fairylands of coloured lights. The people, however, were too worried by the current political situation to give themselves wholeheartedly to rejoicing. 'Instead of jubilation, political gloom cast its shadows on the festivities,' noted Eelco van Kleffens, who had recently been appointed the Dutch Minister for Foreign Affairs.[11]

Two days later came the news of Hitler's invasion of Poland and, on 3 September, our own ultimatum to Germany. It was Sunday and, since no newspapers were published, a blackboard was set up in a shop window near my office in the Plaats on which the latest news of the crisis was written up. Silent, anxious crowds gathered around to read that what they feared so much had in fact taken place. At the legation we received news that Sir Nevile Henderson, our ambassador in Berlin, together with his staff would arrive in The Hague the following day and so preparations had to be made to receive them and for their onward passage to England. Since the Germans refused to allow the party to cross the Dutch frontier until the German ambassador from London reached Dutch territorial waters, the British were held up. 'There was no discomfort or discourtesy about it,' Sir Nevile later recorded, 'as there was fortunately a restaurant car attached to our train. It remained in a siding apart from even the curious, and as I had brought some bridge-cards with me, we were able to while the time away.'[12]

When finally he and his party reached The Hague, it was most interesting to hear of their experiences during these last crucial weeks, as he has subsequently related in his book, *Failure of a Mission*. In order to justify his demand for a Polish emissary with full powers to be sent at once to Berlin, which Henderson had suggested sounded 'very much like an ultimatum', Hitler had explained that it was necessary 'not only on account of the risk of incidents when two mobilised armies were standing opposite one another, but also when Germans were being massacred in Poland'. In this latter connection Hitler had asserted that Henderson did not care 'how many Germans were being slaughtered in Poland'. Apparently this 'gratuitous impugnment of the humanity' of the British

Government was too much even for a highly-trained diplomat like Sir Nevile and the remainder of the interview was 'of a somewhat stormy character'. As the ambassador described the scene to us, he had been instructed to make it clear to Hitler that, if Germany invaded Poland, it would mean war with Great Britain. On being so informed, Hitler worked himself up into one of his towering rages and, dancing up and down like a madman, called the ambassador 'a murderer of women and children', a singularly strange and unwarranted accusation considering we were leaning over backwards in our efforts to prevent war. Advancing towards Hitler, Sir Nevile, who as we now know, was a sick man suffering from cancer of the throat and often in great pain, shot back: 'We will not take that from you, Herr Führer,' whereupon Hitler collapsed like a pricked balloon and became quite normal.[13]

Arrangements had been made with the Batavier line of Rotterdam for the ambassador and his party to take passage in the SS *Batavier V* which was leaving for London at dawn on Thursday morning, 8 September. At the last moment, when arrangements were complete, the minister sent for me and said that Sir Nevile wanted me to arrange for a destroyer escort to meet his ship off the Hook of Holland. I accordingly telegraphed the Admiralty but, since there was considerable delay in the communications with England, I asked for a reply to be sent directly to the consul general's office in Rotterdam. After dinner I set off in my car, together with Captain Richard Shelley RN, our naval attaché in Berlin and the military attaché, Major General Frank Mason-MacFarlane, reaching Rotterdam at 9pm on Wednesday evening. We called in at the consul general's office but there was no message for me, so we went on down to the ship. The ambassador was very disturbed to learn that the Admiralty had not yet replied to my message and, to pass the time, he sat in the saloon with the minister. As 10 and then 11 o'clock struck, he began to get more and more restless. Taking Shelley and me by the arm, he walked us up and down, emphasising that his safety was in our hands and that on no account must the Dutch master of the ship be told the rendezvous until the ship was clear of land. At length he went to lie down. As there was nothing more I could do on board, I decided to return to the consul general's office and wait. Soon after I arrived a telegram from the Admiralty was delivered. The consul general had the code books ready on the table and so, telling his vice consul to write down the groups as he called them out, he tore open the envelope and set to work. I sat down in a chair and lit a pipe.

After some time I got up to look over the vice consul's shoulder to see how the message was coming out. Sometimes there are a lot of corrupt groups which make for a lot of re-checking. Imagine my astonishment when I saw a blank sheet of paper in front of him. I shook him as he seemed to be asleep and he almost fell off his chair. I discovered afterwards that the poor man suffered from chronic headaches and must have taken too strong a dose of the medicine with which he used to try to relieve the pain and it had sent him into a sort of coma. Fifteen precious minutes had been wasted. The consul general and I lifted him onto a sofa and I took his place. In a short time I was on my way back to the ship with the good news that the escort would be there as arranged and I handed Captain Shelley the rendezvous.

Describing the voyage, Henderson later wrote: 'When we went on deck the next morning we were provided with the exhilarating spectacle of three British destroyers, on each side and in front of us, which had been detailed to escort us back home... Every member of our party was affected, as I was, by the sight of these silent but blessed British warships.'[14]

Chapter Twelve

'The race is not to the swift'

How chances mock
And changes fill the cup of alteration
With diverse liquors![1]

1939–40

Until war was declared on 3 September 1939 I had avoided all contact with any organisation engaged in what might be termed purely intelligence work. Once hostilities had begun, I was free to co-operate with such organisations as we had in Belgium and the Netherlands. From that time onwards it was like living out a chapter in a melodramatic spy story. The Germans, needless to say, had built up a large espionage organisation throughout the Netherlands as part of their fifth column activities. They had agents everywhere, especially in the hotels. If one went to the bar and ordered a drink, the inevitable Gestapo agent would take up a listening position behind a pillar. Vigilance was therefore essential at all times. Our press attaché, Captain John Pelham, the Earl of Chichester, was engaged to a charming Dutch girl, Ursula von Pannwitz, whose mother had a large house outside The Hague. One day the Dutch Director of Naval Intelligence sent for me and told me that every word spoken at meals in that house was being passed to the German Legation by the servants. I naturally passed on the warning.[2]

The Germans knew that our Passport Control Organisation was a cover for our intelligence work and set two men to watch the building in which it was housed. As head of the Passport Control Office, Major Richard (Dick) Stevens, an ex-Indian Army officer with a flair for languages and hard work, was covertly working for the British Secret Intelligence Service (SIS). He was a very popular member of the legation staff. One of the first incidents of the war was a raid by RAF aircraft on the German naval base at Wilhelmshaven. The Admiralty was anxious to know what damage, if any, had been done to the German ships. Somehow or other Stevens had managed to get hold of a copy of the German report on the raid. He told me that when the Germans discovered that the information had been leaked they were very angry and Käpitan Besthorn, the German naval attaché, had an unpleasant interview with his minister, news of which we could not help but feel a certain amount of satisfaction.[3]

Meanwhile my French colleagues were busy with their own organisation and were concentrating on obtaining information about the movements of German submarines. As such information was of little use unless acted upon at once we arranged a simple code for use over the open telephone line. One of their staff would telephone me and invite me to lunch or dinner at a certain restaurant at a certain time on a particular day. I would then ask who else was going to be there and they might reply 'no one' or with a series of names such as Charles, Hélène, Fifi, Antoinette and so on. Interpreted this would mean that a certain number of submarines had sailed for such and such a port at a certain time and date. Sometimes we dined out a lot, then for long periods we would remain *chez nous*. Without any disrespect to my French colleagues, I think that most of the information was bogus but I had no means of telling and so back it went to the Admiralty to be assessed.

In one of his stories of the First World War, *The Traitor,* Somerset Maugham refers to the Swiss 'taking their neutrality like a dachshund for a walk with them'. In the Second World War the Dutch wore theirs like a charm to ward off the evil eye.[4] One day I received information that a certain ship was unloading stores at Amsterdam for the German Legation in The Hague. The stores were in wooden boxes marked 'Tea, Sugar, Coffee', etc. but I knew they were cases of sub-machine guns and ammunition which were being steadily imported and stowed in the basement of the legation. The information was so definite that I informed Vice Admiral Johannes Furstner, who was serving as the Dutch Chief of Naval Staff, Ministry of Defence. As he seemed reluctant to believe that the Germans were capable of such a breach of diplomatic privilege I asked him to arrange with the stevedores unloading the ship for a case to be dropped on its end, as if by accident. The admiral thanked me for the information but said it would not be 'correct' to act upon it. (I am glad to record that when the Germans eventually did invade Holland he escaped in a fishing vessel and was instrumental in organising the remnants of the Dutch fleet from London.)[5]

A short time later I was asked to arrange for weather reports from Holland and Belgium for the use of the RAF. We were willing to supply the observers but, although I had no difficulty in arranging reports to be delivered to a certain address twice daily in Belgium, I could not get Dutch approval for placing them where they were required. And so the Germans continued with their plans without let or hindrance on the part of the trusting Dutch. While it is quite understandable that they were anxious not to provoke the German juggernaut into action, I am convinced that had they and the Belgians joined forces to protect their neutrality and taken a tougher line with the Germans they could have made things more difficult for them. Between the two countries they could field two million men under arms and, with co-ordinated action, might have disrupted Hitler's timetable for war more than they did. As the Bible tells us: 'the race is not to the swift, nor the battle to the strong...but time and chance happen to them all'.[6]

There was one Dutchman who had no illusions about the Germans and that was the head of Dutch Military Intelligence, Major General J.W. van Oorschot, who delighted in deflating the arrogant Nazis. There was a story how, on his way back from a visit to Germany just before the outbreak of war he was sitting in his compartment reading a copy of *The Times* when the train reached the German frontier. There was a tramp of jack-boots, the door of the carriage was thrown open and a voice shouted: 'Oorschot'. He carried on reading, the demand was repeated even more loudly and this time the official rapped against the front of the general's paper. Carefully and deliberately putting his paper down, and producing his diplomatic passport, the general asked in fluent German if that was the way distinguished foreigners were treated in Hitler's Reich. Within the limits set by his government, General van Oorschot certainly did all he could to help us and I was relieved to hear that he too managed to escape the clutches of the Gestapo when his country was invaded.[7]

One precautionary measure which the Dutch did take following our declaration of war was to lay protective minefields in the approaches to their naval base at Den Helder. As bad luck would have it, on 8 September one of their minesweepers, the *Willem van Ejwick*, struck one of these mines and sank with considerable loss of life.[8] I was informed that a memorial service was to be held at the base and so the American naval attaché, Captain Kelly, the French naval attaché, Capitaine Guichard, and I expressed a wish to attend as an expression of sympathy on the part of our respective Admiralties. On hearing of our plans, Käpitan Besthorn and Commander Tonaki announced their intention of attending. The occasion remains vividly in my mind.

The news of the sinking on 17 September of HMS *Courageous* by a German U-boat in the Western Approaches off the coast of Ireland had just been announced. Its captain, my good friend, Bill Makeig-Jones, with whom I had served in HMS *Nelson*, had gone down with his ship.[9] Guichard and I drove up together. It was a cold bleak autumn day and, after passing through the town of Alkmaar, famous for its cheese market, the country is barren of trees and the cold north-east wind holds uninterrupted sway. Although Besthorn's grin was more pronounced than ever, we ignored his presence, stamping our feet in an attempt to keep warm.

The Venlo Incident

After devouring Poland, Hitler let it be known that he was willing to make peace (on his terms of course). There were also a number of Germans opposed to Hitler who were making approaches, either directly or through intermediaries, to the British Government. In Holland we were aware of the mysterious comings and goings of a Swedish industrialist, Birger Dahlerus, who passed through The Hague from time to time. One evening Dick Stevens came to see me in my flat. He told me that he had been authorised to get in touch with some German officers who were prepared to organise a *putsch* to overthrow Hitler and make peace provided they were given satisfactory guarantees of safety. Stevens wanted me to meet one of them at lunch, but, wisely perhaps – in view of subsequent events – I declined, considering that my position as naval attaché precluded my involvement.

Contact with the German officers had initially been arranged by a German refugee, Franz Fischer (and known as Dr Franz) in September 1939 with the British agent, Captain Sigismund Payne Best, who was married to a Dutch woman and had been running a bona fide import-export business in The Hague, dealing mainly in pharmaceuticals. Over the next few weeks Dr Franz had managed to convince Payne Best that he and several others formed part of a group which included high-ranking German generals who were interested in overthrowing Hitler, several meetings taking place in different locations. Since Payne Best believed that he was 'on to quite a big thing' he involved Major Stevens in the discussions. The German group had already been infiltrated by Major Walter Schellenberg (alias Captain Schämell), who was reporting directly back to Hitler's head of the Gestapo, Heinrich Himmler. It later transpired that Fischer had agreed to become an agent of the German Sicherheitsdienst (SD-Security Service) in return for which charges of embezzlement, which had caused him to flee Germany, would be waived.[10]

A few days after he had requested me to meet the Germans, Stevens again came to see me and told me that, since there were so many Gestapo agents operating in The Hague, they had asked for their next meeting to take place at the frontier at a little place called Venlo, some 60 miles south-east of Nijmegen. He told me that they had taken Major General van Oorschot into their confidence and he had deputed a Dutch officer, Lieutenant Dirk Klop, to act as liaison officer in this risky mission. We sat talking all night until early in the morning. Stevens was very tense and worried, but he refuted any suggestion that the Germans might be involving them in a trap. Although I was not at all sure about the mission's success, there was nothing I could do to persuade him to the contrary. As he left my flat, I wished him luck. The tragic sequel is well-known.

Two meetings at the Café Backus on the outskirts of Venlo near the frontier on 7 and 8 November passed without incident. At the second meeting, at which only Schellenberg (alias Schämell) was present, he proposed meeting again the following day, promising he would be accompanied by a senior German general. Unknown to Payne Best and Stevens, early on the morning of 9 November, Himmler ordered Schellenberg to abduct the two British agents when they met again at the Café Backus on the afternoon of 9 November.

'Somehow or other,' narrated Captain Sigismund Payne Best, describing the events of 9 November 'it seemed to me that things looked different from what they had on previous days.'

> Then I noticed that the German barrier across the road which had always been closed, was now lifted; there seemed to be nothing between us and the enemy. My feeling of impending danger was very strong. Yet the scene was peaceful enough...I must have rather checked my speed, for Klop called out: "Go ahead, everything is quite all right". I felt rather a fool to be so nervous. I let the car drift slowly along to the front of the café on my left and then reversed into the car park on the side of the building farthest from the frontier. Schämell was standing on the veranda at the corner and made a sign which I took to mean that our bird [i.e. the general] was inside. I stopped the engine and Stevens got out...I had just wriggled clear of the wheel and was following him out when there was a sudden noise of shouting and shooting. I looked up, and through the windscreen saw a large open car drive up around the corner till our bumpers were touching. It seemed to be packed to overflowing with rough-looking men. Two were perched on top of the hood and were firing over our heads from sub-machine guns, others were standing up in the car and on the running boards; all shouting and waving pistols. Four men jumped off almost before their car had stopped and rushed towards us shouting: "Hands up!" I don't remember actually getting out of the car, but by the time the men reached us, I was certainly standing next to Stevens, on his left. I heard him say: 'Our number is up, Best.' The last words we were to exchange for over five years.[11]

Klop, meanwhile, had tried to put up a fight and was fatally wounded, dying later in hospital in Dusseldorf. The kidnapping of the two British agents (and Payne Best's Dutch chauffeur, Jan Lemmens, who was later released) came immediately after a failed attempt on Hitler's life on 8 November at the Bürgerbräukeller in Munich by a disaffected German, Georg Elser. Although Elser insisted that he was acting alone, Hitler realised the propaganda value of claiming that the attack on his life had been orchestrated by British intelligence. Payne Best and Stevens remained as prisoners of war until 1945.

When the news of the kidnap reached us at the legation we were aghast. It showed how little store the Germans set by Dutch neutrality and we mourned the loss of a brave young Dutch officer. Although the Dutch Government asked the Germans for an explanation, none was forthcoming. The capture of our head of intelligence was a distinct feather in the German cap since it virtually put paid to our organisation in Holland.

Meanwhile as the 'phoney' war became reality, daily life continued. That first winter of the war was cold in Europe. In Holland the canals froze and everyone, young and old, took to the ice. It was a pleasant sight on weekdays to see people tumbling out of their offices, when the carillon in the Grote Kerk chimed midday, and betaking themselves to one of the frozen lakes in the woods around The Hague to spend their lunch hour skating. They reminded me of old Dutch paintings when time stood still. At weekends we went for trips along the canals to the neighbouring towns. We would make up a party of six or eight and set out with a log bamboo pole under our arms, all skating in step with the leader, except the last in line who was allowed to rest and be towed along by those in front. We took it in turns to rest, a necessary arrangement when covering long distances. When we came to one of the many low bridges which span the canals, the leader would call out *brug* and down we would all go on our haunches as we shot under the bridge like an express train. At first I quite expected to be decapitated as we were going so fast that if one had struck the bridge it would certainly have been a nasty shock. But, like many of the pleasant things in life, it is the spice of danger which gives added zest to enjoyment. At intervals along the canals little booths had been set up where hot milk and aniseed and cocoa could be bought. While it lasted it was a delightful form of relaxation which made one temporarily forget the war.

Into the middle of this wintry scene stepped an Indian Yuvaraja – an heir apparent to one of India's kingdoms or princely states – complete with his entourage which included a troupe of dancing girls and 300 pieces of baggage. He had been caught by the war while on a visit to England and the Foreign Office, who found his continued presence rather embarrassing, had suggested that if he went to Holland he might be able to charter a ship to take him home. He established himself in one of the big hotels and set his secretary to contact all the shipping lines, unfortunately without success and eventually he moved to the South of France. Meanwhile he was entertained by Sir Nevile Bland, our Envoy Extraordinary and Minister Plenipotentiary; in return he gave a party at his hotel which included a performance by his troupe of dancers. Someone told him that a daily consumption of Dutch gin out of one of those stone bottles was essential to keep out the cold and rumour had it that he became so partial to this beverage that he decided to buy up one of the Dutch factories and transport it back to India.

Although the Dutch would not enter into any sort of military pact with us, we began to draw up plans of action to be implemented in the event of a German invasion. In this connection, I had occasion to visit our vice consul at Flushing, Peter de Bruin. He lived in a sixteenth century house which he had carefully and tastefully restored. The walls of the dining room were still covered with the original handmade wallpaper of the period. After an excellent lunch served by a young lady, attired in the local costume, my host said: 'Let me introduce you to my daughter,' whereupon the serving maid made a deep curtsey! 'You see, we are quite self-contained here,' he continued, indicating a flock of sheep grazing in the paddock outside. 'We grow the wool, my daughter spins it and my wife is wearing it.' As I turned around I was treated to a sight, which that Flushing rope-maker's son and great Dutch admiral, Michiel de Ruyter, must often have seen, of a pretty Dutch girl in local dress at her spinning wheel.

Brussels

On 11 January 1940 I left my office in The Hague and set out by car on a routine visit to the other half of my parish centred on Brussels. From a purely naval point of view, Belgium did not have much to offer since the navy consisted of only a few minesweepers and patrol craft. But Brussels was a good centre of information and it was said, with what truth I would not know, that if you were prepared to' pay the price there was nothing that could not be bought there. I always looked forward to my visits to our ambassador, Sir Lancelot Oliphant, and his wife, Christine, who always made me feel very welcome. Lieutenant Colonel Francis Blake, our military attaché with whom I used to stay, was very hospitable.[12]

After stopping at Antwerp to visit our newly established consular shipping advisers on the staff of the consul general, I continued my journey, reaching Brussels in the late afternoon. I was not in the least surprised to find that Blake was out of town as he was a very busy man. The surprise came when he returned that evening with the astonishing news that a copy of part of the German plan for the invasion of the Low Countries and France had fallen into Belgian hands the previous day. Belgium was at that time sheltering under a declaration made by the German Ambassador on 26 August 1939 which stated that Germany would 'in no circumstances impair the inviolability and integrity of Belgium and will at all times respect Belgian territory'. Following Britain and France's declaration of war against Germany on 3 September the Belgian government had issued a declaration of neutrality. On 27 October, in a broadcast to the United States, King Leopold III of Belgium had declared: 'We cannot believe that the belligerents will fail to respect our neutrality. We have confidence in the promise they made before the whole world.' The witness which the graveyards of Flanders bore to the value of German promises had been forgotten but evidence was at hand that the deception was about to be repeated.

The story as it evolved centred on the activities of Major Helmuth Reinberger, who was adjutant to Colonel Gerhard Bassenge, the commanding officer of Dienststelle Fliegerführer 220, 7 Flieger (Airborne) Division. Reinberger's instructions were to deliver in person two copies of the plan. One copy was to be given to the divisional commander at Münster and the other to the general commanding the 22nd Infantry Division at Cologne. At Münster, Reinberger ran into Major Erich Hoenmanns, who had a private plane in which he offered to fly him to Cologne. They took off at daybreak the following morning. Hoenmanns intended to strike the Rhine and, having got his bearings, go up or down the river as necessary to reach his destination. In the event a low mist covered the ground and he crossed the frozen river without seeing it. Presently he saw some water but, unable to recognise it, came down for a closer look at which moment his engine failed and he was obliged to make a forced landing, damaging the plane, in a field near the town of Mechelen-aan-de-Maas (Malines sur Meuse).

Once the presence of two German officers became known, they were detained and searched by the Belgian police. Reinberger was found to be carrying *sehr geheim* i.e. top-secret documents, outlining Hitler's plan to invade Belgium, the Netherlands and France. Although Reinberger

141

had attempted to burn the documents, what remained was sufficiently legible to divulge their intent: (a) that the German Army of the West was to carry out an offensive across Belgium from the Moselle to the North Sea; (b) that the task of the Sixth German Army was to destroy the Belgian Army; (c) that the men of the 7th Flieger Division were to land between the Sambre and the Meuse. No wonder that this bolt from the blue was as welcome at army headquarters as a downpour of rain at a garden party!

As soon as he had despatched a report of this information to the War Office in London, Blake set out to break the news to General Lord Gort, commander-in-chief of the British Expeditionary Force at British Army Headquarters stationed in Arras. Now that the German intentions had been made plain and the umbrella of neutrality under which Belgium had been sheltering had been blown inside out, I waited anxiously to see what would happen next. No public announcement was made the following day. It appears that the general staff were considering whether the whole thing was a 'plant'. My own mind was firmly made up after a visit I paid that afternoon to the headquarters of our Intelligence Service where I discovered that, ever since the day of the forced landing of the Germans, the telegraph lines between Brussels and Berlin had been working overtime with messages to and from the German Embassy. This plainly showed that the Germans were very disturbed about the affair.

It was not until Saturday, three days later, that the hypothesis of a trick was ruled out and King Leopold told his Prime Minister and the matter was allowed to leak out, albeit in a very attenuated version. Class E reservists were called to the colours on the pretext that rumours of a German attack had been received and certain troop re-dispositions were made. In the hope of eliciting further information concerning the mysterious operation orders (which no member of the British Embassy had, as yet, been allowed to see) former Admiral of the Fleet, Sir Roger Keyes, a personal friend of King Leopold, was directed to ask for a private interview. On arrival Keyes went straight from the airport to the royal palace at Laeken, where the king showed him the partially burnt copy of the captured orders. The admiral was then driven to the embassy, where Blake and I were anxiously awaiting him. In the light of the captured documents, we asked him if he thought that the king would be willing to make capital out of this issue and abandon his policy of neutrality. He told us frankly that he thought this most unlikely.

Writing with the wisdom of hindsight, Winston Churchill, who was First Lord of the Admiralty at the time and had been kept abreast of events, comments: 'It seemed incredible to me that the Belgians would not make a plan to invite us in. But they did nothing about it.' It must be admitted that it was a difficult choice for Belgium. 'Hitler, on the other hand,' continued Churchill, 'as we now know, summoned Göring to his presence, and on being told that the captured papers were in fact the complete plans for invasion, ordered, after venting his anger, new variants to be prepared.'[13]

Farewell to The Hague

On Monday, 15 January 1940 I drove back to The Hague along roads which, in a few months time, were to be blasted with bombs and torn up by machine-gun fire. On arrival I found that, although news of the capture of certain important documents had been communicated to the Dutch Government by the Belgian Government, the Dutch were unaware of their contents. 'Strangely enough the exact contents of these documents was known only to the king and a few of his most intimate advisers,' observed Eelco van Kleffens, the Dutch Minister for Foreign Affairs. Referring to the military precautions being intensified 'with the greatest energy' in Belgium he continued: 'This action by our southern neighbour puzzled us. We on our side had no indication that there was any imminent danger. The season seemed at its most unfavourable for any large-scale military operations. A long spell of frost, which had begun in December, still confined the country in its icy bounds and was particularly severe in Germany, where communication had become difficult... Nevertheless, we decided to increase our vigilance to some extent in order to risk no chance of a surprise attack, but we left it at that, nothing happened and comparative quiet set in again.'[14]

In early February I donned my full dress uniform for the last time when I accompanied Sir Nevile Bland to the opening of the Dutch Parliament by Her Majesty Queen Wilhelmina. Since the Netherlands was still neutral, the Germans and Italians were there in force as well and we glared at each other across the aisle which separated us. Ten days later my relief, Vice Admiral Sir Gerald Dickens – a grandson of the novelist Charles Dickens – arrived.

'I greatly regret Captain Schofield's departure,' Sir Nevile Bland wrote to the Foreign Secretary, Lord Halifax: 'He has been a most valuable member of my staff, and his capacity, energy and devotion to duty have been beyond praise. Not only, moreover, has he made himself deservedly popular in both Dutch and diplomatic society, but he has succeeded, by his tact and good sense, in breaking down to an appreciable extent the hitherto deplorable reserve of the Netherlands Naval Authorities, thus obtaining much useful information and facilitating the task of his successor.'

On returning to England the Admiralty informed me that I was appointed to command a light cruiser, HMS *Galatea,* my appointment commencing on 27 February.[15]

Chapter Thirteen

HMS *Galatea*

Galatea: None of your airs, please. He's the son of Poseidon. There![1]

1940–41

H MS *Galatea*, an Arethusa-class light cruiser of 5,220 tons, was as good looking a ship as any captain with a feeling of pride in his first command could wish for. Launched in 1934, her entire service so far had been as flagship to the Rear Admiral (Destroyers) in the Mediterranean Fleet. Mounting six 6-inch guns in three turrets and four 4-inch anti-aircraft guns, she had a speed of thirty-two knots and was altogether a very handy little ship. When I joined her at the end of February 1940, she had been undergoing a refit at Devonport which was almost completed. At the beginning of March we sailed to join the Home Fleet at Scapa Flow but, since most of the officers and ship's company were new, we were given a month to work up and become efficient. I noted many changes in the bare and defenceless base of the pre-war era. The gaps between the islands had been blocked or strongly protected by nets, and batteries of anti-aircraft guns were springing up amongst the heather like mushrooms after rain. After we had finished working up, we went down to Rosyth where, on 11 March, we hoisted the flag of Vice Admiral Sir Frederick Edward-Collins, commanding the 2nd Cruiser Squadron.[2]

On 9 April Hitler launched his surprise attack on Norway. Our first thought was that this was an attempt by the German Navy to cover the escape of some commerce raiders and the commander-in-chief, Home Fleet, Admiral Sir Charles Forbes, ordered the squadron to join him with the rest of the Home Fleet in a position to intercept the German warships which had been reported crossing the entrance to the Skagerrak. The Luftwaffe were on the lookout for us and gave us a good pasting, happily with very little success. Seeing the great plumes of water thrown up by the bursting sticks of bombs carried me back to the time when, in the *Manly*, we came under fire from the main armament of the German battlecruisers at Lowestoft. I think one feels much more resentment at being bombed than at being shot at but, at any rate, it was my first experience of something which for many people, both in and out of the services, was soon to lose its novelty. We saw no sign of the German Navy and returned to Rosyth.

Norwegian Gold

In mid–April, as part of the Allied attempt to counter the German onslaught in Norway, we were instructed to embark a contingent of soldiers, stores, guns and ammunition. Included in the detachment was Brigadier Harold de Riemer Morgan and the headquarters echelon of 148 Brigade, 49th West Riding Division. Our orders were to land at Åndalsnes, a little village at the head of one of the branches of the Romsdal Fjord, about 170 miles south of Trondheim in Norway. Shortly before 5pm on 18 April we sighted the coast of Norway. Having reached the entrance of the fjord at the beginning of the extended twilight – happily without attracting the attention of the Luftwaffe – we were able to make the long passage up the fjord before darkness fell. The scenery was magnificent. On one side, Romsdals Horn (Romsdalshornet), capped with snow, towered high above us, while on the other a precipitous wall of cliffs and crags rose sheer from the water's edge. Over all there was a sort of eerie stillness, broken only by the swish of our bow wave as we cut through the glassy surface of the water.

We had been told that we would have to disembark the troops and stores by boat so were pleasantly surprised when we found an excellent concrete jetty just long enough to go alongside. The village of Åndalsnes nestled close up to the snow-covered mountains and nothing could have seemed more remote from the horrors of war than the Norwegian community tucked away at the head of the fjord. Our passengers and their equipment were soon ashore and we vacated the berth to allow our sister ship, HMS *Arethusa*, to take our place. Well within the time allowed, the operation was completed and we headed for home.

Less than a week later, we were once again entering Romsdal Fjord bound for Åndalsnes to disembark more troops and stores. As we were about to leave a Norwegian sergeant approached me as I stood on the jetty and asked me, in broken English, if I would take some gold. 'Gold,' I said in surprise. 'Yes, in the tunnel,' he replied. 'Wait, I get it.' A few minutes later a party of Norwegians arrived, pushing a covered railway wagon which they halted in front of the ship. Mustering all hands, the van was soon unloaded although the sailors were mystified as to why the little wooden boxes were so strangely heavy. When it was all safely on board we made ready to cast off. It was broad daylight by the time we reached the entrance and a watchful Heinkel aircraft threw a stick of bombs at us but, as we had just increased speed to twenty-five knots, they missed astern and so Providence was watching over us. We reached Rosyth at midday the following day, 25 April, with our cargo of gold.

Waiting for us on the jetty was a gentleman in a top hat and morning coat, who introduced himself as being from the Bank of Scotland. Having produced his credentials, he said he had come to collect the gold which he understood we had on board and requested me to give him the supply notes so that he could check the amount as it was loaded into a waiting railway truck. The look of surprise on his face when I told him I had no 'supply notes' was worth seeing. When I added that I had no idea whatever of the amount, his expression was one of amazement. He was a little mollified when I told him that, as the boxes were loaded at Åndalsnes, my paymaster had counted them and said he supposed that would have to do. Eventually I received a receipt for just over £2 million, the largest deposit I have ever made! The gold was, of course, the property of the Norwegian Government and I am glad to think that we cheated Hitler out of this bit of loot.

Transportation of the gold was split between three ships, packed into 818 crates of 40kg, 685 crates of 25kg and 39 barrels of gold coins, weighing 80kg each: a total of 53 tons.

The Galatea *arrived back with the first load of 200 crates. Since the Germans were advancing, the remainder was sent by lorry to Molde on the Romsdal Peninsula to be embarked on board HMS* Glasgow *with the Norwegian royal family and then north to Tromsø; having been obliged to take an even more circuitous route, involving being transported in fishing vessels, the remainder was loaded on board HMS* Enterprise *which survived two German air attacks on her way to Scapa Flow.*

The gold was gradually sold in the United States, partly to fund the Norwegian Government in exile. In 1987 ten tons of gold coins were returned to Norway.[3]

On 30 April we were back again at Åndalsnes. But instead of disembarking troops, we had been sent to rescue what was left of Brigadier Morgan's force, plus a party of Royal Marines who had been landed in the area after the disastrous attempt to save Norway. A tragic sight met our eyes as the ruins of the pretty village came into view. It had been completely burnt out and the charred timbers of the wooden houses stood out gaunt and black against the snow. Fortunately, the jetty had not been damaged and we were able to go straight alongside. Admiral Edward-Collins, who was in charge of the evacuation, had some anxious moments as parties of men had sought cover from the bombing all around the fjord and it was only by the winking of a shaded signal light that their presence was known. Naturally he was anxious that none should be left behind, but it was also important that we should be clear of the narrow waters of the fjord before the Luftwaffe recommenced operations at daylight. They had already scored a number of hits on the trawlers and sloops which had remained on patrol in the fjords during the previous fortnight. For my own part, with my between decks packed with men, I was well aware of the shambles, not to mention the loss of life, which would result from a hit. When he was satisfied that everyone had been taken off, the admiral ordered the squadron to depart. I have never seen such exhausted troops. As soon as they were down below they threw themselves onto any bit of vacant deck and went fast asleep. On 1 May, the ship's log recorded: '0400: attacked by 1 enemy aircraft. No hits.'

The Fall of France

On 9 May the Germans opened their offensive in the west and we received orders to go to Sheerness. On arrival we were ordered to the port of Ymuiden (Ijmuiden) at the mouth of the North Sea canal in northern Holland, to take off Their Royal Highnesses, Princess Juliana – Queen Wilhelmina's daughter – and her husband, Prince Bernhard. We arrived after dark and a young Dutch naval officer came on board, bringing with him a portable radio set with which we kept in touch with the harbour master ashore. He told us of the activities of the German fifth columnists, which the German authorities had assiduously nurtured during the previous months, and how the roads behind the fighting area were as dangerous as the front line. After waiting until nearly daylight without any sign of the royal party we returned to Sheerness and repeated the operation the following night. When, once again, we returned empty handed we learned that the whole of the Dutch royal family had made good their escape from the Hook of Holland together with the minister, Sir Nevile Bland, and the legation staff. I was very distressed to learn of the fate which my Dutch friends were having to endure. It was particularly hard for them since, as the Minister for Foreign Affairs, Eelco van Kleffens, later recorded, their 'scrupulous policy of neutrality' had been violated. But, as the Psalmist tell us: 'Many are the afflictions of the righteous.'[4]

As one disaster after the next overtook the Allied armies, we lay at Sheerness at short notice for steam. On 16 May we moved to Portsmouth, returning again to Sheerness a week later. From there we were instructed to lend a hand in the defence of Calais. A Swordfish aircraft of the Fleet Air Arm came out to spot for us and it was not long before the pilot sighted a group of German tanks coming up over the hill above Cap Gris Nez. We gave them a good plastering with 6-inch high explosive and the aircraft reported that all shots were falling in the target area, then tragedy intervened. Two Messerschmitt fighters suddenly appeared and dived on the Swordfish. The difference in speed between the two was so great that the pilot of the Swordfish had only to dive steeply and the bullets of his attackers passed harmlessly overhead, but unfortunately the observer who, in order to get a better view, was sitting on the edge of the cockpit, was unprepared for this sudden movement and fell out and, plummeting into the sea from such a height, was killed. No other aircraft was available and all we could do was to cruise up and down the coast looking for targets but, without knowledge of the position of our troops, we could not open fire unless we were certain that what we saw was enemy.

Then came the miracle and agony of the evacuation of British and French troops from Dunkirk which began on 26 May. The Admiralty decided that we were too big to be of any assistance and we had to stand idly by at Sheerness, 'hands employed cleaning ship' or 'washing down upper deck'. My ship's company were desperately keen to lend a hand

and it was not easy to explain to them why we could not do so. By 4 June over 300,000 men of the British and French armies had been evacuated, Winston Churchill – who had succeeded Chamberlain as Prime Minister on 10 May – making a stirring speech in the House of Commons, emphasising the importance of the Royal Navy:

> We shall go on to the end, we shall fight in France, we shall fight on the seas and oceans, we shall fight with growing confidence and growing strength in the air, we shall defend our Island, whatever the cost may be, we shall fight on the beaches, we shall fight on the landing grounds, we shall fight in the fields and in the streets, we shall fight in the hills; we shall never surrender, and even if, which I do not for a moment believe, this Island or a large part of it were subjugated and starving, our Empire, beyond the seas armed and guarded by the British Fleet, should carry on the struggle...[5]

In readiness for this struggle, on 16 June we proceeded to Plymouth, the 2nd Cruiser Squadron now under the command of Rear Admiral Alban T.B. Curteis, who had succeeded Vice Admiral Edward-Collins at the end of May.[6] We were not left long to enjoy the beauties of the Devonshire coastline as, soon after our arrival, instructions came for us to go to Arcachon on the west coast of France to take part in Operation Ariel: the evacuation of Allied forces and civilians from ports in western France. Our orders were to evacuate the British Ambassador, Sir Ronald Campbell, and his staff who had followed the French Government when they moved out of Paris. We could not enter the harbour of Arcachon and had to remain cruising up and down outside. I lowered the motor boat and sent my commander in to reconnoitre. His first haul was a party of ambulance drivers from the Hadfield-Spears Unit, set up by Lady Hadfield and now run by Mrs Edward Spears (better known as the American novelist Mary (May) Borden). They had been driving night and day across France and were badly in need of restorative treatment. I placed my after cabin and bathroom at their disposal. Whatever they may have left behind in France they had not forgotten their bath salts and for weeks to come I was reminded of the fragrant presence of these brave ladies.[7]

At dusk, since there was no sign of the embassy party, the motor boat returned. We were being used as a mobile transmitting station by the

Admiralty to pass the thousand and one messages covering every phase of human activity which a crisis of the dimensions we were witnessing calls forth. When, the following day, there was still no indication of when our guests would arrive, the admiral decided that we had advertised our presence to any interested U-boat for long enough and so we moved down to St Jean de Luz, our place off Arcachon being taken by a Canadian destroyer, which was instructed to bring the ambassador and his party to us as soon as they arrived. They reached us that evening and I shall never forget the look of surprise on the faces of my old friends of the Paris embassy staff when they looked up and saw me at the top of the gangway waiting to receive them! It was one of those happy coincidences which lightens even the most sombre moments. In addition to the ambassador, the ministers for Canada and South Africa had joined the party and so I had to transfer the ambulance drivers to one of the transports anchored in the bay. I was glad to learn that they all reached home safely. The admiral temporarily transferred his flag to HMS *Calcutta* and just after midnight I set sail for Plymouth, which, by travelling at a speed of twenty-eight knots most of the way, meant that I was able to disembark Sir Ronald and his party before nightfall the same day, 24 June.

After the fall of France and the signing of the armistice with Germany at Compiègne on 22 June, the French Government, under the authority of Marshal Philippe Pétain, moved to Vichy in the unoccupied 'free zone' which included France's colonial empire. The British Government was concerned that the French Navy would fall into the hands of the Germans or Italians who had entered the war on the side of Germany on 10/11 June. As part of Operation Catapult, British officers were ordered to take possession of French ships already in British ports, many of which were undergoing repairs following the evacuation from Dunkirk. Among those at Plymouth, under Amiral Lucien Cayol's command, were the battleship Paris, *the large destroyer* Le Triomphant *and the destroyers,* Mistral *and* Ouragan, *as well as sloops, a torpedo boat, submarines and four submarine chasers.*[8]

On the morning of 3 July we were ordered to take over two French destroyers, the *Mistral* and *Le Triomphant*, anchored in the Sound in accordance with instructions which had been issued by the Admiralty.

Surprise was to be achieved at all costs. There must be no time for effective resistance to be organised. The crews must awake from their slumbers to find that we were in control of their ships and this, it was hoped, would assist them in reaching a dispassionate decision whether to return to their defeated homeland or to stay and continue the struggle with us. I detailed my gunnery and torpedo officers each to take command of a boarding party and I arranged that, if the situation got out of hand, they were to fire a red Very light and help would be sent. It was still quite dark when the two motor boats, each towing a cutter, left the ship (at 4am). The admiral and I stood on the quarterdeck listening to the phut-phut of the motors growing fainter as the dark outline of the boats merged with the silhouette of the destroyers. It turned into a lovely summer morning above the hills as a faint glow of light heralded the approach of dawn. The admiral's steward appeared with a pot of tea which he placed on the after capstan. When Admiral Curteis had helped himself, I poured myself a cup and was about to raise it to my lips when the red trace of a Very light soared skyward from the northernmost destroyer. 'Better go and see what's up,' said the admiral. I ran down the ladder into the motor boat in which a platoon of Royal Marines was waiting at the ready. I gave the coxswain orders to move off and in a matter of seconds we were on our way. As we approached one of the destroyers, the *Mistral*, I noted that she was beginning to list but otherwise all seemed quiet on board.

'What's the matter, Guns?' I asked, as I stepped over the side. 'It's the captain, sir, I can't do anything with him. He's given orders to scuttle the ship and he's behaving like a lunatic.' I walked towards a figure leaning on the guardrails looking over the side. '*Bonjour, mon Commandant*,' I said to the captain, Guillaume de Toulouse-Lautrec (a cousin of the famous artist). He wheeled around and I observed that he was a young man in his thirties. 'You will give orders immediately to stop the sinking of your ship,' I continued in French. He looked at me for a moment, then, without replying, he deliberately turned his back on me. 'Very well, my friend,' I said, 'if this ship goes down, you're going down with it,' and I ordered the sergeant of the marines, who was standing close behind me, to take him below. Then the verbal dam burst. Turning on me with a look of unbridled anger, he loosed a torrent of abuse comparable to that of a thwarted Thames bargee. Even the burly sergeant was momentarily stunned, but, pulling himself together he seized the infuriated officer's arm in a vice-like grip and led him below.

The *Mistral*'s list was noticeably increasing and so I sent an urgent request for a salvage vessel. As there was no sign of the rest of the ship's company, I sent Guns forward to roust out the crew and walked aft to try and raise some of the officers. Putting my head down the first hatch I came to, I called out in French. 'Hullo, down there. Come up on deck at once.' A few minutes later four or five sleepy officers appeared and I sent the ship's first lieutenant down to reason with his captain while I explained to the remaining officers what was happening. Presently he returned to tell me that the captain had countermanded the flooding orders and that he wished to speak to me. Then Guns came aft with a report of astonishing scenes being enacted on the mess decks. It appeared that some of the sailors had broached the officers' wine store and were carousing in no uncertain manner. Telling him to do his best to get them on deck, I prepared to receive the French captain. Evidently he had repented of his folly and I could not help feeling sorry for him.

'So, *mon Commandant*, you wish to speak to me?' His manner was as truculent as ever. 'I saved many of your soldiers at Dunkirk and you treat us like this.' I explained to him the reason for the action we had been obliged to take. I praised the spirit which had prompted him to bring his ship here rather than let her fall into the hands of the Germans. Finally, I told him that if any of them did not wish to continue the fight with us they would be repatriated. 'Fight with you!' he repeated. 'Bah! I'd sooner fight against you.' I saw that I was wasting my breath and that I had no alternative but to keep him under arrest and deal with his more co-operative first lieutenant.

Meanwhile, the salvage ship had arrived and had started pumping. The next step was to disembark the crew, a tricky operation as the wine had deprived many of them of the use of their legs. In the event only two of them fell overboard and were soon rescued. Most of them went happily over the side singing and clutching their few precious belongings. Then, just as the tug in which they were embarked was leaving, the fiery captain slipped his escort and, rushing to the ship's side, bade his men farewell with a few stentorian shouts of '*A bas l'Angleterre – A bas l'Empire Britannique!*' which were answered by the sailors in the tug with roars of '*Vive la France!*'

I had arranged for the captain and officers to land separately from the crew but, after his outburst, I decided to segregate him from the rest of the officers. These filed quietly down into the waiting boat. The final act of this matutinal drama took place a few moments later with the captain's departure with his Royal Marine escort. As the boat left the gangway he stood up and gravely saluted his late command, and then sitting down, he put his face in his hands and wept like a child.[9]

Resistance was also encountered at Plymouth from the submarine, Surcouf; *during the struggle the ship's engineer and three British servicemen were killed and the captain severely injured. Meanwhile unsuccessful discussions had been taking place in relation to the powerful French naval squadron at Mers el Kebir in French Algeria, under the command of Admiral Marcel-Bruno Gensoul on board the* Dunkerque. *To conduct the negotiations Vice Admiral Sir James Somerville, in command of Force H in the western Mediterranean, had sent Captain Cedric Holland, who, after the fall of France, had left the British embassy in Paris to take command of HMS* Ark Royal *in the Mediterranean. The choices offered were as follows: to join British naval forces in the fight against Germany; to sail with reduced crews to a British port and hand the ships over to British officers; to sail them to a French port in the West Indies where they could be disarmed. Failing agreement to any of these 'fair offers', Holland had been instructed to inform Gensoul that he would be requested to scuttle his ships. If this was not done then the French admiral was warned that the British Government would use whatever force was considered necessary to prevent them falling into German or Italian hands. But prevarication (and a reluctance to meet a junior officer) on the part of Gensoul meant that valuable time was lost and no agreement reached. Once the British ultimatum had passed, on the evening of 3 July the Royal Navy attacked, sinking the battleship,* Bretagne, *and damaging several others, including the* Strasbourg *which managed to escape to Toulon, while the* Dunkerque *ran aground; 1,297 lives were lost.*

Elsewhere at Alexandria, Dakar and the French West Indies, French ships were either handed over or taken by force, eliminating, as Churchill observed, the French Navy 'as an important factor at almost a single stroke'.[10] Within days, with virtually all northern Europe subjugated, Hitler turned his attention to the invasion of Britain. On 16 July Operation Sea Lion was launched.

The Battle for Britain

After the fall of France all thoughts were now turned to the possibility that Germany would attempt to invade Britain. On 4 July the 2nd Cruiser Squadron was ordered to Immingham in the north-east of England. The shallow water in the approach to this estuary was particularly suitable for the employment of the new types of ground mine which the Germans had developed and which they were laying in ever-increasing numbers, principally by aircraft. We had, however, been degaussed (i.e. the magnetic field had been neutralised by encircling it with a conductor carrying electric currents) and an efficient force of minesweepers was at work and so we went in and out on our business for quite some time without any trouble. One fine morning we were returning from a night patrol and rounding Spurn Point at the north entrance to the Humber at a speed of twenty knots when a gigantic explosion took place just off my starboard bow. It threw up a great column of water, most of which descended on the bridge. Although the ship was badly shaken, the damage was not great and, after a week in dock at Immingham, we were ready for sea again. At the beginning of September we were ordered to return to our old base at Sheerness at the entrance to the Thames.

Throughout this period, as the German Luftwaffe made a determined effort to gain air superiority over the RAF, our skies were full of planes. On 7 September in an attempt to undermine morale an unprecedented attack was made on London, signifying the beginning of the 'Blitz' (which continued until May the following year). From Sheerness we had to counter the possibility of a sea attack. A reconnaissance of the French ports had revealed a concentration of barges at Boulogne and, on the night of 8 September, we were ordered to bombard them, taking care to do as little damage as possible to the town. The weather was anything but propitious and, as we passed Dover, an electrical storm of astonishing intensity burst upon us, making me recall Hesiod's lines describing the war of the gods:

> *A dreadful sound troubled the boundless sea*
> *The whole earth uttered a great cry*
> *Wide heavens, shaken, groaned*
> *From its foundation far Olympus reeled.*[11]

Torrential rain reduced visibility to a few hundred yards and the masts and yards glowed with the light of what sailors call St Elmo's Fire – when luminous ionised air emits a glow in a strong electrical field in the atmosphere, named it is believed from a corruption of the name Erasmus, the patron saint of sailors. Navigating by dead reckoning, we reached a position which we believed to be off Boulogne, but we could not open fire without a point of aim and, in the murkiness and low cloud, star shell would have been useless. After cruising up and down for some time in case the weather should improve, we threaded our way back through the course of minefields and headed for home. Dawn was just breaking. Suddenly (at 5.25am), with a muffled roar, followed by a huge bang, a mine exploded close off the starboard bow. Once again the hull damage was not serious, but that inside the ship was greater. The boilers suffered the most and the majority of the turbine feet were broken. We steamed slowly back to Sheerness and resumed our place in the front row for the Battle of Britain. After a thorough inspection had been made it was decided that we would only be ordered to sea in the event of an invasion being launched. Each night the ship was darkened, air raid warnings were a regular occurrence together with the order: 'Repel Aircraft'.

During the air raids we would watch the German bombers soaring high overhead and through our glasses we could see our fighters harrying them as best they could. Every now and then one of the bombers would haul out of formation, catch fire and come hurtling down in a sheet of flame. Sometimes they were just winged and, losing height, would turn around and head back for base. My anti-aircraft gunners were ready and waiting for them and they were certainly 'stormed at with shot and shell' if they came anywhere near us.[12] We had recently acquired some Bofors guns and the crews of these quick-firing weapons, with the red tracer shells, were always on the look-out for a target on which to try out their new and very lethal armament. Sometimes their enthusiasm got the better of them and they kept on firing long after it was obvious the aircraft was going to crash.

While we were in dock I encouraged the ship's company to take any opportunity for exercise which was offered. There is quite a good golf course at Sheerness and one day several officers went onshore for a game. It so happened that they were out on the course during an air raid. I was on the quarterdeck when they returned and I noticed that they were looking rather perturbed. 'What happened?' I enquired, addressing one of them. 'Did you lose a lot of balls?' 'It wasn't question of losing balls, Sir', he replied. 'We nearly lost a number of our mess. The senior [engineer] and I were peacefully putting on the seventeenth green when a hail of shell started to plough up the ground behind us. We threw ourselves flat in a bunker and when the firing ceased I found my bag had been hit, three of my clubs smashed and, as if that was not enough, my opponent's ball had been blasted into the hole!' 'Yes,' said the senior, 'I'm staying on board in future. It's safer!'

He could have spoken too soon. Soon afterwards the admiral and I were taking the air on deck when a German bomber suddenly appeared low over the Isle of Grain, just opposite Sheerness, heading east. We were so used to them by that time that we did not take much notice until a warning shout from the quartermaster caused me to look up. Out of the corner of my eye I saw a stick of bombs coming down. Shouting out 'Lie down everyone!', I fell flat on my face and so did the admiral as three bombs burst with loud reports only a few yards astern. We had again been lucky. It is surprising that, of all the hundreds of German bombers which passed over our heads during that period, this was the only one which appeared to be deliberately attacking us. The harbour was at that time packed with a large number of anti–invasion vessels of all kinds so that a heavy air attack would undoubtedly have caused considerable damage, but Göring's Luftwaffe had other objectives in mind.

By mid–October the invasion of Britain seemed no longer a practical proposition and we went up to Chatham for a refit. My ship's company enjoyed some well-earned leave as I did myself. I remember enjoying playing thirty-six holes of golf on one of those lovely autumn days, when the air is cool and clear and the sun shines on the russet and gold leaves of the trees and one wonders what demon is it in man which drives him to seek death and destruction rather than the peace, contentment and beauty which nature offers in endless variety? The repairs to the ship were found to be more extensive than was apparent at first and this, combined with a decision to replace our single 4-inch guns by twin mountings, kept us out of action until the middle of January.

The commander–in–chief, Home Fleet, Sir Charles Forbes, sent for me to act as the prosecutor at a series of courts martial at Scapa Flow and

I made the long journey up to the Orkneys by train and stayed on board the flagship, HMS *Nelson*. It was as if the wheel had turned full cycle and I was back where I had left off in 1939.

By the end of October 1940 the German High Command had to concede defeat in the skies, signifying the end of The Battle of Britain – traditionally commemorated on 15 September. Having abandoned his plans to invade Britain, Hitler focused on the Balkans as well as preparing for Operation Barbarossa: the invasion of the Soviet Union.

I rejoined the ship in early February 1941. During my absence, after her refit, the *Galatea* had proceeded to Scapa Flow. Soon after my return the squadron went on patrol south of Iceland which was to be my last exercise at sea in the *Galatea*. I had been informed that I was to be relieved to take up the appointment of Director of the Trade Division at the Admiralty. Having just got the ship back into fighting trim, I was not too enamoured of the idea. No one likes the prospect of an office desk when compared with the command of a ship. But, as Plutarch says: 'In human life there is constant change of fortune and it is unreasonable to expect exemption from the common fate.'[13]

My remaining weeks were spent at Scapa carrying out practices and training the new ratings who had joined during the refit. On 2 March I handed over the ship to Captain Edward William Boyd Sim. My last view of the *Galatea* was from the Scrabster ferry which carried me over to the mainland to catch my train south. In August the *Galatea* was transferred to the Mediterranean and on one bright moonlight night, on 14/15 December, as she was about to enter the harbour of Alexandria, she was struck by a salvo of torpedoes from a U-boat and sank in under a minute with heavy loss of life. Captain Sim, aged 42, went down with his ship as did many of the officers and men it had been my privilege to command.[14]

Chapter Fourteen

'Sail on O Ship of State!'

Sail on O ship of State!
Sail on O Union, strong and great!
Humanity with all its fears,
With all the hopes of future years,
Is hanging breathless on thy fate![1]

1941

To the uninitiated the name of the Trade Division might suggest some marketing organisation within the salty precincts of the Admiralty. In fact it was so interpreted by our American Allies in the early part of the war and the misunderstanding took some eradication. Any regrets which I may have had on leaving the *Galatea* were soon forgotten as I came to realise the responsibility of my new assignment. My predecessor was Captain Maurice Mansergh, who had had the difficult task of expanding the division from its peacetime nucleus and putting it on a war footing. I was fortunate indeed in taking over from such an able and gifted officer. I was also lucky in retaining the services of his secretary, Paymaster Lieutenant Commander Claude Millson RNR who was a tower of strength to me during the whole of my period in office.[2]

The function of the Trade Division was to initiate and execute Admiralty policy for the protection of merchant shipping in time of war. This included the organisation for the convoying and routeing of merchant ships, as well as for arming them. Since the Admiralty's functions did not include the chartering and general running of these ships, which was carried out mainly by the Ministry of War Transport (formed on 1 May 1941 from the merger of the Ministry of Shipping and the Ministry of Transport), there had to be a close link between the two departments and between the Admiralty and the principal shipowners. I am glad to say that, on the whole, our relations with these various bodies were excellent. Shipowners are justly proud of their ships and jealous of the high standard of management which they have built up. When government departments step in and take over their ships, it is rather like asking a father to entrust his children to the care of a stranger. On the outbreak of war, therefore, it was wisely decided to establish a committee known as the Shipping Defence Advisory Committee, comprising the director of the Trade Division as chairman and representatives from the Chamber of Shipping, who met once a month in the Admiralty. This enabled me – as the director – to keep the shipowners informed of Admiralty policy regarding the defence of their ships and they, in turn, could question me on matters about which they were disturbed. It was a very satisfactory arrangement and I used to look forward to these meetings with great pleasure.

The Trade Division operated through a large staff of naval officers, established in all the principal ports of the world and known as Naval Control Service officers in British and Allied ports and Consular Shipping advisers in neutral ports, all of whom were an important part of the organisation. These officers gave the masters of ships instructions for their voyage based on the latest information issued by the Admiralty. They checked that they had the latest code books and that the ship's armament was in good order. Where there was no representative of the Ministry of War Transport they arranged for watering and bunkering and similar needs and so their responsibilities, especially at convoy assembly ports, were great. They were appointed by a section of the Trade Division and I was told that, just before the outbreak of the war, when the retired officers who were to fill all these posts were receiving their instructions at the Admiralty, the scene resembled the Stock Exchange on a busy morning! An impassive captain sat at a table dispersing these 'old gentlemen' to the four corners of the earth, while, in the lobby outside, big business was being done swapping Buenos Aires for Bordeaux or Madeira for Mozambique, according to the prejudices and preferences of the nominees. It all sorted itself out and when the gun was fired the organisation went into operation without a hitch. As the merchant ships' principal antagonist was the U-boat, we were closely connected with the Anti-Submarine Division and the two divisions were represented on the naval staff by a rear admiral with the title of Assistant Chief of the Naval Staff (Trade), later changed to (U-boats and Trade).

I had not long taken over – in April 1941 – when a fine refrigerated ship on her way home from the River Plate with a valuable cargo of frozen meat was torpedoed and sunk on leaving the Canary Islands, where she had called for bunkers i.e. fuel oil. She was a fast ship and outside the limits for convoy (fixed at a maximum speed of 15 knots) and was travelling along the route given to her, but her owners could still exercise their prerogative of arranging where she should call to take on fuel. Here was a case of lack of co-ordination which had cost us dearly. A thorough enquiry revealed that the Admiralty had not yet received all the information necessary to ensure the safety of independently-routed ships. We requisitioned the premises below our offices and installed seventy 'ancient mariners' still capable of plying parallel rulers and dividers (the essential tools of a cartographer) and set them to work on large charts on which, by means of numbered and coloured pins, we could record the noon position of every Allied merchant ship in the world. The information was obtained from Lloyds' daily summary of merchant ship movements, a section of which was established in these new offices. These charts provided a visual picture of the flow of shipping in every ocean and enabled instant action to be taken to divert any ships threatened with attack from enemy submarines or commerce raiders.

Some of the German raiders were disguised as neutral or Allied ships and would approach their quarry flying the distinguishing signal of the ship they purported to be. When they got within range the guns would be exposed and the trusting merchant ship was added to the bag. We instructed the masters of ships that, if they were in any doubt as to the identity of a ship they encountered, they were to ask the Admiralty for a check. By means of these plots we were able to tell at once if the ship sighted was true or false. On one occasion we got the answer back to a ship in the South Atlantic within ten minutes of receiving her enquiry.

Over 200 convoy routes existed in the war, over a quarter of which were hit by U-boats. Each route was known by two or more letters which usually (but not always) indicated the departure and destination harbours. In the North Atlantic 'UR' meant from the UK to Reykjavik. In the South Atlantic and Indian Ocean 'CD' meant Capetown to Durban and in the Mediterranean 'GTX' signified Gibraltar to Tripoli and Alexandria, while 'HG' meant Homeward from Gibraltar.

The South Atlantic

While Axis forces were tightening their hold on Europe with Hitler's invasion of Greece and Yugoslavia in early April and an airborne invasion of Crete in May, together with establishing a presence in North Africa, U-boats had begun making a deadly appearance in the South Atlantic. The port of Freetown in Sierra Leone on the west coast of Africa was our southernmost convoy assembly port. Ships from South and West Africa or those coming around the Cape of Good Hope from ports further east arrived independently to await the sailing of the next northbound convoy. Southbound ships not calling at Freetown were released from convoy off the port to sail independently to their destinations. In order to find out what the Commander-in-Chief, South Atlantic Station, Admiral Sir Robert Raikes, was doing to combat what had become a serious situation, Admiral Sir Dudley Pound, the First Sea Lord, instructed me to fly to Freetown.[3] The Air Liaison in the Admiralty informed me that a Sunderland flying boat, which had flown home from Freetown for a periodic overhaul, was due to return there the following day, so I packed a grip bag and, leaving my deputy – Captain George Allen – in charge of the division, I took the train to Southampton and presented myself at the Naval Air Station at Calshot on the Hampshire coast. Due to a slight hitch we did not take off until the following evening, flying low over Devon so that the pilot could wave goodbye to his wife who was staying in a farmhouse on the edge of Dartmoor. Reaching the Scilly Isles at dusk, we continued onwards to Gibraltar which we reached without incident early the next morning.[4]

We refuelled and took off again in the late afternoon, reaching Bathurst (Banjul), the Gambia's capital, in time for breakfast. I was interested to see this small and not often visited Crown Colony which extends for 300 miles inland along the banks of the sluggish and muddy river which gives the colony its name. It is like a finger reaching into French Senegal and, at that time, there was a certain amount of nervousness because of its close proximity with Dakar but, for the duration of the war, the Vichy French did not attempt to molest the colony in any way. We took off again after breakfast and reached Freetown in the early afternoon. I was agreeably surprised to see the commander-in-chief's barge cruising near by when we alighted and I told the RAF tender, who met us, to put me on board. The flag lieutenant and I had twice been shipmates and I appreciated the admiral's friendly gesture in sending him out to meet me. But, as soon as I got on board, I found that the barge had been sent to collect King Peter II of Yugoslavia and his entourage, who were expected about the same time, having recently fled from Yugoslavia. Before I could disembark, the tender had already left and so it was a case of *j'y suis, j'y reste*. When the Royal party arrived I explained my mistake and we all went ashore together.[5]

Freetown is an excellent anchorage but it had taken a war to stir it into activity which inevitably exposed its deficiencies. There were no deep water berths for ships to load and discharge alongside. Everything had to be put into lighters and towed to or from the ship and manhandled by local labour. The climate is not such as to induce great activity and so it was little wonder that, as soon as any pressure was brought to bear on this tranquil scene, something resembling chaos ensued. Yet, in true British manner, much was being done with the little there was. One of the first things which I noticed on landing was a veritable mountain of empty beer bottles. Since there was an acute shortage of bottles at home I suggested that ships returning in ballast might load up with some. One or two masters acted on the suggestion, but, alas, they found great difficulty in disposing of them on arrival in England.

Understandably Admiral Raikes was extremely worried about the way in which the U-boats were picking off merchant ships in the approaches to the port. Since there was a great shortage of surface escorts – not only at Freetown but elsewhere – we could not immediately apply the obvious remedy which was to extend the convoy system to the port of Takoradi on the Gold Coast (Ghana). The Admiralty believed that the four or five Sunderland aircraft stationed at Freetown would be more effective in keeping the U-boats down and restricting their movements, but, as I saw for myself, the persistent haze and general climatic conditions greatly reduced their value. Another problem arising from the numerous sinkings was the lack of accommodation for the survivors. Grim stories had reached us in England about the conditions under which they were living. Having inspected all the camps, I was able to make recommendations for improving their lot until such time as ships became available to take them home.

The only two spare rooms in Admiral Raikes's residence were occupied by the convoy commodores, who were resting while the convoy turned around, and so the chief justice kindly offered me a room. One of the commodores told me that he considered I was very lucky because the admiral's garden was infested with snakes, a cobra having lodged itself in his bedroom doorway that morning! After completing my investigations, I was anxious to return to my duties at the Admiralty but enquiries from the officer commanding the Royal Air Force in Freetown revealed that there was no prospect of a plane back for several days and so I had to employ my time as best I could. I visited the airfield under construction at Hastings and had talks with a wide range of people, which meant that by the time I left I was fully acquainted with life in Freetown.

To make the long hop from Bathurst to Gibraltar against the prevailing northerly wind and avoiding Vichy-held territory in North Africa, we had to carry a large tank full of petrol amidships even with which the margin of endurance was not great. The pilot decided that the risk of a fusillade from the French was to be preferred to a forced landing in the Atlantic and so, as soon as we had passed Dakar, he turned inland and cut across the westerly bulge of Africa on a straight course for our destination. Due to our extra load of petrol and the hot tropical air, we were unable to gain much height and it seemed that we were literally skimming over the surface of the desert. Every now and then I could see the fires of some Arab encampment flickering in the darkness and the shadow of the aircraft, cast by the bright moonlight, swept across the country like some giant black beetle.

We landed safely at Gibraltar in the early morning and the pilot announced that we could take off again at 4pm. I went ashore and after breakfast did some shopping, read the papers in the garrison library and lunched with some friends, arriving back on board the flying boat in good time. We cast off and taxied out of the harbour. The water of the bay was like a sheet of glass and the pilot announced that, in order to get sufficient run for the heavy load we were carrying, we would have to go right across to Algeciras. With our four engines thrumming away we made stately progress across the bay, the German agent (who reputedly sat in the Reina Cristina Hotel in Algeciras reporting on everything that went on in Gibraltar) no doubt observing our passage. We wheeled around, the engine throttles were opened and the great flying boat slowly gathered way. Our direction was towards the northern end of the north mole of the harbour so that, when we were airborne, we could pass over the airfield and around the northern face of the Rock without infringing Spanish neutrality. As we gathered speed, the boat lifted a little but showed no signs of leaving the water. Faster and faster we skimmed along the surface and larger and larger loomed the solid mass of the north mole. I watched the pilot frantically working the stick. He had already given the engines the extra boost reserved for emergencies. I then heard the engineer's warning, his eyes glued to the dials in front of him. 'Starboard outer, getting hot' – 'Port outer, overheating'. The pilot swore under his breath and muttered imprecations, then, just as it seemed that nothing could save us, the great machine rose in the air and we zoomed over the mole with a foot or two to spare! 'Phew! That was a close shave,' exclaimed the pilot, wiping his brow. 'I wonder what the devil made the old bus so nose-heavy?' 'I think I know, sir', volunteered the sergeant, putting his head up through the hatch which led to the lower deck. The explanation for the heavy load was a wooden packing case which had been loaded at Gibraltar. From its weight when we subsequently tried to move it, I think it must have contained books or bars of gold!

The broad Atlantic was as smooth as a mill pond and we reached the Scilly Isles the following morning. To avoid the attention of any German fighters which might be close we came down to within a few feet of the water and, almost like a ship, we sailed into Plymouth Sound and alighted. 'Everything seems very quiet here,' I remarked to the attendant who served me breakfast in the RAF Mess at Mount Batten outside the town. 'Quiet? Sir,' he replied, 'if you'd been here earlier, I reckon you'd have met the whole Luftwaffe. Fair flattened the place out, they have.' How flat it was I saw on my way to the train station. Practically all my favourite haunts and landmarks had been wiped out. Places I had known since I was a cadet had disappeared in heaps of burning rubble. I felt sick and angry;

but this was war. It took me longer to get from Plymouth to London that day than it had to get from Gibraltar to Plymouth.

Although the Luftwaffe's main focus of attention during the Blitz was on London, other cities were targeted, Plymouth suffering some of the worst damage between 21–29 April.[6]

Sinking the Bismarck

Back at the Admiralty, the news of the escape into the Atlantic of the German battleship, *Bismarck* and the heavy cruiser, *Prinz Eugen*, in late May 1941 caused us great anxiety. Earlier in the year the *Scharnhorst* and *Gneisenau* had taken a heavy toll on shipping during their incursion into this area and now we had another and more serious threat to our vital supply line. The war room in the Admiralty was spread with charts on which every scrap of information which came in was recorded. The movements of all our own forces were carefully plotted and estimates made of the Germans' most probable course of action. When, on 24 May, HMS *Hood* was sunk while both she and HMS *Prince of Wales* were in pursuit of the *Bismarck* at the Battle of the Denmark Strait, there was a tense, set look on everyone's faces, revealing a grim determination to avenge the loss of our gallant comrades, over 1,400 of whom had perished on board including Captain Ralph Kerr, leaving only three survivors.[7]

When, two days later, after having eluded her pursuers for over twenty-four hours, the *Bismarck* was again located, the excitement, although guarded, was intense. That evening after dinner the First Lord of the Admiralty, A.V. Alexander, and the First Sea Lord, Admiral Pound, were sitting at a table poring over the charts. I was standing close behind them when I noticed the door at the end of the room open and there, framed in the doorway, stood the Prime Minister, Winston Churchill. Clad in his signature zip suit and with the customary cigar in his mouth, he advanced slowly towards the table. The First Lord and First Sea Lord were deep in discussion and were not aware of his approach. Like Moses dividing the waters of the Red Sea, he lay a hand on each of their shoulders and they parted to admit him. I produced a chair and the discussion continued almost without interruption, so great was their concentration of mind. Four hours later, when Churchill left the room, he believed 'that Admiral Pound and his select company of experts were sure that the *Bismarck* was doomed'.[8]

Late on 26 May air strikes by planes from HMS Ark Royal *jammed the* Bismarck's *rudders. During the night British destroyers shadowed the ship. On the morning of 27 May the British battleships HMS* King George V *and HMS* Rodney, *supported by the heavy cruisers HMS* Norfolk *and HMS* Dorsetshire, *the light cruiser HMS* Sheffield, *and several destroyers, began attacking her. After nearly two hours the* Bismarck *sank from the combined effect of shellfire and a deliberate decision to scuttle her. Over 2,200 men went down with the ship including Admiral Günther Lütjens and Captain Ernst Lindemann, of which 115 men were rescued; the senior surviving officer was the fourth artillery officer, Kapitänleutnant Burkard von Müllenheim-Rechberg.[9]*

Casualties and Statistics

One section of the Trade Division was known as the casualties section, run by Commander Norman Holbrook, who had the distinction of being the first submariner to win the VC in 1914 for his action in sinking the Turkish battleship *Mesudiye* in the Dardanelles.[10] A better choice for the post could not have been made. He possessed in full measure the tact, sympathy and understanding necessary for dealing with one of the most human problems of the war at sea. The master or senior survivor of any merchant ship lost by enemy action or attacked and subsequently salvaged was always invited to visit the Admiralty. On arrival he would be taken to the casualties section where Holbrook would offer him a drink and a smoke. When he was comfortably settled, he would be asked to describe his experiences. The story was taken down verbatim and copies were sent to the First Lord and other members of the Board of the Admiralty and to the Ministry of War Transport. Some of these brave men who manned our merchant ships and those of our Allies had tales to tell of hardship and endurance equal to any in the history of human experience. They described voyages in open boats under scorching tropical sun, or in the stormy seas of the Atlantic, of tankers torpedoed and instantly engulfed in a sheet of flame, of desperate struggles to bring in a damaged ship and of personal bravery more often than not masked by a natural modesty. It is a very moving record. These reports were carefully scrutinised, not only for what they might reveal of enemy tactics but so that we might remedy any defects in our organisation. The ministry, which was responsible for the provision of life-saving equipment, boats, rafts, radio sets, food, etc., also studied them and many improvements were made on the recommendation of men who had learnt what was required from practical experience.[11]

The casualties section had another function which was to record the details of tonnage, cargo and all other relevant statistics of all ships sunk, for the statistical section, headed by Sir William Elderton and his assistant, P.N. Harvey, who were marvels at interpreting the very close and guarded statements with which I supplied them.[12] Every Monday morning I had to take the list of the tonnage lost in the previous week to the First Lord so that he might be fully briefed on it for any questions which the Prime Minister might ask him. Very often they were Black Mondays indeed and the First Lord would cross-examine me on every detail to see if a nought too many had not slipped in. But my statisticians never let me down, although they had no adding machines and all their work was laboriously done by hand. (Later, during a visit to Washington, I was shown a machine in the Navy Department which would analyse data recorded on cards in a matter of minutes and deliver the answer all neatly typed out. As I knew that the Prime Minister was particularly interested in this problem I asked his scientific adviser, Frederick Lindemann, Lord Cherwell, to witness a demonstration in the hope that this might lead to the purchase of some of these machines, which nowadays are used extensively both in government departments and in business, but alas, nothing came of it and we continued to ply our pens as before!)[13]

These statistical records played a very important part, not only in recording the losses we were suffering but in enabling forecasts to be made of the amount of shipping likely to be available for future operations. It is not too much to say that, in all the major conferences and discussions on the conduct of the war, shipping was always one of the primary matters for consideration. These forecasts were produced by the Ministry of War Transport in consultation with the Admiralty and, as can be imagined, called for a good deal of crystal ball gazing on our part.

On 21 June 1941, reneging on the non-aggression pact signed between Germany and the Soviet Union in 1939, Hitler ordered German forces to invade the Soviet Union. The British Government at once offered assistance to the now beleaguered Russians.

The Atlantic Charter

Towards the end of July I was instructed to prepare for a three-week voyage and to bring with me all the data relevant to our convoy organisation, tonnage losses and shipping protection generally. I was to present myself at platform 4, Marylebone station, at 12.30pm on Sunday 3 August. It was all very mysterious but I knew better than to ask questions. I was glad to discover that Commander Michael Goodenough, Plans Division in the Admiralty, had received similar instructions and so I should have a pleasant travelling companion. In July 1940 he had been awarded the DSO for 'good services in successful operations which prevented much war material from falling into the hands of the enemy' during the Allied evacuation from Northern Europe.[14]

At Marylebone a long, brown train was drawn up in the platform but there seemed to be very few passengers. I caught sight of Colonels Hollis and Jacob from the Ministry of Defence and then I saw the First Sea Lord's secretary, Paymaster Captain Brockman and so I asked him where his boss was. 'Joining later,' came the reply. A sleeping car attendant then showed us to our berths. Evidently we were bound for Scotland. The whistle blew, we pulled out and soon afterwards lunch was announced. We had just returned to our compartment when the train slowed down and pulled up at a little wayside station – Wendover. Glancing out of the window I saw the Prime Minister standing on the platform accompanied by Admiral Pound, the First Sea Lord, together with the Chief of the Imperial General Staff, General Sir John Dill, the Vice Chief of the Air Staff, Air Chief Marshal Sir Wilfrid Freeman, the Prime Minister's secretary, Sir Alexander Cadogan and Lord Cherwell. They boarded the train and, as soon as we were again moving, Pound sent for Goodenough and me to meet the Prime Minister and the other members of this distinguished company.[15]

The Prime Minister had changed out of the navy blue yachting suit in which he had been dressed on the platform and was now in his favourite siren suit. He looked extremely pleased. I then heard our destination. We were bound for Scapa Flow where we were to board HMS *Prince of Wales*; we would then sail to Argentia in Newfoundland where the Prime Minister was to meet the President of the United States, Franklin D. Roosevelt, and his chief staff officers. Goodenough and I returned to our carriage quite excited to be taking part in such an historic event.[16]

It was raining when we reached Thurso the following morning. The newly commissioned O-class destroyer, HMS *Oribi,* had been detailed to take us across the Pentland Firth to Scapa. Admiral Pound followed the Prime Minister onto the bridge while Goodenough and I and the rest of the party took shelter in the wardroom. I went up on deck again as we entered the Sound of Hoxa and, as we came round into the Flow proper, I caught sight of the *Prince of Wales.* I was anxious to see one of the new King George V-class of battleships, about which I had heard a great deal. Laid down in 1937, she had been launched in 1939 but only completed at the end of March 1941, having been damaged by German aircraft while she was in dry dock in 1940. Her most recent action was with HMS *Hood* against the *Bismarck* in May; but shortly after the *Hood* was sunk she sustained several hits and had had to disengage. Her appearance was impressive. She had nice lines, although I should have liked to have seen the fo'c'sle raised a little more. Her captain was an extremely able officer, John Leach; one and a half years my senior, we had been at Osborne and Dartmouth together and had known each other intermittently for twenty years. He was an athlete of the first order but despite his many successes he remained a modest, unassuming and delightful companion. As Churchill later wrote: 'I took a great liking to our captain, Leach, a charming and lovable man and all that a British sailor should be.'[17]

I had been allocated a cabin in the fore superstructure under the bridge which meant that when we ran into heavy weather twelve hours after leaving Scapa, I was still able to carry my scuttle and enjoy fresh air while the rest of the ship was battened down. The First Sea Lord was in the chief of staff's sea cabin opposite; having found the admiral's quarters aft distinctly uncomfortable at sea, it was not long before the Prime Minister joined us in what came to be known as 'Snob's Alley'. It was a busman's holiday for me and so I amused myself by making a thorough tour of inspection of the ship. To a professional sailor a new ship full of the latest gadgets holds tremendous fascination. I was disappointed to find that the ship only mounted 14-inch guns. My first big ship had mounted 12-inch guns and the next one 15-inch. The two Nelson-class ships, HMS *Nelson* and HMS *Rodney,* carried 16-inch guns and not being a gunnery specialist, unlike Captain Leach, I thought the 14-inch ones were a retrograde step. He explained to me, however, that the new gun with its higher muzzle velocity and more rapid rate of fire really packed a more powerful punch than the older gun of a larger calibre. Another feature I did not like was the quadruple turret, of which two were mounted in these ships. An unlucky hit could put two-fifths of the main armament out of action at one fell swoop, but it was done, as I later learnt, to economise on weight.

We left Scapa Flow on 4 August. The Prime Minister had ordered a map room to be fitted on board, similar to the one we had in the Admiralty and on which the movements of all shipping in the Atlantic were shown by coloured tags, appropriately marked, and so, during the voyage, I was able to watch the progress of my precious convoys as they slowly fought their way across the Atlantic. Captain Richard Pim, Operations Division, Naval Staff, who headed the map room in 10 Downing Street, was in charge of the maps and they became a regular feature of every subsequent voyage which the Prime Minister made during the war.[18] The journalist H.V. Morton captures well the atmosphere on board ship: 'Although Mr Churchill was not always visible to the ship, evidence of him was bellowed all over the battleship by loud-speaker. Men in the engine room, sailors on the mess decks, Marine sentries and others smiled with delight as they heard unaccustomed orders shouted, such as "Will Mr Martin please go at once to the Prime Minister on the bridge"; or "The Prime Minister requests the presence of Brigadier Dykes upon the bridge." Hearing such orders the crew caught a reflected glory and knew that this voyage was like no other.'[19]

Each night we had a film show in the wardroom, the films kindly provided by the Prime Minister. On one occasion, I was sitting just behind him and the film was the one in which Raymond Massey movingly portrays the famous American abolitionist, John Brown, in the 1940 film *Santa Fe Trail*. It will be remembered that Brown was captured after his seizure of the arsenal at Harpers Ferry in West Virginia in 1859 while attempting to initiate a slave revolt. During a pause while the reels were being changed, the Prime Minister asked Dill, who was sitting next to him, if he could recall what subsequently happened at Harpers Ferry during the American Civil War following the incident we had just seen. General Dill had to confess that he did not remember, whereupon Churchill gave us a resumé of the campaign in which, in September 1862, the Confederate general, 'Stonewall' Jackson obliged over 12,000 Union troops to surrender.[20] Another film, only just released, was Alexander Korda's *That Hamilton Woman*, starring Laurence Olivier and Vivien Leigh telling the well-known story of Admiral Lord Nelson's love affair with Emma, Lady Hamilton.

On the morning of Saturday 9 August we reached Placentia Bay, one of the largest of the southern indentations in that tattered piece of territory which John Cabot discovered in 1497. I had not been back to Newfoundland since 1919 and I was glad to renew my acquaintance with this attractive country which held pleasant memories of excellent trout fishing in the fast-running streams flanked with pine trees. The land was shrouded in mist, as it so often is, and it was not until we had almost reached our anchorage off Argentia that we could see the United States' ships assembled to meet us. There were two cruisers, the *Augusta* and *Tuscaloosa*, the battleship *Arkansas* and several destroyers. Word went around that the President was on board the *Augusta* and, looking through my binoculars, I spotted him sitting under an awning that had been erected over the forward turret. The American ships looked very spic and span with their glossy paint and shining brass work compared to the dull war paint worn by the *Prince of Wales*. They were still at peace. We had been at war for almost two years. The words of William Blake came readily to mind:

> *I will not cease from mental fight / Nor shall my sword sleep in my hand /*
> *Till we have built Jerusalem / In England's green and pleasant land.*

Nine years later I was to hear 3,000 American voices in Annapolis Chapel sing that moving anthem with an élan which brought tears to my eyes.

After the first formal meeting between the President and the Prime Minister which took place on board the *Augusta*, we got down to work and a series of meetings and conferences between the staffs was arranged. The First Sea Lord took Goodenough and me over to the *Augusta* for a meeting between him and Admiral Harold Stark, Chief of Naval Operations (CNO), at which that remarkable man, Admiral Ernest J. King, Commander-in-Chief, US Atlantic Fleet, was present. Although, beneath his grim and sour look, King had a sense of humour, many a verbal tussle did we have in the days to come with this hard bitten old – at nearly 63 – man of the sea.[21] The purpose of our meeting on the *Augusta* was to study a paper which the British Chiefs of Staff had prepared, reviewing the political and military situation throughout the world. It was a most comprehensive document and evoked a good deal of praise from our American friends. One particular item which remained in my mind was that referring to the possible shortage of rubber and tin, should Malaya be overrun by the Japanese. 'Tins,' joked Stark, 'why the greatest problem in our country is how to get rid of the darned things!'[22]

On Sunday 10 August that most memorable British–American service was held on the quarterdeck of the *Prince of Wales*, attended by the President and the Prime Minister, together with their staffs and by a number of United States officers and men with the officers and ship's company of the *Prince of Wales*. This was the first of many meetings between the men on whose shoulders would lie the task of forging victory out of disaster and what could have been more fitting than that they should seek God's blessing on their endeavours, '...that we being armed with Thy defence may be preserved evermore from all perils, to glorify Thee, who art the only giver of victory'. So ended the prayer for the victory of Right and Truth. The service concluded with the sailors' own hymn, suggested – I believe – by the President: 'Eternal Father strong to save'. As that combined chorus of British and American voices echoed across the still waters of the bay, it was impossible not to feel deeply moved and spiritually uplifted. 'It was a great hour to live,' Churchill wrote. 'Nearly half of those who sang were soon to die,' when, on 10 December 1941 the great ship in which we stood, together with HMS *Repulse*, was sunk off Singapore, Captain Leach going down with his ship.[23]

President Roosevelt lunched on board in the wardroom which was on the same level as the quarterdeck obviating any difficulty about moving him up and down ladders. After lunch he and the Prime Minister adjourned to the ante-room and we were brought up one at a time to be introduced to him. I knew, of course, all about his heroic fight to overcome the after-effects of infantile paralysis which he had developed aged 39 and I was not surprised to see in his face the traces of that grim struggle which he had been waging for twenty years. My lasting impression of the President was that of a man who had acquired strength through suffering. Although he was a very forceful man, he was kind, as the food parcels, one for every man on board, which he sent over to the *Prince of Wales*, bore witness.

Over the next two days further meetings were held, during which what became known as 'the Atlantic Charter' was drafted and agreed. On Tuesday evening we sailed. The Prime Minister had expressed a wish to visit Iceland and so, having rounded Cape Race, the southernmost point of the island, we steered to the north-east. On Friday morning, Admiral Pound sent for me and informed me that he intended to tell Captain Leach to steer the ship so that it passed between the columns of the eastbound convoy which it was expected we would overtake that evening to permit the Prime Minister to see it. I was delighted at the opportunity of seeing one of my convoys at such close quarters and went immediately up on the bridge. I regret to say that the first thing we sighted was a column of smoke which is one of the most tell-tale advertisements of its presence which a convoy can give to a prowling U-boat and which was a subject constantly under investigation by the Admiralty and the Air Ministry.

Soon the ships themselves began to appear over the horizon. There were seventy-three in all in six columns, five miles long at intervals of a mile between them so they covered a huge expanse of ocean. They had an escort of eight corvettes which was the maximum number we could muster in those days. As we drew close the Prime Minister and Admiral Pound came up on the bridge. Churchill was greatly impressed by the sight of these slow-moving ships of every sort and condition, rising and falling to the long Atlantic swell and loaded with vital supplies for our island fortress. 'How long will the convoy take to get across?' he asked. 'Another ten days, Sir', I replied – 'given good weather,' I added as an afterthought because Atlantic gales used to play Old Harry [the devil] with some of our convoys. Just at that moment the short foremast was dressed with flags spelling out 'Good voyage, Churchill'. A faint cheer rose from the men in the merchant ships as the signal was decoded. Some captains tried to sound the V sign in reply, but the inherent weakness of steam sirens of the period when called on suddenly to perform, resulted in a muffled hissing sound of escaping steam and water, bearing little resemblance to the dots and dashes of the Morse code. But the Prime Minister took the will for the deed and waved back, making the V sign with the first two fingers of his right hand.

After we had passed the commodore's ship in the van of the convoy, Churchill asked Pound if we could turn around and return between another pair of columns. The captain was told and around we went to repeat the inspection. This time the sirens in the merchant ships were more successful and they covered the whole gamut of sound from the deep base notes of the larger ships to the shrill treble of some of the smaller ones. It was indeed, as Churchill later recorded 'a heartening sight'. It was one which I shall never forget. The officers and men who manned these merchant ships and hundreds like them contributed every bit as much to our victory in the Battle of the Atlantic as did those equally dauntless heroes who manned the escort forces and the aircraft, which hunted down and destroyed the U-boats. The Prime Minister remained on the bridge until the convoy was lost to view in the gathering dusk.

We reached Iceland early the following day with the sun shining out of a clear blue sky on the barren red volcanic rocks of Hvalfjord in which we anchored. A destroyer came alongside and embarked the Prime Minister and the rest of the party visiting Iceland's capital, Reykjavik. I took the opportunity of meeting and conferring with my Naval Control Service officers there; when our business was concluded, they took me on a tour of the city, which, with 30,000 inhabitants, boasts a cathedral and a university and is the home of the Icelandic parliament. During my visit my attention was chiefly concentrated on the shops, which were bountifully supplied with the luxuries which had long since disappeared from those at home. Among other things, I purchased 4lbs of butter, which I think was the most welcome present of all.

We sailed again that evening and reached Scapa Flow safely on Monday 18 August. The Prime Minister's special train was waiting for us at Thurso just as we had left it two weeks previously. By the following morning I was back at my office in the Admiralty. The Atlantic Charter had been written and would take its place beside the other great charters of human hopes and aspirations like the Magna Carta and the Declaration of Independence. In addition, personal contacts had been made which were to prove of inestimable value in the difficult and testing years to come.

The Atlantic Charter was originally called the Joint Declaration by the President of the United States and the Prime Minister, but when addressing Parliament on 24 August 1941, Churchill used the name 'The Atlantic Charter'. Although the United States had not committed to enter the war, the leaders deemed 'it right to make known certain common principles in the national policies of their respective countries on which they base their hopes for a better future for the world'. Outlining eight major areas of co-operation, it was significant that the United States, still a neutral country, was prepared to stress the importance of 'the destruction of Nazi tyranny' after which the two countries would jointly work towards establishing a peace which would give all nations 'the means of dwelling in safety within their own boundaries', the right of people to choose the form of government under which they will live, the lowering of trade barriers, working towards freedom of the seas, global economic co-operation and the advancement of social welfare. Dated 14 August, no final version signed by both Churchill and Roosevelt exists.

On 7 December the Japanese bombed Pearl Harbor bringing the United States into the war. Field Marshal Sir John Dill assumed the position of Chief of the British Joint Staff Mission and senior British representative on the Combined Chiefs of Staff in Washington DC, Field Marshal Sir Alan Brooke becoming Chief of the Imperial General Staff. Admiral King was appointed Commander-in-Chief, United States Fleet, his reaction (wrongly) recorded as follows: 'When they get into trouble, they call for the sons-of-bitches.' Although King denied having made the remark, he confessed: 'if I had thought of it, I would have said it.' In 1942 he succeeded Stark as CNO, being the only officer to hold the combined command.[24]

The Arctic Convoys

Meanwhile plans to assist the Soviet Union were under way. As soon as Stalin realised that Britain was in no position to afford him the direct military help for which he was asking, he concentrated on formulating demands for the maximum amount of armaments and raw materials which he trusted Churchill would make available to him. Delivery of course had to be by sea and it was the Admiralty's intention to run convoys to north Russia on a 40-day cycle.

The risks were great and the conditions gruelling. After assembly in a Scottish port or in the bleak harbour of Hvalfjord, the convoys were routed through the Norwegian and Barents Seas to Russia's only ice-free port, Murmansk, at the head of the Kola Inlet. When ice conditions allowed, use was made of the White Sea port of Archangel (Archangelsk). The area through which the convoys sailed was notorious for blizzards, fog, and gales of great intensity, and the high northern latitudes produced a winter of perpetual night, changing gradually to a summer of continuous day – circumstances which had a profound effect on the operation of the convoys. The Northern Lights or Aurora Borealis, regarded in ancient times as portents of disaster, stretched their brilliantly coloured filaments of light across the night sky like the talons of some aerial monster clutching at the heavily laden merchant ships as they ploughed their way through the icy seas. Even under the most favourable conditions, once east of the meridian of Greenwich, they could not avoid coming within range of the German aircraft stationed in north Norway, the port of Murmansk lying only 90 miles from the nearest enemy airfield; even Archangel 450 miles further east was not beyond their reach.

The first of the famous PQ series of convoys (the initials being those of Commander Philip Quellyn Roberts in the Admiralty's Operations Division, the return journey being classified QP), sailed on 28 September from Iceland bound for Archangel, where it was due to arrive on 12 October. It comprised ten merchant ships and was escorted by the cruiser *Suffolk* and two destroyers; included in the cargo were twenty tanks and 193 fighter aircraft. Its passage was uneventful and the convoy arrived a day ahead of schedule.[25]

Chapter Fifteen

'The peril of the waters'

But ships are but boards, sailors but men; there be land-rats and water rats, land thieves and water thieves – I mean pirates; and there is the peril of the waters, winds and rocks.[1]

1942–43

The year 1942 was a grim one in the Trade Division. Despite the entry of the United States into the war in December 1941, the U-boats, which had moved closer to North America, were reaping a rich harvest amongst the many ships sailing independently in those waters. It was not until the middle of May that a fully organised convoy system was introduced on the American coast. This created problems for us in linking up these convoys with our own trans-Atlantic ones in order to minimise the delays to shipping. By the end of the year a fully interlocking system was evolved. When the halcyon days for U-boats off America came to an end, they moved to new and distant hunting grounds off the Cape of Good Hope and even as far as the Mozambique channel and off the coast of Brazil. In the latter half of the year they once again joined battle with our ships in the Atlantic, operating mainly in an area just beyond the reach of the shore-based air cover from Newfoundland and Iceland. Coastal command lacked the very long range aircraft necessary to cover this area and, in view of the heavy demand for bombers, there seemed to be little prospect of the deficiency being made good for some time.

Meanwhile a steady flow of convoys was being sent to the Soviet Union. To date only one outbound ship had been lost (in PQ7) out of a total of 103 which had made the passage to Archangel or Murmansk. But German resolve in preventing the flow of munitions to the Soviet Union was intensifying. In January Hitler had moved his only (but stronger than any we possessed) battleship, *Tirpitz*, to Trondheim. This was followed by the arrival of the heavy cruisers, *Admiral Scheer* and *Admiral Hipper*. In March PQ13 lost five ships out of nineteen which sailed and in May PQ16 lost seven. Then, in early July, disaster struck, when, sailing from Hvalfjord to Archangel, PQ17 was repeatedly attacked by German U-boats and Luftwaffe aeroplanes. Only eleven out of the original thirty-six ships reached their destination, while twenty-three were lost and two turned back. This was the worst loss in the history of the Arctic convoys, described by Winston Churchill as 'one of the most melancholy naval episodes in the whole of the war'. To me Claudius's remarks in Shakespeare's *Hamlet* were most apt: 'When sorrows come, they come not single spies, but in battalions.'[2]

The order given by Admiral Pound for the convoy to 'scatter' remained controversial as did his decision to withdraw the escort ships in order to go in pursuit of a reported (though subsequently erroneous) threat from the Tirpitz. *Although for political reasons Pound was not blamed, Soviet–Allied relations were impaired, Stalin unable to believe that so many ships could be lost in one convoy. The Americans were likewise critical of the decisions taken. After PQ17 the convoys were suspended until perpetual daylight ended. They were resumed in September with the departure of PQ18 from Loch Ewe on 2 September. Although not as disastrous as PQ17, thirteen out of forty ships were lost.*

The Arctic convoys were not the only ones to suffer. With the defence of the Atlantic Ocean divided into British and American 'strategic' zones, between January and July 1942 the US had lost 113 ships in its strategic area (and a further 406 along the North and South American coastlines, especially in the Caribbean), while 49 ships had been lost in the British strategic area.[3] So desperate did the situation appear that, in November 1942, Churchill set up a new Anti-U-boat Warfare Committee. One decision taken was to withdraw the radar-carrying Liberator from action for a period in order to carry out improvements which would lengthen its range.

Another measure, arising from a meeting which I had with the Director of Merchant Shipbuilding, Sir Amos Ayre, was the conversion of a number of tankers and bulk grain ships, already under construction in Scottish dockyards, to enable them to be fitted with flat decks. This would not impede their normal use but would enable them to operate several Swordfish anti-submarine aircraft and so provide air cover to the convoys in which they sailed throughout the voyage. These merchant ship aircraft carriers were christened the 'MAC-ships' and all bore Scottish names. After a great deal of heart-searching by the Naval Law department of the Admiralty it was agreed that they should fly the Red Ensign, the risk of the pilots being captured and treated as *franc-tireurs* [partisan fighters] being considered small. The first to be launched was the grain ship, *Empire MacAlpine,* in December 1942 followed by the *Empire MacAndrew* in May 1943. As Churchill recorded: 'The merchant ship had now taken the offensive against the enemy instead of merely defending herself when attacked.' The MAC ships did invaluable work, remaining in service until 1945. A proper naval vessel, the escort carrier, was also developed.[4]

By the time the convoys to the Soviet Union were resumed in November their codename had been changed from the ill-fated PQ to JW; with greater escort protection all sixteen ships in JW51A and all fourteen in JW51B reached Molotovsk and Kola Inlet safely in December 1942.[5]

Casablanca

In the first week of January 1943 I received another summons to prepare for a voyage into the unknown. On the appointed evening I presented myself, as directed, to the north-west door of the Admiralty where I was joined by Captain Charles Lambe, the Director of the Plans Division in the Admiralty. We entered a waiting car and set out along the Bath Road. Reaching Marlborough, we stopped outside an inn and Charles rapped on the door which opened cautiously to admit us. In the lounge we found Admiral Pound, General Sir Alan Brooke, Dill's successor as CIGS, Frederick Leathers, the Minister of War Transport, and a large number of staff officers who had preceded us, our late arrival caused by car trouble on the way. When the party was mustered and correct we re-entered our cars and drove to Lyneham airfield where we were received by the Air Commodore and his staff.[6]

After being briefed on what to do in case of a forced landing in the sea and being fitted out with parachutes and flying kit, we were taken onto the airfield where a number of Liberator bombers were drawn up. We squeezed ourselves in through the loading hatch and settled ourselves in the bomb bays; around midnight we took off. It was the most uncomfortable night I can remember. Somewhere, quite unlocatable, there was a small hole through which a blast of icy cold air played around my head the whole night long. Opposite me Admiral Pound seemed to be faring a little better for he appeared to doze off from time to time; best of all was an air marshal who sat bolt upright all night reading Sir Arthur Bryant's book, *The Years of Endurance*, with as little concern as if he were in his London club. I still had no idea where we were going although I realised that the choice was limited to North America or North Africa.

When – on 13 January – we touched down some nine hours later and emerged from the dark belly of the aircraft, I caught sight of a camel and knew that the latter was correct. We entered the waiting cars and soon found ourselves in a heavily-guarded barbed wire compound which had been erected by the United States Army around the Anfa Hotel and its neighbouring bungalows about four miles outside the town of Casablanca. I had been allocated a cabin on board the headquarters ship, HMS *Bulolo*, lying in Casablanca harbour. Immediately after breakfast I drove down to the ship.[7] There were still signs of the American assault a few months previously when, in November 1942, American and British forces had attacked Vichy-held Casablanca as part of their planned landings in North Africa codenamed Operation Torch. Outside the French admiral's office in the dockyard stood two unexploded shells from the USS *Massachusetts* on which, with typical French humour, had been written, *Cadeau des Américains*; alongside the quays American ships were unloading stores and supplies not only for their troops but also for the civilian population. Having called on Captain Richard Hamer (who had received a DSO for a successful attack on German U-boats in June 1940) and deposited my suitcase, I returned to the Anfa Hotel, where a high-level conference, codenamed Symbol, was to take place between Roosevelt and Churchill and between their combined chiefs of staff. Also present were the leaders of the Free French, General Henri Giraud and General Charles de Gaulle. Stalin was absent on the grounds that the battle for Stalingrad was reaching its climax and it would be unwise for him to leave the Soviet Union.[8]

It was indeed a pleasant spot as the Prime Minister remarked when I met him walking in the gardens with Sir Charles Wilson (later Lord Moran), his personal physician, the next morning. There were palm trees and flowering shrubs and the warm North African sun was very enjoyable after the murk and gloom of wartime London in winter. The Americans had laid on every comfort at the hotel. The bar was well-stocked and everything was 'on the house'. They had thoughtfully provided an assortment of toiletry requisites like razor blades and soap which were scarce at home as well as an unlimited supply of 'candy'. The hotel itself was a modern building on top of a hill and commanding a good view of the surrounding country and the town of Casablanca. It had a flat roof which formed a veritable suntrap and here Admiral Pound, Captain Lambe and I used to foregather after lunch each day to discuss matters arising from the conference. The scene in the lounge of an evening was historic. In one corner Generals Montgomery, Alexander, Eisenhower and Marshall might be exchanging soldierly reminiscences; in another, General Brooke, Air Marshal Tedder and General Giraud (a likeable character with a keen sense of humour) would be discussing his recent escape from being held as a prisoner of war by the Germans. Admirals Pound, Cunningham, Mountbatten and King might be grouped around a table swopping yarns, while the Prime Minister, Air Chief Marshal Portal, Lord Leathers, General Arnold, Harry Hopkins and Air Marshal Jack Slessor surveyed the scene with evident satisfaction. One well directed bomb and the whole higher direction of the war would have gone west![9]

On one occasion the Prime Minister was called in to resolve a deadlock which had arisen between the British and American chiefs of staff. Glancing down at the glum faces on either side of the table he is reported to have said: 'So Gentlemen, you are only little brooms, you can only sweep away pebbles but I am the big broom, I can sweep away boulders,' which he promptly did! On another occasion we had urged Admiral Pound to ask Admiral King to allocate more of the new United States' destroyers to the Battle of the Atlantic as we had gained the impression that the majority of their new construction was going to the Pacific. He said he would raise the subject during a walk which they were to take together that evening. They set off down towards the beach after tea and we waited anxiously for their return. Dusk was falling as they re-entered the hotel. 'Any luck, Sir?'

we asked. The First Sea Lord shook his head. 'Every time I got around to the subject he picked up a nice flat stone and sent it skimming over the waves and the only answer I got was – got five that time! See if you can beat it.' Such were the periodic communication lapses with our allies!

By the end of our deliberations many important decisions had been reached, the most significant of which was the Casablanca Declaration, stating that the Allies would only accept 'unconditional surrender', a phrase suggested by President Roosevelt which General Ulysses S. Grant had used during the American Civil War.

The main point of contention was Churchill's preference to attack the 'soft underbelly' of the Axis alliance in the Mediterranean by invading Sicily and moving northwards through Italy as opposed to Roosevelt's wish to begin the cross-channel invasion of Northern Europe. Eventually the leaders had reached a compromise: Roosevelt agreed to the attack on Sicily, while Churchill promised greater assistance for the war in the Pacific, which meant a renewed focus on winning back Burma.

Once the conference concluded on 24 January, we of the staff packed up our books and papers for the return trip to England, while Churchill, accompanied by President Roosevelt, took off for what he called the 'Paris of the Sahara' – Marrakesh – and some of the chiefs of staff went to Algiers.[10] We flew first to Gibraltar where, because of adverse weather reports, we were delayed for two days. We finally took off in three Liberators, one of which crashed in Cornwall the following morning, killing amongst others, Brigadier Guy Stewart, the Director of Planning at the War Office.[11] My plane landed safely at Lyneham in poor visibility. I was standing on the tarmac talking to the air commodore when a plane passed overhead. 'There goes Joan of Arc', he said. 'They've missed the airfield. I shall have to send a fighter after them.' And so he did, and General de Gaulle was retrieved!

Shipping and Tonnage

I had only been back in my office about six weeks when I was instructed to go to the United States with a committee which was to examine and report on the shipping position, which remained a decisive factor. Not only was it a question of how much tonnage would be available on a given date when losses, new construction and essential imports had been allowed for, but the military problem, of how many men with the necessary stores and equipment could be packed into a given number of ships, had to be agreed with our American allies. The other members of this committee chosen for the task were Harvey from the Ministry of War Transport's statistical section, Mr Picknett, deputy director of sea transport and Brigadier W.D. Williams from the movements section of the War Office.

In the hope of reaching our destination quickly our passage was booked by Pan American Airways, which, at that time, ran a flying boat service from Foynes in Ireland to New York by a circuitous route which took us first to Rabat, Bathurst in the Gambia, Trinidad and finally New York! The trip was scheduled to take four days but it took eight. First we were held up in Ireland for two days waiting for a gale to moderate and then for another two days in Trinidad because of bad weather over New York. It was a crisp, cold morning when we circled over Long Island and alighted in the Sound. As we drove along the busy streets between the towering skyscrapers I found it hard to believe that over twenty-three years had elapsed since I had last set foot in this remarkable city which seemed all so familiar.

After we had bathed and shaved in a luxurious suite which had been reserved for us at the Waldorf Astoria Hotel on Park Avenue, we went to call on Sir Ashley Sparks, the Ministry of War Transport's representative in New York, and whose investiture I had witnessed on board HMS *Renown* in 1919. With the introduction of convoys on the United States coast, his job of ensuring the rapid flow of munitions, raw materials and food to Britain had become more difficult and I was anxious to hear first hand how things were going. Sir Ashley was a man among men and he possessed that rare gift of being able to inspire his subordinates with his own dynamic spirit, tackling and surmounting all difficulties with energy and enthusiasm. I left his office after this – the first of many meetings – thinking how fortunate we were to have him at the helm on this side of the Atlantic. That afternoon we travelled to Washington. It was dark when we arrived and it was not until the following morning that I was able to take in the beauty of this capital on the shores of the Potomac River. Most cities look their best in spring but Washington is specially favoured by the number of handsome trees which line the avenues and particularly by Rock Creek Park, which runs through the city. I was reminded of Paris, which is not surprising since a Frenchman, Pierre L'Enfant, was responsible for the design. But, as I soon discovered, the atmosphere was very different from Paris.[12]

The heart of the greatest war machine ever fashioned for the defence of human rights was beating with a distinctly audible throb. From the bureaus and offices orders were going out to factories and shipyards, mobilising the tremendous resources of the country so that everything that was needed to win the war could be produced quickly and in great quantity. In his office in the Navy Department overlooking Constitution Avenue, gaunt, ascetic-looking Admiral King drove his staff with relentless pressure. Already the tide in the Pacific had begun to turn and sweep the Japanese back to their homeland. Everywhere I went there was a sense of urgency in the air.

I went immediately to report to Admiral Sir Percy Noble, head of the British naval delegation to Washington. I also went to see Sir Arthur Salter, who headed our shipping mission in Washington.[13] The problems we had come to resolve were not difficult, provided agreement could be reached on a basis for calculation. My job was to estimate the probable losses and work out whether we could take care of the shipping involved, while my colleagues had to decide how much shipping was required and find out if it would be available. There were also a number of matters which I wished to discuss with the US Navy Department. To give them the benefit of our experience, I had sent them one of my most experienced convoy officers from the Trade Division, Captain Peter Morey. He had done good work as a liaison officer and introduced me to Rear Admiral Ralph Metcalf USN and his staff who were in charge of the convoy and routeing section and I benefited from many useful discussions.[14]

During our visit Sir Arthur hosted a cocktail party at which Admiral King was one of the guests, as well as the principal American shipping officers, among whom was the industrialist, Henry Kaiser, whose Kaiser Shipyards had greatly increased production even before the US entered the war. He immediately tackled me about the shipping losses; in particular he was disturbed about the hardships suffered by the crews of torpedoed ships and he made the suggestion that every ship should tow behind it a specially equipped lifeboat. We had had this matter under constant review in London and, with the help of the ministry, who provided and equipped the ships, we had collected a small number of 'rescue ships', of about 1,200 tons, which were operated out of Scotland by the Rescue Ship Service. Sailing with the convoys to pick up survivors and providing medical attention, their presence had already helped to improve the survival rates of those whose ships were sunk. Our objective was to include one in each convoy, but there were not enough to go around.[15] Having heard of the speed with which ships were being built in American shipyards, I thought this might be an opportunity to get some more of these ships. All this I explained to Kaiser and he seemed greatly interested.

'How many more would you be wanting?' he asked. 'Oh, about thirty,' I replied, pitching the number a little higher than our actual requirement.

'Thirty', he repeated. 'Thirty, did you say? Once I got a yard all tooled up for a job like that I couldn't take an order for less than three hundred.' It was not for nothing he was called the 'father of American shipbuilding', his adaptation of production techniques enabling him to build his 'Liberty ships' in forty-five days, a record being set when a faster 'Victory' ship was built in just over four days.

While I was in North America, I planned to visit Ottawa where, in addition to being director of naval intelligence on loan to the Royal Canadian Navy, my friend, Captain Eric Brand, had been entrusted with the formation of a Trade Division at Defence Headquarters in order to handle the Royal Canadian Navy's contacts with the merchant shipping of all nations. A year junior to me, we had met when he entered Dartmouth in 1911; like me, he was a navigator and had been an instructor at HMS *Dryad*.

As an instructor on the pilotage course Brand taught how to take the sun's meridian altitude with an innovative 'astronomical spotting table'. This involved another officer leaning out of an upstairs window and pulling the brass gong (which normally stood in the entrance to the wardroom) attached to a piece of string up the side of the wall, thereby enabling his students standing in the courtyard outside to use their sextants to measure the maximum altitude of this artificial 'sun' from the artificial 'horizon' of the white-washed wall!

Paymaster Rear Admiral Sir Eldon Manisty, a founder member of the Trade Division in the First World War, currently serving as head of the convoy section in the Ministry of War Transport, had arrived in Washington and we decided to travel to Canada together on the overnight passenger train, the Montrealer. When we changed trains at Montreal in the early morning and I sniffed the cold, clean air I could have imagined I was in Scotland. Spring had not yet come to this part of Canada and the river was in full flood with water from the melting snow. The buds on the trees, still closed and deep red, were awaiting the warm sun to burst them open and disclose the young folded leaves inside. Accommodation had been reserved for us at the Chateau Laurier Hotel, itself not unlike a highland castle, and we spent two days discussing affairs of common concern, Canada having made a magnificent contribution to the Battle of the Atlantic. The work of her corvettes, many manned by men who had never seen the sea before, is worthy of the highest praise.[16]

On my return to Washington I found that little progress had been made to resolve the problem for which we had crossed the Atlantic, an unbridgeable gap remaining between the British and American figures for tons per man to be used in estimating the amount of shipping required for the re-entry into France. The American figure was much higher than ours and, if accepted, the concern was that the operation could not be mounted with the resources available. We reported the deadlock to our various heads of mission and the matter was referred back to London. Meanwhile I busied myself with obtaining American support for a fast tanker convoy direct from Trinidad to the United Kingdom. It was agreed that the matter would be placed on the agenda for the next chiefs of staff meeting. Unfortunately, either Admiral King forgot to read his brief or this item had been omitted in error, since when it came up, in his usual abrupt manner, he looked angrily around the table, declaring: 'Someone's holding a pistol to my head, but whoever it is, he's the guy that's going to get shot.' I was just behind Admiral Noble and I watched him as he leaned forward and in the calmest possible voice said: 'I may be mistaken, Admiral, but I thought it was the Germans and Japanese we were aiming at, not each other.' There was a pause, then King's face relaxed and he went as far as he ever did to smile and replied: 'I guess you're right, Admiral,' and the discussion continued.

During our stay Sir Arthur Salter asked me to accompany him to New York to witness a demonstration of a helicopter landing on a ship under way, which was being staged by the inventor, Igor Sikorsky. Although helicopters had been under production for some years, full-scale production had only begun after Sikorsky, who had already developed the first Pan American Airways flying boats, had pioneered the rotor configuration. Again travelling overnight by train, we reached Pennsylvania Station early the following morning. Crossing to Grand Central Station, where we breakfasted, we caught another train which took us to Bridgeport where we embarked in a US Navy tanker. A platform about twelve feet square had been rigged in the after part of the vessel and on this a helicopter with large floats was perched. As soon as we were under way, a young colonel of the US Air Force put the machine through its paces. I was greatly impressed with the ease with which he manoeuvred this strange looking craft, the modern version of which looks like being our greatest asset in the struggle against the high-speed submarine. By the time I got back to Manhattan the sun was setting in a blaze of gold over Jersey City as we drove down Riverside Drive. That evening I dined at the Diamond Horsehoe, established by the legendary theatre owner, Billy Rose, in the basement of the Paramount Hotel in Times Square, with Colonel John Llewellin. As Minister for Aircraft Production, he later worked with the Americans to oversee the development of the atomic bomb.[17]

The following day I again conferred with Sir Ashley Sparks. I also spent a good deal of time with Captain Harold Auten RNR, our chief naval control service officer to the port, who had won a VC in 1918 for 'coolness, discipline and good organisation'.[18] For the weekend Sir Ashley had kindly invited Sir Eldon and me to his home in Oyster Bay Cove, Long Island, where we spent an enjoyable forty-eight hours in beautiful surroundings away from the immediate concerns of war. Sir Ashley was an excellent host and a great believer in early morning tea. On Sunday morning he woke me in person with the biggest cup of tea I had ever seen, which he described as a 'basin-full'! I was especially glad of the opportunity our stay afforded me of meeting his daughter, Amy, the widow of Captain Edward Sim who had relieved me in command of HMS *Galatea* and had gone down with the ship in December 1941. Amy had been left with a young

189

daughter, the image of her father. (Subsequently I learnt that in 1945 Amy had re-married.)

Trident

On my return to Washington Admiral Noble greeted me with the news that another conference – the third Washington Conference, codenamed Trident – would shortly take place between the Prime Minister, the President and the Combined Chiefs of Staff. The custom was that, on 1 May, all the services changed into summer uniform. Since I had not expected to be away for such a long period, I was left in a quandary because I had not brought my summer uniform with me. Now that I had to remain in Washington I had to obtain some suits. Admiral Noble was well-known for his sartorial perfection and I was anxious to live up to his standard. The American white naval uniform was at that time much better cut than our own and made of better material and so I purchased two of their suits and borrowed some RN buttons and shoulder straps. When I appeared before Admiral Noble, he at once remarked: 'That's a very smart white suit you are wearing, where did you get it?' Having informed him of my recent purchase, he looked at me more closely. 'You shouldn't put things in your pockets,' he proffered. 'It spoils your appearance. You see I always have mine sewn up to enable me to resist the temptation!'

The Prime Minister and his party reached Washington on Tuesday 11 May. The following day we received instructions that a solution to the problem – the discrepancies in our estimates and those of the Americans regarding the amount of shipping required for the invasion of Northern France – must reach the White House no later than noon the next day. A full conference was summoned for that evening; with the added weight of Lord Leathers and Lewis Douglas, deputy administrator of the United States' War Shipping Administration, a solution was reached at 5am after an all-night sitting. General Gros, who had held out for so long to ensure, as he put it, that 'his boys did not go short' finally capitulated. On the basis of the agreed figure for tons per man we were able to assure the chiefs of staff that there would be sufficient shipping to mount the operations which they had in mind.[19]

One night Admiral Pound, who was staying at the new Statler Hotel just north of the White House on 16th Street, sent for me at about 10pm.

It was very hot and the management had provided what looked like a small bath full of ice which was standing on the floor of his sitting room. Sticking out from among the blocks of ice were the necks of bottles containing almost every known variety of liquid refreshment, which the First Sea Lord was contemplating with amusement. 'If you're thirsty,' he said, 'go ahead and help yourself.' Suitably refreshed, we began our meeting!

For the next two weeks the Allied leaders discussed plans for what was hoped would be the concluding stages of the war. While the President and Prime Minister met on alternate days, the military leaders met almost daily in the Board of Governors Room in the Federal Reserve Building on 20th Street and Constitution Avenue. Both Roosevelt and Churchill adhered to the principle – adopted at Casablanca in January – of unconditional surrender. Discussion also focused on the Allied invasion of Sicily, the date for the invasion of Northern Europe, as well as the conduct of the war in the Pacific. Once the conference concluded, Churchill took off for Gibraltar; the rest of us embarked in Liberator aircraft for England, by way of Gander in Newfoundland and Prestwick on the west coast of Scotland. These aircraft had been adapted for passenger use and so we did not have to endure the same discomfort as on the voyage to Casablanca.[20]

By the end of May 1943 I was back in my office after an absence of eight weeks. Soon afterwards my relief, Captain Derek Stephens, was appointed.[21] I handed over to him in late July, having been informed that, in the King's Birthday Honours, I had been appointed Commander of the Military Division of the British Empire – CBE – 'for distinguished service'. It had been a very memorable two years, covering the crucial phases of the Battle of the Atlantic. The fortunes of the Arctic convoys had improved. Despite continuing offensive action by the Germans, there had been no more losses by the time the convoys were again suspended in March 1943 during the summer of perpetual daylight (until the following November). The division had grown steadily and now numbered over 360 naval officers and civilians – both men and women, nearly twice what it was when I took over in 1941. Among those I worked with was my very good friend, Captain William Beswick RNR, whose help and advice I found of the greatest value.

On my departure from the Admiralty Admiral Pound wrote me a personal letter of thanks: 'Director of Trade Division is not an easy appointment to fill because you have to deal with so many outside people, and it is all the more credit to you therefore that you have made such a great success of it. Hence you can leave the Admiralty with the knowledge that you have earned a good seagoing appointment.'[22]

Chapter Sixteen

From *Duke of York* to *Dryad*

There is no felicity upon earth,
Which carries not its counterpoise of misfortune.[1]

1943–44

I joined HMS *Duke of York* at Scapa Flow on Friday, 6 August 1943. I could not have wished for anything better. Flagship of Admiral Sir Bruce Fraser, Commander-in-Chief of the Home Fleet, and commissioned in 1941, she was one of the five new 35,000-ton battleships of the King George V-class. My predecessor was my Osborne and Dartmouth contemporary, George Creasy, who had been promoted rear admiral in July; our paths were to cross again during the planning of the Allied invasion of northern Europe. For my arrival, he had kindly sent the ship's amphibious Walrus aircraft to Wick airfield. After crossing the Pentland Firth and landing alongside the ship, I had the unusual distinction of joining my ship by being hoisted in over the side!

I was greeted by the news that His Majesty King George VI was scheduled to make a three-day visit in a week's time and would be taking the Home Fleet to sea for exercises. I had never handled a ship of this class before and so I was naturally a little anxious about doing so for the first time with the Royal Standard flying. On the appointed day – 12 August – His Majesty came over from the mainland in a destroyer and, after being received with the customary honours, took tea in the admiral's after cabin. It was a pleasure to see how genuinely delighted he was to be with the fleet again. When Admiral Fraser told him that I had only just assumed command of the ship and had not yet taken her to sea, the king laughed and asked me if I was nervous. I answered, of course, that I was not!

That evening the king gave a dinner party on board to which all the other flag officers present were summoned to attend. The menu included plum pudding and, undoubtedly because of the royal occasion, the admiral's chef had added a few extra sixpenny pieces. The chief steward brought in the flaming delicacy and handed it to His Majesty but when he transferred a helping to his plate there was a noise like the emptying of a money box as silver pieces tumbled out. The king was much amused and to commemorate the occasion Admiral Fraser suggested that two of the sixpenny pieces should be mounted as presents, one for each of the princesses. To this the king readily agreed so they were handed over to me. Two little ebonite boxes were made in the ship's workshops and a well burnished coin mounted on the top of each.

The next day was wet and stormy but the king, quite undaunted, carried out a full programme of visits to other ships, including two ships I had served in, the *Renown* and the *Malaya*, and shore establishments. When he arrived back on board in the dog watches it was still raining hard. As the quarterdeck was awash, I suggested that, instead of going aft to the admiral's hatch, he should go down the hatch by the wardroom which was abreast of the gangway. The king agreed and, preceded by the master at arms, we went below and aft under cover. To reach the admiral's cabin we had to pass between the gunroom and the midshipmen's quarters and, at that time of day, several young officers in various states of undress were in the passage on their way to or from the bathroom. The horrified master at arms slammed shut every door in advance of our arrival, at the same time as chasing away any loiterers in the gangway. The king suddenly stopped and turning to me said 'Your master at arms seems to think that I am the Mikado, flag captain. I don't in the least mind being seen by the boys.' I immediately told the master at arms that his precautions were unnecessary and we proceeded along to the admiral's cabin.

That night I had the honour of sitting next to His Majesty and we talked a great deal about our term mates at Osborne and Dartmouth and what had become of them. I took the opportunity of describing to the king some instances of the heroism of our merchant seamen which had come to my notice as director of the Trade Division. The king showed the greatest interest in these stories and this led on to a question which had been raised just before I left the Admiralty, of giving the title royal to the Merchant Navy. The consensus of the opinion in the Admiralty and in the Ministry of War Transport opposed the idea but I have no doubt that, had his ministers tendered other advice, the king would have been only too pleased to grant it.

The following day we got under way and the king took the fleet to sea, as his father had done when Admiral Beatty was commander-in-chief of the Grand Fleet in the latter part of the First World War. His Majesty took a keen interest in the various gunnery and other practices carried out and he was particularly impressed by the spectacular rocket practice of the naval carrier-borne aircraft. So far everything had gone well, but on the way into harbour and passing between the gate vessels of the boom where there was a strong cross set, I thought for a moment we were going to hit the one on the port side. I cracked on speed and we shot safely through the gap! On the day of the king's departure a demonstration was given of the air defences of Scapa. It would have been a brave and foolhardy German pilot who would have attempted to penetrate the barrage of high explosive which these defences were now capable of putting up.

Not long after His Majesty had left, the United States' aircraft carrier, *Ranger,* and two cruisers, the *Tuscaloosa* and *Augusta*, together with several destroyers, joined the Home Fleet and we were thus able to carry out some harassing operations against the Germans in Norway. In late September we received a visit from a delegation including the Secretary of the US Navy, Colonel Frank Knox, whom I had met in Washington, and who had been an ardent opponent of the US's prior isolationism. The Americans had received a tremendous buffeting crossing the Pentland Firth in the destroyers which had been sent for them. Knox was quite *hors de combat* on arrival and had to be revived with a stiff scotch and soda. Admiral Fraser jokingly remarked that it was fortunate that he was not on board one of his own American ships, whereupon we fell to discussing the pros and cons of prohibition on board US warships. At one moment I quite thought we had convinced Mr Secretary that, as Iago says in Shakespeare's *Othello*: 'Good wine is a good familiar creature, if it be well used', but we were reminded of the opposition such a measure was likely to meet in Congress and there the matter rested. Nevertheless, I know that many American naval officers would welcome some relaxation of the restriction which would enable them to return hospitality in kind when abroad. Knox's premature death in April 1944, after a series of heart attacks, came as a great shock.[2]

I had already learnt a little about the King George V-class battleship from my trip in the *Prince of Wales,* now tragically at the bottom of the sea off the Malayan peninsula in the South China Sea. I began a critical inspection of my ship in order to submit a report which the commander-in-chief had requested regarding modifications necessary to render the ships suitable for operations in the tropics. There were a number of things with which I and the other captains found fault and some lessons had been learnt from the survivors of the *Prince of Wales.* A curious weakness, which I discovered, had its origin in the desire of every commander of a ship for a smooth side devoid of excrescences, like scupper pipes. This had resulted in these being kept inside the ship down to the level of the water line. There was a large number of these pipes on both sides of the ship and they discharged overboard through a cast iron fitting on the ship's side. Cast iron fractures very easily as the result of an explosion, hence a near miss by a bomb or a shell could cause the compartments concerned to be flooded without the ship herself having been hit. Another issue was the temperature reached in the ship's galley when the oil-fired stoves were in use. Even in winter in home waters temperatures of over 100 degrees Fahrenheit were normal, so what they would have been in the tropics can be imagined. The Walrus aircraft, while useful as a taxi, was a serious fire risk and, with the advent of radar, aircraft spotting was no longer a necessity.

After a period at sea undertaking exercises in early October, we spent a week in Rosyth before returning to Scapa Flow. Storms often blow up when least expected and the comparative tranquillity of our existence at Scapa was broken not by the elements, nor by the enemy, but by an innocent Wren (i.e. WRNS) rating who drove the commander-in-chief's car from Inverness to the naval base at Thurso on his return from a visit to the Admiralty. Learning that she had never been on board a ship, Admiral Fraser brought her over to Scapa on his destroyer; sending her to the WRNS' quarters at Lyness, he told her that she could see around the flagship the following day. By so doing he unwittingly contravened the WRNS regulations which stipulated that Wrens were only allowed on board ship in organised parties and on certain days.

When news of the commander-in-chief's action reached the desk of the Director of the WRNS, Vera Laughton Mathews, she felt obliged to present herself on board the ship to remind the commander-in-chief of the rules. On arrival she was received with the honours due to a flag officer and we then started on what she describes as a 'truly royal tour of the ship'. She stood up magnificently to the strenuous programme I had arranged which included visits to each of the officers' messes; as she later recalled, the 'highlight' was visiting the ship's galley to stir the Christmas puddings which 'started with 80 lbs of raisins. The commander-in-chief and I both poured in jugs of rum and sixpences and stirred with boat paddles.' But she never forgot for one moment the purpose of her visit. When, after lunch, the chief of staff, secretary, flag lieutenant and I excused ourselves, she said to Admiral Fraser in a voice full of meaning: 'And now Admiral we can have our little talk.' I knew that a solution was to be hammered out on the unyielding anvil of the WRNS regulations. And so it was, as Dame Vera later recorded: 'After we had thrashed things out for about an hour' Admiral Fraser 'more or less agreed to everything we wanted namely, not to give instructions direct to Wrens and not to have Wrens on board except in organised parties arranged through the senior WRNS officer ... Having jotted the "agreement" down on a signal pad and got the Commander-in-Chief's signature to it, I felt I had really achieved something.'[3]

I was thoroughly settled and happy in my new command when I was suddenly faced with a great personal crisis. I reported the situation to the Admiralty and it was decided that it would be best if I were relieved of my command.[4] On 9 December 1943 I handed over to Captain the Hon Guy Russell. A short time later he took the *Duke of York* into action off the North Cape of Norway. Although the *Tirpitz* had been immobilised following attacks by midget submarines in September and did not re-appear until the following March, the *Scharnhorst*, which had joined the *Tirpitz* in early 1943, was still at large. Her sinking on 26 December was one of the most successful surface actions of the war in home waters. For a naval officer, whose training is fashioned towards taking part in a great sea battle, the aptness of the Right Reverend Jeremy Taylor's words at the beginning of this chapter will now be appreciated.[5]

HMS Dryad

On 19 January 1944 the Admiralty, with great consideration, appointed me in command of HMS *Dryad*, the Navigation School which was within easy reach of my home. The old school to which I have referred in previous chapters had been bombed and the establishment was now housed at Southwick House, an old Victorian manor standing in a park of 300 acres north of the Portsdown hills and about nine miles from Portsmouth. In 1941 the house had been requisitioned from its owner, Colonel Evelyn Thistlethwayte, who had already been offering overnight accommodation to the officers of the Navigation School at Portsmouth during the frequent air raids. I had not been there very long when Major General Freddie de Guingand, Chief of Staff to General Bernard Montgomery, 21st Army Group, called to see me. He told me in strict confidence that he was looking for a suitable headquarters from which the forthcoming invasion of France could be directed. Codenamed Overlord, the operation had been in the planning stages since 1943. After I had shown General de Guingand around the house and grounds and he had seen what excellent cover there was in the park, he departed.[6]

Shortly afterwards I was informed by Admiral Sir Charles Little, Commander-in- Chief, Portsmouth, that the matter had been decided and that I was to arrange for the transfer of the officers studying navigation to the Royal Naval College at Greenwich. On 3 April the Navigation School moved out. Only the Action Information Training Centre (AITC), currently engaged on the high priority industry of preparing to equip the fleet being assembled to join that of the US in the war against Japan in the Pacific, remained as a self-contained unit in what had formerly been the old stables. Admiral Sir Bertram Ramsay, who, as Vice Admiral Dover, had overseen the evacuation of Dunkirk in 1940, was appointed Commander-in-Chief (Navy) of the Allied Naval Expeditionary Force, while Rear Admiral George Creasy was appointed as his chief of staff. I immediately went to see Admiral Ramsay at his London headquarters; my suggestion was that, since he and his staff must be very preoccupied with the tremendous task of working out the logistics of transporting thousands of men and tons of heavy equipment across the Channel, he would require someone to organise and administer his headquarters. Admiral Ramsay heartily approved of my proposal and so I entered on a new phase of activity, which involved converting the old house into a headquarters with all the necessary communications.

There was not a great deal of time. First the supply of electric power was inadequate. The water supply which came from a well had to be augmented and so had the drainage facilities, which had been barely adequate for the Navigation School. Teleprinter and telephone lines galore had to be laid and extra buildings erected. Almost every day I was informed of some additional requirement so that the place grew like a bed of mushrooms. The last of the nissen huts went up only about forty-eight hours before Admiral Ramsay and his staff took up residence towards the end of April, Ramsay occupying what had formerly been my office on the first floor. Their arrival was followed soon afterwards by that of the Supreme Commander, General Dwight Eisenhower, and General Montgomery with their respective staffs; they parked their caravans and tents under the now luxuriant foliage of the trees of Southwick Park. Every tree and copse was alive with men but the greenery was so abundant that an aerial photograph of the estate revealed no sign of anything but a country house set in the peaceful surroundings of the English countryside. This camouflage proved a little too effective for one major general whose caravan had been located in the wilderness shrubbery. The morning after his arrival he awoke to find himself completely wired in, the Royal Marines, who had been entrusted with the task of securing the area with barbed wire, having failed to see him!

Inside the house, the long drawing room, with its gilt mirrors and Victorian trappings, was turned into an operations room, while the library, soon to be the scene of the most fateful of all conferences, became a mess for the admiral and his staff. In a nissen hut equipped with teleprinters, the meteorologists, chief among them Group Captain Dr James Stagg, applied themselves to a study of the weather upon which the whole success of the operation was to depend. Then followed those few weeks of expectancy with everyone poised waiting for D-Day, when the amphibious assault on the beaches of Normandy (codenamed Neptune) would begin.[7] Scheduled for Monday 5 June, as the day approached, I sensed an increased tenseness in the air. The look on General Eisenhower's face as he came and went, although as enigmatic as that of the Sphinx, reflected the weight that lay on his shoulders.

By 3 June the decision was becoming critical. In the early hours of Sunday morning, the following day, a conference of naval, military and air commanders presided over by Eisenhower was held in the library. The weather forecast was so unpromising that it was decided to postpone launching the operation on a day to day basis. I was standing in the porch looking up at the clear morning sky. The news of a 24-hour postponement had just been whispered around, yet it seemed hard to believe that the most fickle of jades, the weather, was to play us false. Although I was in no way connected with the great decision which was pending, I shared the feeling of suspense which permeated the whole building. I think that Sunday was the longest twenty-four hours I have ever known. The forecasters pored over their charts, weighing every scrap of information reaching them from ships and shore establishments. By the afternoon, grey clouds covered the sky and the trees in the park bent to the rising wind. That night, with the rain beating down on the shuttered windows of the old country house, General Eisenhower, his commanders-in-chief and their chiefs of staff met again in the library.

While the conference was in progress, I again stood at the entrance watching the trees in the copse opposite swaying and the clouds scudding across the previously clear sky, harbingers of the depression which the meteorological experts had forecast would travel up the Channel that night but which would be succeeded by a short spell of better weather on Tuesday 6 June. Even so conditions seemed most unpropitious and the same thought was in the mind of the groups of staff officers gathered in the hall waiting the outcome of the conference. When Stagg joined us, everyone looked at him expectantly, but only Eisenhower could make the crucial decision. Moments later he appeared and strode towards the front door. Catching sight of Stagg he smiled and said 'we're laying it on again and please no more bad news' (or words to that effect). Then acknowledging my salute, he walked towards his waiting jeep, jumped in and drove off. The following day, after another meeting in the early hours, General Eisenhower's brief command 'OK. Let's go!' triggered off the greatest combined operation in history.

Covering one end of the operations room a large wall map had been erected on which the positions of the many convoys converging on the Normandy beachheads could be shown. Until the invasion was actually launched, the preparations had been kept closely hidden. Now, like the opening of a dramatic scene in a theatre, the curtain was drawn aside and the players went into action. Stretching over a fifty-mile area from Cherbourg to the mouth of the River Orne, American forces would land on beaches codenamed Utah and Omaha, while British, Canadian and French forces would land on sectors codenamed Gold, Juno, and Sword. Following D-Day, came D+1, D+2 and so on until by the end of June over a million men had been landed. Despite the carefully guarded secret, the German response, under the leadership of Field Marshal Erwin Rommel, was swift, American losses being particularly severe on the section of the beach codenamed Omaha.[8]

With the launching of the invasion came the V-1 flying bombs, the first attack on London on 13 June coming one week after the Allied landings. While the majority were directed at London, quite a number of them were aimed at the Southampton area and we were in the direct line of fire. I never ceased to admire the calmness of the WRNS officers in the war room who used to plot the position of these dangerous missiles from the time they left the French coast until the rhythmic throb of the motor could be plainly heard approaching. A direct hit on that brick stucco mansion would have brought it down in a heap of rubble but these women never turned a black, brown or golden hair. On one occasion a bomb failed to clear the Portsdown hills behind which we were located and went off with a loud report that shook the old house to its foundations, but mercifully that was the only one which fell anywhere near us. At their height more than 1,000 V-1 bombers were launched in one day, making a total of nearly 10,000 which were despatched, until eventually the sites from which they could be launched were overrun by the Allies. By the beginning of July Caen had fallen, opening the way to Paris which was surrendered to the Allies on 25 August.

The purpose for which HMS *Dryad* had been commandeered had come to an end and in early September Admiral Ramsay and his staff left for France. Before leaving he handed me a letter in which he recorded that 'Dryad's contribution to the success of the operation has been a very real one of which you may all be proud'. It came as a great shock to all of us who knew him to hear of his untimely death in an air crash outside Paris on 2 January 1945 while he was en route to a meeting with General

Montgomery in Brussels. He had rendered very distinguished service to his country and besides being a great leader, he was a great gentleman.

One year after the war was over and two years after the landings, on 7 August 1946 the Wall Map of H-Hour (6.30am) – the time the invasion was launched – was unveiled by Admiral Ramsay's chief of staff, Rear Admiral George Creasy. Alongside was a plaque, inscribed as follows: 'Presented to HMS *Dryad* by Admiral Sir Bertram Ramsay KCB KBE MVO, Allied Naval Commander-in-Chief, Expeditionary Force.' A note below explains how 'this Wall Map, in its present position, was used as the main tactical plot on which were shown all naval movements before, during and after the invasion of the Continent which led to the liberation of Europe. This room was used as the Naval War Room and here the Supreme Commander General Dwight D. Eisenhower watched the progress of events of D–Day, 6th June 1944, as the Assault was launched.'

While these momentous events were taking place at Southwick House, a purely domestic change affecting the future of the Navigation branch of the Royal Navy had been inaugurated in the old stables. The war both in Europe and in the Pacific had given prominence to the need for warships to be able to direct the fighter aircraft, which gave them overhead protection, onto any attacking aircraft shown up by the ship's radar set. This system of direction called for a special technique and officers and ratings had to be trained in its use. The Admiralty decided to make it a function of the Navigation branch, which would be known as the N/D (Navigation and Direction) branch. To carry out the training it was necessary to construct models of the operations rooms of various types of ship and, as this was closely related to the continuance of the war against Japan after the defeat of Germany, as mentioned, it had been agreed that this work should go on *pari passu* while the main building was used as a headquarters.

After Admiral Ramsay had moved to France and the establishment reverted to its normal function, I raised the question of its post-war location with the Admiralty. So many new buildings had been erected that the idea of restoring the property to its new owner, Colonel Thistlethwayte's nephew, Frank Borthwick-Norton, in the condition in which it had been taken over, did not commend itself on the grounds of expense. It was impracticable for the school in its new guise to return to the old building in Portsmouth's dockyard and so I had no hesitation in recommending that an offer be made to purchase Southwick House as a permanent home for the Navigation and Direction School. I was supported by Admiral Little, Commander-in-Chief, Portsmouth, and by the Director of Navigation, Rear Admiral William Gordon Benn (who, as captain of HMS *Royal Oak*, had survived when she was torpedoed and sunk by the German U-boat in Scapa Flow in September 1939).[9] Despite a certain amount of opposition from various quarters, eventually the purchase was agreed and HMS *Dryad* became an establishment of which all past, present and future N/D officers could be proud.[10]

In the autumn I visited Rouen in France to preside over a series of courts martial which sadly were necessary in the concluding stages of the fighting in France. I was thus able to see something of the aftermath of war on land. At sea, when a ship sinks the ocean closes over her and leaves no trace, but ashore the shattered buildings, torn and twisted bridges and mounds of debris remain for months and even years as a monument to the senseless destruction caused by war.

Chapter Seventeen

The *KGV* and the Pacific

War made in earnest maketh war to cease,
And vigorous prosecution hastens peace.[1]

1945–46

My next appointment was to take command of HMS *King George V.* The first of the King George V-class battleships to have been built, commissioned in 1940, she had been engaged in the action to sink the *Bismarck* in 1941; more recently, as the flagship of Vice Admiral Sir Bernard Rawlings, second-in-command, British Pacific Fleet and commander of the British task force operating with the US Pacific Fleet, the *King George V* had been undertaking operations against the Japanese. My official letter of appointment, signed by the Lords Commissioners of the Admiralty, was dated 12 April 1945 – which, for those of us who had been closely in touch with our American allies, was notable since, on that day, President Franklin D. Roosevelt died, his successor being the Vice President, Harry S. Truman.[2] My orders were to depart at once for Sydney, Australia, where the British Pacific Fleet had its headquarters, taking passage in the Dutch liner, *Nieue Amsterdam*, which had been converted into a troop transport.[3]

We sailed from the Clyde in almost summer weather on 23 April; I was fortunate in having a cabin to myself considering we were carrying over 6,000 officers and other ranks, most of whom were packed as tight as sardines in a tin. The master of the ship was the commodore of the Holland-Amerika line and he kindly made me an honorary member of the ship's officers' mess. I spent many hours in his company listening to his wonderful stories and experiences and tasting once again 'Oud Geneva', as the Dutch call their favourite gin. Sailing west of Ireland, we entered the Mediterranean and passed through the Suez Canal, making for Western Australia without any intermediate stops. We were already halfway across the Indian Ocean when we received news of Germany's surrender on 8 May known as VE Day. Although all troopships were officially 'dry', from the depths of the hold enough alcohol was produced to enable everyone on board to celebrate the occasion in a fitting manner. The following morning a service of thanksgiving was held and, although we still had one more enemy to defeat, it was a tremendous relief to know that our loved ones at home could dwell in safety.

I was looking forward to seeing Australia. The first sight which greets most people is the island of Rottnest, lying some ten miles west of Fremantle; then come the low-lying sandy beaches, which stretch for miles north and south of the port. It is not surprising that the early Dutch navigators, who were the first Europeans to sight this part of the world, did not bother to investigate it more closely, for there is little sign of vegetation. (Now, thanks to the tenacity and hard work of the early settlers, the beautiful city of Perth has arisen beside the banks of the Swan River and the surrounding country is fertile and prosperous.) Travelling onwards, on a bright, sunny morning towards the end of May, we passed between Sydney Heads and I thought I had never seen such a fine harbour since I sailed into Rio de Janeiro in the *Renown* in 1919. The many creeks and bays reflecting the blue of the sky, the green scrub coming down to the water's edge and the red roofs of the white houses made a most striking picture. Soon the city, with its fine buildings, came into view, nestling mainly to the south of the famous Sydney Harbour bridge and this too was an imposing sight.

On arrival I called on Admiral Sir Bruce Fraser, who had taken command of the British Pacific Fleet in December the previous year. He informed me that HMS *King George V* – or the '*KGV*' as we familiarly called the battleship – would not be in for another ten days. In the meantime he invited me to attend his daily conferences so that I could get myself up to date with the war in the Pacific. As was evident, the Japanese were reeling under a series of mighty blows delivered by the overwhelming United States' sea, air and ground forces. At the end of 1942 the US Navy had one serviceable aircraft carrier in the Pacific; now more than 100 of such ships, capable of launching 5,000 aircraft, were in operation.⁴ Supporting the carriers was a vast fleet of battleships, cruisers, destroyers and submarines, all of which were kept supplied by an immense fleet train comprising tankers, supply ships, ammunition ships and replenishment carriers.

Compared with this huge armada, the United Kingdom's contribution was modest. We had not yet been able to divert all our forces from the European to the Pacific theatre. The operating task force consisted of four aircraft carriers, two battleships (the *KGV* and HMS *Howe*) and a number of cruisers and destroyers. Our fleet train was of a decidedly makeshift character and consisted of a variety of tankers and merchant ships of several nationalities, with varying speeds and capabilities, taken up by the Ministry of War Transport through the Director of Sea Transport. We had never followed the American practice of building a proper fleet train because, with our many bases scattered all over the world, we had never envisaged the need. With the loss of Hong Kong and Singapore, we found ourselves compelled to improvise a fleet train since our base at Sydney was too far away from the scene of operations to be of value as an operational base. One notable difference between the British and American methods of conducting operations was the freedom of action given to American admirals at sea. This obviously stems from the greater distances with which they have to deal, but we shall be foolish if we think that we shall ever again be able to exercise the centralised control practised by the Admiralty during the war.

The British Pacific Fleet's main focus of operations was against the Sakishima Islands in support of the Americans fighting to capture the strategically important Okinawa Islands to the north; during these operations they had come up against the deadly kamikaze, the name given by the Japanese to their suicide pilots who formed part of the Special Sea Attack Force (SSAF) created in late 1944 out of the remnants of the Imperial Japanese Navy Air Service. How deadly they were is indicated by post-war records: for an expenditure of 2,550 aircraft (and pilots), they scored 474 hits. Fortunately, the British carriers had armoured decks so that when hit by a kamikaze, the damage was not as great as that suffered by some of the US carriers, which were not so well protected. Nevertheless, due to the need for repairs and replenishment with spare parts and stores not yet available in the fleet train, Rawlings had to bring his force back to Sydney for a short spell and this included his flagship, HMS *King George V.*[5]

It was a great moment when, on 4 June, I stood on the jetty at Woolloomooloo, east of Sydney, and watched my ship come slowly in. I could hardly wait to get on board. After three weeks in dock, undertaking exercises and bringing on ammunition, on 28 June we set sail on the long trek back to the scene of operations, averaging just under 400 miles each day. This time we were the only battleship in the British task force, the *Howe* having had to return for a refit. HMS *Duke of York* and HMS *Anson*, which had been detailed to join the BPF, had not yet arrived from England. Our Chaplain, Canon James Bezzant, whom I came to know well, was one of the fortunate survivors of HMS *Repulse* in 1941.[6]

On 4 July we reached Manus, one of the group of Admiralty Islands which lie just south of the Equator. Having topped up with fuel and stores we continued north to rendezvous with the United States Third Fleet under the command of Admiral Bill (Bull) Halsey in his flagship USS *Missouri*, which – after finally taking Okinawa on 22 June in a bloody battle lasting three months – had retired to the Philippine island of Leyte, taken from the Japanese the previous October in what was probably the largest naval battle in the Second World War.[7]

By the beginning of July the time had come to shift the full weight of our attack to the Japanese mainland, operations by US Navy aircraft beginning on 10 July. A week later we joined in the operations. The weather was pleasantly warm, but the sky was grey and cloudy. At first light, like a swarm of angry bees, nearly 1,000 aircraft took off from the British and American carriers and disappeared over the horizon. We were about 100 miles off the Japanese coast so we could see nothing of what was going on. We steamed to and fro at high speed awaiting the return of our aircraft and keeping a watchful eye on the radar plot for signs of Japanese retaliation. Presently terse reports from the aircraft began to come in, but it was not until the strike had landed that a picture could be obtained of the damage inflicted on the Japanese.

Meanwhile, a second strike had been launched and so it went on all day. Overhead fighter aircraft stood by ready to intercept any enemy aircraft which might try to attack; so good had this interception technique become that it was rare for our guns to have anything to shoot at. But the Japanese were desperate. We knew that they had recruited over 4,000 kamikaze pilots, each one determined to immolate himself on the altar of sacrifice to the emperor and so we had to be constantly on our guard. The frequency with which Japanese reconnaissance planes were shot down led them to release a small radio transmitter on a parachute over or near the fleet for the kamikaze pilots to home on. Seeing one of these boxes floating down for the first time, one of my bridge lookouts was heard to remark to his pal: 'Cor lumme Bill, see that? Must be his luggage for the next world', as the aircraft releasing it was shot down in flames.

Every two or three days we had to rendezvous with our respective fleet trains in order to re-arm, refuel and take in any stores that we required as well as the mail flown from home. This perpetual motion was something quite new to me since of course we could not stop engines out in the open sea. We moved about inside our protective screen of destroyers from tanker to storeship, to ammunition ship, while the whole force advanced at a steady eight or ten knots. On one occasion we took in ammunition from a little Danish freighter of about 3,000 tons. She was so small compared with the *King George V* that I felt I could have hoisted her inboard. She was not fitted with a gyrocompass (to enable her to find geographical direction automatically) and, as I knew her magnetic compass would be of little use in such close proximity to our 35,000 tons of steel, I had a gyro repeater (which would automatically indicate true north) passed across to her bridge on a long lead. The master looked at it for some time, listened to it ticking, then pulled out his watch and compared it with the compass. He then gravely shook his head and sent the repeater back!

Sometimes at night, while the carriers withdrew, we in the *King George V* would be ordered to join the American battleships and carry out a surprise bombardment of targets such as steel works and factories on the Japanese mainland. How effective these bombardments were it was impossible to tell, but the sight and sound of a dozen or so big battleships blazing away with their main armament at comparatively close range must have contributed to the shaking of Japanese morale. They never knew where we would strike next. On the night of 29 July we closed to within four miles to take part in a night bombardment of Hamamatsu, on the south coast. More than a thousand tons of heavy calibre ammunition were flung at shore installations. Soon fires could be seen illuminating the darkness ashore as salvo after salvo thundered out. It must indeed have been a terrifying and humiliating experience for the citizens, who, like the people of Britain, had been brought up to rely upon their Navy to protect their shores. There was no opposition and after fifteen minutes of shattering noise we ceased fire and withdrew as swiftly and silently as we had come. By the end of the month American and British aircraft had sunk the last remnants of the Japanese fleet. With their much-vaunted Imperial Japanese Navy lying at the bottom of the sea, the Japanese must have felt very defenceless.

On 5 July a general election had been held in the United Kingdom. When the results were announced on 26 July, giving the Labour Party led by Clement Attlee (Deputy Prime Minister in the Coalition government during the war) a landslide victory, Churchill – together with Truman and Stalin – was at Potsdam discussing the administration of post-war Germany. During the meeting Truman revealed that the United States possessed a 'powerful new weapon'.[8]

Victory over Japan

We were continuing our systematic destruction of the Japanese capacity to wage war when, on 6 August 1945, the American B29 bomber, *Enola Gay*, dropped the first atomic bomb on the city of Hiroshima, instantly killing an estimated 60–80,000 people. Three days later the city of Nagasaki received the only other atomic bomb then in existence and an estimated 40,000 more Japanese were slain, thousands more dying later from the effects of radiation. Those who question whether these bombs should ever have been used might reflect that the United States had already sustained 300,000 casualties in the fighting in the Pacific and that, had the invasion been carried out against a fanatical foe, the cost was estimated to be at least a million more. These two devastating and terrifying explosions brought home to the Japanese government that it was useless to continue the war.[9]

On the day that we received the news of Japan's surrender on 15 August, I was talking to Admiral Rawlings on his bridge which was just below mine, while watching the signalman bend on the flags signifying 'Cease hostilities against Japan', when the Fleet Fighter Direction Officer,

Commander Pollock RNVR, warned us that there was a Japanese aircraft overhead presumably getting into position for his death dive. Somehow, he had sneaked in unobserved. I rushed back to my bridge and alerted the anti-aircraft guns and we stood by ready to greet him with a fusillade as he came down. Suddenly a couple of American Corsair aircraft appeared in answer to our call and promptly shot down our would-be attacker, who fell into the sea on our starboard quarter. It was a timely example of allied co-operation.

When we received permission from the Admiralty to splice the main brace – giving every man on board a tot of rum in celebration of VJ Day – victory over Japan, we were fuelling from one side of an American tanker; on the other side of the tanker was Admiral Halsey's flagship, the USS *Missouri*. The thought of our American commander-in-chief having nothing stronger than orange juice with which to celebrate such a great victory was more than the admiral, chief of staff and I could bear and so we sent across a small keg of rum from the 'Limeys' (the nickname by which we were generally known on account of our supposed preference for lime juice, originating, I believe, from the enforced consumption of citrus fruits to prevent scurvy on long sea voyages in the previous century).

While the final negotiations were taking place we remained cruising at sea, ready to strike again if necessary. On 22 August the weather in the operational area turned patchy with light mist and occasional rain squalls and visibility at two miles. We were manoeuvring independently of the US fleet and were steaming on a northerly course at a speed of twenty knots when I sighted, on my port bow, one of the American task forces, comprising the usual assortment of carriers, battleships, cruisers and destroyers, steaming towards us on a nearly opposite course. It looked as if the two forces would perform what used to be known as the grid-iron manoeuvre, the ships of one force passing between those of the other on opposite courses. Suddenly over the radio came the order to the American force to turn 180 degrees left together. We were closing rapidly and at the time the signal was made the leading US carrier, the USS *Bon Homme Richard*, was less than a mile away on my port bow. Unless the signal was executed instantly she would not have had sufficient room to turn across my bows. I had just given the order 'Hard a port', reversed my port engines and sounded two blasts on my siren when the American force was ordered to turn. By the time the great 36,000 ton carrier had started to answer her helm, I could have tossed my cap onto her as she swept down on my starboard side. Whenever I am asked to relate the most frightening moment of my life, I have no hesitation in saying that was it!

On 27 August we sighted the coast of Japan for the first time in daylight. Off the island of Oshima we embarked Japanese pilots and an interpreter, who had charts of the minefields. Just before sunset we came to anchor in Sagami Bay under the shadow of Mount Fuji and I gave the order to stop engines for the first time in two months. From Admiral Fraser, Commander-in-Chief, British Pacific Fleet, came the momentous signal, 'The Fleet has anchored in Japanese waters.' Two days later the great Anglo–American fleet got under way again, the long lines of grey and sea-stained ships slowly threading their way through the minefields in the Uraga Channel. On 30 August we anchored in Tokyo Bay. The sun of militaristic Japan had set.

The formal signing of the Instrument of Surrender took place on board the USS Missouri on 2 September; among the many Allied ships present in Tokyo Bay were the King George V, the Duke of York and the Anson; the Japanese Foreign Minister, Mamoru Shigemitsu, was the first to sign. As Supreme Commander Allied Powers, General Douglas MacArthur signed on behalf of all Allied Nations, Admiral Chester Nimitz on behalf of the United States Navy and Admiral Fraser on behalf of Great Britain. Representatives on behalf of the Commonwealth also signed the document.

Three hundred men of the ship's company took part in the landing operations covering the occupation of Japan. HMS *King George V* also helped in the evacuation of released prisoners of war and internees. Outwardly the surrounding country looked green and peaceful and there were few signs of damage. But when Admiral Rawlings and I landed and drove in a jeep from Yokohama to Tokyo, we passed through the most fearful scenes of destruction I have ever beheld. There were no houses standing the whole way and even in Tokyo itself only the modern concrete buildings had survived the ordeal by fire to which the city had been subjected. Rawlings, who had been naval attaché in Tokyo from 1936–38, found himself completely lost. Grubbing among the ruins we located the site of the former English church by the stone steps which alone remained. Passing the Japanese in the streets they eyed us curiously. What they thought one could not tell. Only the police averted their gaze, pretending not to see us as we passed, because they had been ordered to salute all Allied officers.

The British Embassy, which is situated a short distance from the centre of the city, had survived with very little damage. The caretaker let us in and we were surprised to find the visitors' book lying open on the hall table just as it had been left in December 1941. Nothing had been touched, a thick layer of dust bearing testimony to the passage of time. The royal portraits looked down on us from their gilt frames and the escritoire in the ambassador's study was still stocked with notepaper and envelopes. As we were leaving, the caretaker asked if I could spare some European food. The following day I sent a couple of midshipmen up with a box of comestibles of various kinds. They returned with a small parcel. I took it down to my cabin and opened it. Inside was a note from the caretaker, thanking me for the provisions, and, carefully wrapped in rice paper, was a long piece of exquisite Japanese embroidery which was one third of his wife's wedding obi. This is the ceremonial sash worn around the waist by Japanese brides and is specially woven for the occasion. In his letter he told me that, although his wife and their small son had spent a terrifying night in a slit trench when, on the night of 29 July, we had given the town of Hamamatsu – where she had gone to visit her parents – a thorough pasting with our big guns, she bore us no ill will and wished me to accept the obi as a peace offering in gratitude for the food we had sent. It is a beautiful piece of embroidery and hangs in my drawing room as a memento of a very polite gesture. On 4 September the commander-in-chief, Admiral Fraser, visited the Embassy (detailed as a shore establishment of the Royal Navy and named HMS *Return*) and made the historic gesture of signing the visitor's book; Vice Admiral Rawlings and I also signed it, and, in the days to come, so did several others from the ship.[10]

The official re-opening of the embassy took place on Sunday 16 September when the Union Jack was re-hoisted, while members of the ship's company and a detachment from the Royal Marines took part in a changing of the guard ceremony. Although a typhoon warning had been received, the warm sun and blue sky seemed to give the lie to this ominous threat. When we re-embarked that evening after the ceremony the first signs of the approaching storm could be seen in the sky and the barometer began to fall precipitately. We raised steam, let go a second anchor and veered cable. I was not worried so much about dragging my anchor as about the possibility of some other ship in this crowded harbour being swept down on top of me. The storm reached its height early the following morning, the wind rising to nearly 100 miles an hour and accompanied by torrential rain. Added to the spray whipped off the tops of the waves, visibility was reduced to a few yards. Every now and then I caught sight of one of the big American aircraft carriers anchored on my port beam. She offered great resistance to the wind and was yawing about a good deal, but she held fast. Several landing craft to windward broke loose and were swept down and quite a number went ashore, but the great fleet rode out the storm, the centre of which passed some fifty miles to the westward. By 4pm the wind had dropped to a gentle breeze and the sun was breaking through the cloud. On 18 September Admiral Halsey and his chief of staff, Rear Admiral Carney, were able to fulfil their engagement to come on board and dine with Admiral Rawlings.

The Japanese naval dockyard at Yokosuka, lying some fifteen miles south of Yokahama, had been occupied by British and American forces and I landed there one day to visit the seamen and Royal Marine detachments which had come from my ship. I was received by my gunnery officer, Lieutenant Commander H.C.O. Bull, and the senior Royal Marine officer, Major Northcote. After I had inspected the men's quarters they led me to a large shed on the floor of which were a number of shells, bigger than any I had ever seen for a naval gun. On measuring one of them we discovered that it had a diameter of eighteen inches. This was the first indication we had that guns of this size had been mounted in the two big Japanese battleships, *Musashi* and *Yamato*, which had been sunk by the US carrier pilots in October 1944 and April 1945. These ships had been built in such secrecy that very little was known about them. But although they were larger than any ships in the British or American fleets, they had not been able to save the Japanese Navy from defeat. On my return to England, I brought one of these shells back and presented it to the Gunnery School, HMS *Excellent*, at Portsmouth.

Above Yokosuka, on the top of a hill, lies the grave of the English navigator, William Adams, who was born at Gillingham, Kent in 1564. He came to Japan as pilot of a fleet of Dutch ships for the Dutch East India Company. Only one ship had reached Japan and Adams was one of the survivors who settled there, becoming one of the first Western samurai. As advisor to the Shogun, he taught the Japanese how to build seagoing ships as well as facilitating the establishment of trading factories by both England and the Netherlands. Ever since his death in 1620 his grave had been tended with care by the local inhabitants. While anchored at Yokosuka, Admiral Rawlings had a meeting with the mayor, an elderly Japanese, who, with two others arrived on board ship, dressed in ceremonial white kimonos, their sandaled feet making a clopping noise on the wooden deck. Having received them formally on the quarterdeck, the admiral asked the mayor why Japan had made war on England. 'I don't know, your Excellency,' he replied, bowing so low that he swept the deck with his long white beard. 'You won't ever do it again, will you?' continued the admiral. 'No, Excellency, never', the mayor responded, emphasising his words with repeated bows. The admiral then asked if Will Adams's grave had been looked after during the war. 'But of course, your Excellency', came the reply. 'Very well,' remarked the admiral, 'this afternoon I will send a deputation to pay my respects to his memory.' The grave was found to be in perfect order.[11]

We were sorry when the time came to bid farewell to our American friends and allies. We were proud to have formed part of that vast American fleet which, when fully deployed, covered 200 square miles of ocean, to have fought alongside them and then been able to rejoice with them in our common victory. After three weeks in Japanese waters, on 20 September we weighed anchor to return to Sydney where we received a great welcome. On Thursday 11 October I celebrated my fiftieth birthday, one of the Australian newspapers noting that I had been in the 'RN since a boy'. It was a sad day for all of us in the *King George V*, when, on 26 October, the flag of Admiral Rawlings was hauled down and he and his staff returned to England. We were immensely proud to have had the honour of being in his flagship and of serving under his command. Ably assisted by his chief of staff, Commodore Peter Reid, he led us with a spirit which never flagged and an enthusiasm which was infectious.

We knew the Japanese were being beaten, but we were under the critical eye of another navy, better equipped than ours and, despite our logistic weakness, it was due to his personality and drive that the whole force acquitted itself so well. Mention must also be made of our US liaison officer, Captain Eddy Ewen USN. Eddy had a sense of humour which never failed even in moments of crisis and he had an endless fund of stories. His hearty laugh echoing up the voice pipe from the admiral's bridge was Homeric. I am glad to say that our paths crossed again several times after the war.[12]

The ship was badly in need of a refit but before this began Admiral Fraser suggested that we should visit Melbourne, which suggestion was gladly accepted by the local authorities. Our presence would also resume a tradition, begun in 1883, when an earlier HMS *Nelson* visited the city for the famous Melbourne Cup. We scraped and polished all the brightwork – the exposed metal and varnished wood – which had been painted over during the war and removed the stains of long steaming with a new coat of paint. As a journalist accompanying us to Melbourne reported: 'From Sydney the ship sailed with portholes open that had not previously been unsealed. Lights burned at night and no armament was "closed up" as the Navy paradoxically describes the preparation of guns for action.'[13]

On 29 October, we steamed up the wide bay of Port Phillip to our berth alongside the east side of Station Pier. We were the first large British warship to visit Melbourne since HMS *Hood* and HMS *Repulse* as part of the Special Service Squadron in 1924, our arrival recorded by a 'special' reporter who came on board from the pilot steamer:

We were four miles out from Station Pier. The ship slowed down to less than a crawl. The Union Jack was broken from the fore jackstaff. 'Fall in the top men! .... Fall in the spare hands!' Crisp orders from the bridge. Swift, orderly movement of sailors in their 'clean Rig of the Day' on the fore peak and quarter deck. The whistle of bosuns' pipes. Bugles blowing 'ipes Out' and then the 'Extend'. A civil and a military plane roared overhead, a welcome message blinked from the USS *Birmingham*. Launches played around the battleship's sides. '*Tooranga* to the starboard bow', the pilot [Captain R.B. Denniston] megaphoned from the bridge as the tugs fussed in. *Tooronga* took the bow hawser, belching smoke and threshing water as she endeavoured to overcome the seeming irresistible force of the battleship. *KGV*'s bow swung ominously to the pier. But *Tooronga* strained and panted, churning a maelstrom of mud and foam as the *Euro* went round the stern to pull the great hull parallel to the pier. Amidships, on the starboard side, the *Eagle* and the *James Patterson* shoved their buff noses against 16in of armour plating and slowly nudged her in.[14]

On arrival I left the ship to make official calls on Rear Admiral C.E. Van Hook USN, who was flying his flag in the USS *Birmingham*, berthed at Princes Pier. I also called on His Excellency, the Governor of Victoria, Sir Winston Dugan, the Chief Justice, Sir Edmund Herring, and the Premier of Victoria, Ian Macfarlan, as well as the Lord Mayor, Councillor F.R. Connolly. Almost immediately my calls were returned by the Governor, the Lord Mayor and Admiral Van Hook. The following day a civic reception hosted by the Lord Mayor was held in the town hall which I attended together with fifty officers and 150 men. That evening I attended the Royal Navy Victory Ball, to which fifty officers from the ship were invited. Another event was the march past of 1,000 men from the ship. Throughout our stay the people of Melbourne gave us a tremendous reception, making our ten-day visit the most strenuous socially I have ever spent. It was my first experience of being a 'public' figure and my photograph was in the paper every day in some way or another. I had to give interviews and make speeches which I found quite alarming although I survived somehow! I shall always remember the many kindnesses shown to me and to my ship's company by the citizens of Melbourne. They subsequently presented the ship with a set of bugles and drums which I flew from Sydney to receive at the hands of the Lord Mayor in the Town Hall.

HMS *King George V* was to be open to the public on Saturday and Sunday, 3 and 4 November. Although we expected a good number of visitors, we were not prepared for the crowd of over 30,000 that thronged the pier and fought and jostled each other to get on board, seriously endangering the 8,000 who had already been admitted. With great presence of mind, and much to the disappointment of the crowd, Commander Dick White (who had the distinction of being awarded a DSO and two bars during his wartime service) had to close the gangways. Using a loud hailer or megaphone, he explained that this step was necessary as life was being endangered by the press of people.[15] Had the rails of the pier given way, as well they might, many would have fallen into the dock and been drowned. The following day, in view of the events of the previous day, it was decided not to attempt to open the ship to the public in the afternoon as had been originally planned, but to avoid disappointment to the large crowd which was expected to visit the pier, a working demonstration of a 14in turret, a 5.25in turret, pom-poms and searchlights, was laid on at half-hourly intervals together with a running commentary on the loud hailer. This demonstration proved most popular and it is estimated that it was witnessed by about 80,000 people, a far larger number than could ever have visited the ship in the time available.[16]

Although we were unable to receive all the general public on board, large numbers of them were shown over the ship in organised parties during our stay including 30 blind children. Of particular interest to all visitors was the chapel in which the late King George V's personal Bible was kept. This Bible had been presented by his son, His Majesty King George VI, and in the letter which accompanied it, and which was kept in a frame beside the Bible, the king had described how his father was wont to read a chapter from this copy of the Bible every day of his life.

Tuesday 6 November was the Melbourne Cup. All men in uniform were admitted free to the course and officers of commander's rank and above were given passes to the members' enclosure. After the first race I had lunch with Sir Winston and Lady Dugan, following which they kindly invited me to witness the races from their box. Having had a modest and successful stake on an earlier race, I went down to collect my winnings. While waiting in the queue I asked the man next to me who was, of course, a complete stranger, what he fancied for the cup. To my surprise he replied: 'Why, my horse, of course!' I asked him the name: 'Rainbird' came the reply. I drew my winnings and staked them on the stranger's horse which I am glad to say won at odds of twelve to one![17]

Before leaving Melbourne we loaded 100 tons of food, which was part of a consignment purchased by the Government of Victoria for shipment to Britain. We intended to sail at 3pm (i.e. one hour before high water) on 8 November. This would have enabled Port Phillip Heads to be cleared before dark. But in the morning a strong northerly wind got up. In view of the low power of the tugs and the shallowness of the water which prevented utilising the full power of the engines and the fact that, had anything gone wrong, the ship had a short distance to go before grounding, I decided, after consultation with the local pilot, to postpone sailing until the next high water early on the morning of the following day. The decision was also influenced by the forecast of a south-westerly wind during the night, which direction was far more favourable for turning the ship in the very confined space available.

On our return to Sydney we docked in the new graving dock named after Captain Cook at Woolloomooloo. While repairs were being carried out to enable us to steam home, we enjoyed the glorious summer weather and bathing on the famous beaches. Thanks to the kindness of Major General Bert Lloyd, who was then commanding the Australian Second Army headquartered at Parramatta, I was provided with a car and a driver while we were in dock and this made a great difference to my enjoyment. I visited Katoomba in the Blue Mountains when the jacaranda and Japanese cherry trees were in full bloom. I spent Christmas on a farm about thirty miles inland with a daytime temperature of close to 100 degrees Fahrenheit (nearly 38 degrees Celsius).[18]

The refit over, we prepared to sail for home. I had wanted to bring the ship back via South America as I considered it was a most appropriate moment for showing the flag there, but my suggestion was not approved and it was decided that we should return via the Cape of Good Hope. Before sailing, the Royal Art Society Women's Auxiliary, in collaboration with the citizens of Sydney, presented the ship with an oil painting, showing her passing through Sydney Heads. They presented me with a personal memento of our stay in the form of an oil painting of the Blue Mountains by the distinguished Australian artist, Robert Johnson, called 'Harmony in Grey'. The ceremony took place in Sydney Town Hall, the presentations made jointly by the Lord Mayor, Alderman Bartley and Lady Braddon, President of the Royal Art Society. In return I asked the Lord Mayor to accept two 5.25in brass cartridge cases, which had been suitably inscribed and belled out to form flower stands.

Homeward bound

We sailed on a perfect day on 7 January 1946. Since the Governor General and his wife – Their Royal Highnesses, the Duke and Duchess of

Gloucester – together with their young sons, Prince William and Prince Richard, were taking passage in the ship to Hobart in Tasmania, we went out flying the Royal Standard and all ships paraded a guard and band and saluted as we passed. It was a great honour to have them on board. Prince William, who had just passed his fourth birthday, thoroughly enjoyed running around the ship. Fearful lest harm befall him, I instructed a Royal Marine sergeant to look after him and I understand that they became great friends. It was a lovely evening when, on 9 January, we anchored off Hobart under the shadow of Mount Wellington and Mount Nelson (the former, I regret to say as a sailor, being the higher!) Early next morning we went alongside the Ocean Pier and Their Royal Highnesses left the ship for a month's holiday on the island.[19]

HMS *King George V* remained anchored in Hobart for five days, the officers again being hospitably entertained by the local residents and which included a visit from His Excellency the Governor of Tasmania, Admiral Sir Hugh and Lady Binney. One resident, Dr William Crowther, (whose niece had just married my navigating officer, Lieutenant Commander Charles Cree, in Sydney) presented me with two whales' teeth on which some sailors of long ago had etched pictures of the ships in which they had served. My joiner mounted them on two pieces of Australian oak in the form of bookends and so the teeth of Leviathan are now pillars of learning.

Before leaving Hobart, as at Sydney, we took on board many gifts of 'Food for Britain' for those at home including a consignment of fifty dozen eggs, donated by Miss Lillian Overell. As I learnt when she first contacted me, she had a large number of chickens and had, for some time, been wanting to donate eggs to Britain's blind soldiers but had been unable to find a method of transport. After a certain amount of correspondence, I agreed to bring them home and ensure that they reached St Dunstan's Home for the Blind.[20] From Hobart we set course for Fremantle where we made another short stay and completed with fuel. I called on the Mayor, Frank Gibson, whose kindness to ships of the Royal Navy calling at the port was famous throughout the fleet. He drove me around the city of Perth and out into the surrounding country. What is noticeable about all Australian cities is the acreage which they can cover. Nearly all the houses are single storey and each has an attractive piece of garden so the effect is to produce a city of flowers.[21]

With perfect weather, our sixteen–day voyage across the Indian Ocean was a veritable yachting trip! I spent the long hours reading and playing deck tennis and going around every conceivable hole and corner in the ship. Having been given a complete set of carving tools by my mother, during the long hours a captain has to spend alone, both at sea and in harbour, I occupied my spare time in wood carving, for which I appeared to have some aptitude. One carving I did was of the ship's crest in silky oak and another one of the ship in maple to give to a school in Scotland, which had been very good to the ship during the war. I should imagine these carvings are unique as battleship captains do not usually carry a complete set of carving tools with them![22]

We reached Capetown on the morning of 7 February. When, the following day, I called on the Governor General, Gideon Brand van Zyl, he kindly invited me to dine with him that evening and informed me that the Prime Minister, Field Marshal Jan Christian Smuts, would be present. For me this was a great piece of good fortune. I had read a great deal about him and, despite his reported arrogance, had formed a mental picture of one of the great men of the age. I was not disappointed, his steely blue eyes still having such a twinkle even at the age of seventy-four. When the ladies retired, the Prime Minister came and sat next to me. With that easy manner of his, he began a conversation, every word of which I should have liked to record. He talked about the war, told amusing stories of some of his meetings with Prime Minister Winston Churchill, discussed the administration of South West Africa (Namibia) and through it all ran the wisdom of a truly great man, whose intellect soared above the petty squabbles of party politics. It was one of the most memorable evenings I have ever spent.[23]

Our stay was so short that I did not have time to see much of the surrounding country but I enjoyed being taken for a drive through some of the wine-growing districts inland. The ship's company busied themselves buying gifts and food for their families and friends at home. After a stay of only two days, we headed north for Freetown, Sierra Leone; I remember it as terribly hot. Passing by Tenerife, the island was a lovely sight against the setting sun.[24]

Peacetime routine

Arriving at Portsmouth on 2 March 1946, crowds lined the quayside to welcome 'the famous battleship' which, as the local papers reported, had 'come home without a scratch' despite the actions in which she had been engaged in the Pacific. The ship was detailed to become the flagship of the commander-in-chief, Home Fleet and, on 10 April, we hoisted the flag of Admiral Sir Neville Syfret.[25] It seemed strange, after such great happenings, to settle down once again to the Home Fleet peacetime routine which I knew so well. We spent two months at Portsmouth, during which time we received a number of visitors, including the Emir of Transjordan, Abdullah bin al-Hussein, on 7 March. He had come to Britain to sign a series of treaties culminating in the Anglo-Transjordanian Treaty signed on 22 March, which gave full independence to what became the Hashemite Kingdom of Jordan, after which he became King Abdullah I.[26]

On 6 May we left Portsmouth for Spithead, arriving in Guernsey two days later to take part in the celebrations commemorating the liberation of the island a year previously. It was a simply wonderful day, with a cloudless blue sky, brilliant sunshine and no wind to speak of. Included in the festivities was a cavalcade, the sailors marching very well. There was a great deal of ingenuity in the decorated cars and lorries. One horse-drawn cart was a vision of flowers and even the wheels were decorated with roses and red rhododendrons. At night we had a firework display, the ship looking lovely outlined in green, red and white lights, the effect made by sailors standing the whole length of the ship holding the lights in their hands. We left Guernsey five days later in mist and rain and when we got out into the Channel it was blowing hard. It was very tricky coming into Portland as the wind was in the worst possible direction for picking up the buoy but we managed it all right in the end. When the sun came out the Dorset cliffs looked as attractive as ever with the green of the downs behind them. We remained at Portland until the beginning of July with the exception of a five-day visit to Torquay in early June, when the ship was opened to members of the public, including a party of forty schoolboys and forty schoolgirls. At night I had obtained special permission from the Admiralty to have the ship illuminated, requiring over two miles of wire and 5,000 lamps for a ship of her size.

We began our summer cruise up the west coast of Britain on 3 July; over the next two months we stopped at Falmouth, Aberystwyth, Bangor (County Down), and Oban on the coast of Scotland, returning via Fleetwood on the Lancashire coast, having spent about a week in each location and during which time the ship was opened to visitors. Everywhere we went we were most hospitably entertained by the local authorities. At Aberystwyth, our recreational activities included a mayor's ball, luncheon at the King's Hall, tea for the ratings, dancing on the promenade, cricket, bowling and golf matches. The Royal Marine camp at the coastal village of Borth lent us some DUKWs and I had the unusual experience of being taken from the ship to the golf club by one of these amphibious craft! In the absence of a pier on the open beach, they also proved very useful for landing and embarking libertymen who had been given permission to go ashore. To discourage the inevitable misdemeanours, like drunken behaviour or petty theft, I started publishing a list of the week's offences and punishments under the heading 'Is it worth it?' (After our visit to Guernsey I had had to see seven defaulters for breaking their leave, two of whom were petty officers who should have known better. There was also the case of a stoker who was married with a small baby, but who had got mixed up with a married woman in Sydney and was trying to return to Australia).[27]

The Governor of Northern Ireland, Vice Admiral Earl Granville, was a former Harwich Force captain and I enjoyed meeting him again when we visited Bangor. He and the Prime Minister, Sir Basil Brooke, challenged the commander-in-chief and me to a game of golf. In the end we split up and I played with the Prime Minister against the other two. If my memory serves me right we were beaten, I having developed an incurable slice!

At Oban Admiral Syfret invited his personal friends, Jervis and Islay Molteno, of Glenlyon, Perthshire, and three of their five daughters, Deirdre, Loveday and Penelope with another friend, Anne Hetherington, on board. After lunch Captain Schofield was able to 'bow out', since the C-in-C had deputed four lieutenants to look after 'les' girls! The

Moltenos had lost their only son, Major Donald Ian Molteno, serving with The Black Watch, 51st Highland Division in northern Europe in February 1945.[28]

There was a great deal of rain during the rest of the cruise which is a common feature of summer on the west coast of these islands. After a week in Portland, we returned to Portsmouth. 'It is a lovely day,' I noted on 15 August, 'quite the best we have had for weeks & this great ship is steaming along at 14 knots under a cloudless blue sky and on a calm sea. It is sad to think that this probably will be the last time I shall take her to sea but I am glad, if that is so, that it is such a beautiful day.'[29] Soon afterwards, I received a letter from the Naval Secretary informing me that my relief would join in September and that I would be required for temporary duty at the Admiralty. I had thus reached what most naval officers consider to be the hardest moment in their career: to have stood on the bridge of the ship that they have commanded and said 'Stop Engines' for the last time. Even those who are fortunate enough to fly their flags at sea as admirals can never again experience the satisfaction of achievement which alone comes from being in command of one of His Majesty's Ships.

> *Ah! What pleasant visions haunt me*
> *As I gaze upon the sea!*
> *All the old romantic legends,*
> *All my dreams come back to me.*[30]

Chapter Eighteen

Glad Waters

I count myself in nothing else so happy
As in a soul remembering my good friends.[1]

1946–50

My next appointment was as chief staff officer to the President of the Fighting Instructions Committee, Vice Admiral Sir John Edelsten, whose last wartime appointment had been with the Pacific Fleet as Rear Admiral (Destroyers). We were given six months to put together in book form the tactical lessons learnt during the war. It was an exercise which had its origins in the seventeenth century, embodying the tactical principles on which the Royal Navy has trained since that time. In the event, we did not go to press until the end of June 1947. It was most interesting work which I enjoyed, including, as it did, a visit to Washington to compare notes with our opposite numbers in the United States Navy who were engaged on a similar task. Washington in the spring is a lovely sight and I was glad to be back. I did not know then that I would shortly be returning for quite a long spell. Our work completed, the admiral and I spent a pleasant weekend with my friend, Sir Ashley Sparks, at his Long Island home in Oyster Bay Cove. It was good to see him again and to talk about the problems of the war now happily behind us.[2]

While waiting for the proof sheets of our book to be ready it was agreed that we should all take some leave. I greatly wished to revisit France and Italy and to see how some of the places I knew had fared under the scourging hand of war. A few days before I was due to start my leave, I was notified by the Admiralty of my promotion to rear admiral, effective 12 August, so that the pleasure of my trip was enhanced by the knowledge of my great good fortune and also by the presence of my present wife, a former WRNS officer, to whom I had been married a short time previously.[3] We went by train via Lausanne and Stresa to Florence where I was relieved to find that the damage was not so great as I had feared it might be. It was sad to see Bartolomeo Ammanati's beautiful Ponte Santa Trinita lying in ruins on the bed of the Arno (happily reconstructed in 1958), but a joy to see again the many superb works of art for which this lovely city is justly famous. From Florence we went to Venice which, of all the Italian jewels, I love best and from there to Rome, where there is so much history in stone one would need a lifetime to study it all, to say nothing of the pictures. We returned by way of Paris, not at its best under a hot summer sun, but nevertheless enchanting.

When the book was finally completed, the RN College, Greenwich claimed me once again, on this occasion as a student at the senior officers' war course.

Washington DC

In the New Year – 1948 – the First Sea Lord, Admiral of the Fleet Sir John Cunningham, offered me the post of chief of staff to the admiral, British Joint Services Mission (Navy) in Washington, DC. I had hoped to be offered a sea appointment but, with our much-reduced Royal Navy, these were hard to come by. In any case the appointment appealed to me for several reasons, not the least of which was the fact that my chief was to be Admiral Sir Henry Moore, under whom I had served twice before, when he was chief of staff to the C-in-C, Home Fleet in the late 1930s and when he was vice chief of naval staff at the Admiralty and I was director of Trade Division from 1941–43. I was also glad of the opportunity I would have to get to know the United States, for whose people I had already developed a great liking.[4]

We sailed for New York in March on board the *Queen Elizabeth*, and then travelled by train to Washington. The nation's capital in peacetime was very different from the city I had known in 1943. Its natural beauties were the same, but the social round was what my French friends would call *formidable*. In the first seven weeks we attended fifty-six parties of various kinds! Among our British Embassy friends in Washington was Admiral Earl Jellicoe's son, George, and his wife, Patsy; he had served with distinction in the Coldstream Guards during the war, being awarded a DSO during operations in Crete in 1942. We also developed a lasting friendship with Rear Admiral Erhard Qvistgaard and his wife Rose. Qvistgaard had been sent to Washington as naval attaché with responsibility for leading the Danish delegation during the planning of the North Atlantic Treaty Organisation (NATO), later becoming Chief of Defence and Chairman of NATO's military committee.[5]

One of the Americans I came to know well was Rear Admiral Thomas B. Inglis, who was the chief of US naval intelligence when I arrived; another was Arleigh Burke, who had served in the Pacific during the war. Promoted rear admiral in 1949 he took up the position of Navy secretary on the Research and Development Board, Department of Defense, becoming chief of naval operations after the Korean War. The current US chief of naval operations was Admiral Louis Denfeld, a man of a very different temperament from Admiral Ernest King, with whom I had interacted during the war. I was sorry when, in early November, he was obliged to resign his post on account of the fight which developed between the US Navy and the Air Force on the subject of the super-aircraft carrier. His successor was Admiral Forrest Sherman, the youngest man to date to take up the position. He too had served in the Pacific, having been deputy chief of staff to the Pacific Fleet Commander, Admiral Nimitz.[6]

Known as the 'Revolt of the Admirals', the dispute related to President Truman's desire to reduce military expenditure by placing reliance on the use of strategic nuclear bombing by the US Air Force in preference to enhancing the US Navy. Cancellation of the construction of both the USS United States *and her sister ships contributed to the public argument. Although Truman's view prevailed, the Korean War revealed that aircraft carriers were still necessary and four new Forrestal-class 'supercarriers' were laid down in the 1950s; the first, the USS* Forrestal, *was commissioned in 1955.*

Soon after settling into our new home, an attractive and business-like young lady called at our house and announced that she was the Welcome Wagon Hostess and started to unpack a large basket containing an assortment of tinned goods and a number of vouchers which could be exchanged for goods at the store named. She explained that the custom had originated in Texas in the early days when some of the immigrants trekking westward were waylaid by those who had already settled there. In order to induce them to go no further, they sent their most attractive girls with baskets of delicacies to prove the fatness of the land. While it is now obviously a custom with a business motive, it is of great help to the newcomer.

For the first eighteen months I had an office in the Pentagon which, being fully air-conditioned, was a comfortable place in which to work in the humidity of a Washington summer. This remarkable building, with its attendant car parks and occupying a 34-acre site on the south bank of the Potomac, houses 32,000 workers of the United States Defense Department. It is completely self-contained with cafeterias, restaurants and shops to meet every need. Whether you want to have your suit cleaned, your watch repaired or send flowers to your girlfriend, you can do it all from the concourse by which name the shopping centre in the basement is known. I was sorry when a shortage of space for their own people obliged our American hosts to move the British Joint Services Mission to offices in the old Navy Department on Constitution Avenue, where there were no such facilities.

In a land in which the search for the latest and most modern in everything is predominant, the historic old suburb of Georgetown is like an eighteenth century antique shop in the midst of a twentieth century block of flats. The area was already home to an active community when George Washington invited Pierre L'Enfant to design the layout for the federal city. Its old houses and quaint walled-in gardens give a picture of America during the Civil War period. Old coach lamps ornament the doorposts and the doors themselves wear attractive well-polished brass knockers and there is much wrought iron railing and traceries. In summer the shady narrow streets, with their uneven red brick pavements, give a quiet air of peace and old worldliness to this select residential area. It was in the music room of one of Georgetown's lovely mansions, Dumbarton Oaks, that, in August 1944, the first meeting took place between representatives of the great nations and at which the foundation stone of the United Nations was laid. Since Admiral Moore and his successor as head of the British Joint Services Mission (Navy) in Washington, Admiral Sir Frederick Dalrymple-Hamilton, both resided in Georgetown, I came to know this village within a city very well indeed.[7]

In post-war America, cars were scarce, production not having yet overtaken demand and I was glad to have been able to purchase a car from my predecessor. Coming from Britain, where we still had rationing, certain aspects of life were novel. For example, travel by car appeared easy. Excellent meals could be obtained at any wayside restaurant. I once stopped at a small restaurant in the Adirondack mountains and was surprised at the variety on the menu. On enquiring, I was informed that the dishes were already prepared, cooked and frozen and all that was necessary was to heat up whatever the customer selected! Petrol, tyres and other accessories were all obtainable simply by producing a credit card from the oil company of your choice. The bill would then be sent to one's home address once a month. During my time in Washington, I drove up to Canada twice, the first time by way of Niagara Falls to Montreal, Quebec and Ottawa in the early summer, experiencing beautiful weather all the way. On the second occasion I had to give a lecture in Montreal and drove directly there in pouring rain, but the roads were so good that driving was a pleasure.

On another occasion, when two of our destroyers were visiting Key West, I benefited from the opportunity to see this well-known US Naval base, at the tip of Florida, for the first time. Having arrived by plane, I could well appreciate President Truman's fondness for this coral island jutting out into the warm waters of the Gulf of Mexico, with its bright flowers, waving palms and sea on all sides. While in Key West I managed to put in a day at sea which I naturally much enjoyed. The ship's companies of the two ships had been warned that the Puerto Rican police were inclined to treat any offenders rather more roughly than they might normally have been accustomed. To date the sailors had behaved so well that there had been no incidents, but one evening two stokers, who had hoisted in rather more than they should have, decided to sleep it off in a car they saw parked on the roadside. The car was locked and the noise they made trying to open the doors roused the owner, who, much to their surprise, opened his window, drew a gun and fired, wounding one of the men. When the police arrived, they took the wounded man to the hospital but the other man was put in jail. We eventually managed to square the whole matter up, but one of the local inhabitants was heard to remark: 'You see, these guys don't realise that Florida is still a frontier state and every man carries a gun.'

Key West is well known for its excellent sea-fishing. Keen anglers go in search of big fish like marlin and tunny, but the waters also yield the most delicious lobsters which, when freshly caught and cooked in Creole fashion, are a dish fit for a king. My lasting memory of this subtropical island is one of colour; hibiscus, orchids, frangipani, poinsettia and poinciana all produce a riot of colour and scent not easily forgotten. During my stay I encountered one of my old midshipmen from the *Renown* at a cocktail party, who, having always been of a literary turn, was running a local bookshop. The trouble was that he could never bring himself to sell a book which he had read and of which he did not approve, and so I gathered that his business was not doing too well!

One of the highlights of the United States Armed Forces' social calendar, which dates from 1890, is the annual Army-Navy football match between the Army Black Knights of the US Military Academy at West Point and the Navy Midshipmen of the US Naval Academy at Annapolis. Allowing for the difference between 'American' football and British soccer, I was expecting the match to resemble our own similar contest held at Twickenham. Since the match was due to take place in Philadelphia, we travelled by special train which was one of many which converged on the gigantic municipal stadium which stands outside the town. The midshipmen from Annapolis and the cadets from West Point were there in force and, before the game started, they marched onto the field with their bands playing in an impressive array. Once in their seats they came under the spell of their organised cheer leaders and gave tongue when called upon in true American fashion.

During the interval a mock battle took place between non-playing members of the opposing camps. This took the form of an engagement between a tank and a battleship and ended with the pair of them blowing up to reveal a couple of jeeps. Despite the sunshine, there was a cold wind blowing and some of our neighbours had brought flasks of the spirit that cheers and warms and from which they took nips as the game continued. Perhaps this had a little to do with the exuberance of the onlookers, for I have never seen nor heard a more enthusiastic crowd of spectators. The match was close and, with each point scored, the excitement increased in intensity. Towards the end of the game, my neighbour on my left waved his now empty flask of Bourbon in the air and threatened to crown with it any 'son of a gun' who allowed the Army to score another point. When the whistle finally blew for a drawn match, he kissed all the ladies within range. I could not help wondering what reaction there would have been in the grandstand at Twickenham.

Another assignment took me back to New York. The admiral had received a letter from the Admiralty saying that a recording had been made of the unveiling ceremony of the wall map at HMS *Dryad* which had taken place in August 1946. A copy had now been sent to be presented to General Eisenhower who, since 1948 had been serving as the President of Columbia University. Since I had been so closely connected with these events, the admiral kindly suggested that it would be appropriate for me to make the presentation. I made a date with the general and he invited me to lunch. As I walked across the campus of this great seat of learning, I was struck by the severity of the buildings which have little of the grace of Oxford or Cambridge, but I was still conscious of being in one of the most important educational establishments in the country (originally founded by royal charter of George II as King's College in 1754). After climbing the stone steps leading up to the entrance of the main building, I was shown into the president's office, a large room which was sparsely furnished and less luxurious than I had expected.

General Eisenhower greeted me warmly and I handed him the recording, telling him how happy I was to make this presentation on behalf of the Admiralty. Recalling those anxious days at Southwick House before the invasion of Normandy in June 1944, we also talked of his work at the university and the responsibility he believed we all have for making our knowledge and experience available to the youth of the next generation. As we walked across the campus to his private residence, the general apologised that we should be alone for lunch. No apology was needed since I was only too pleased to have an opportunity to talk to him alone! We discussed many of the people who had made their mark in the war including of course our respective leaders, Churchill and Roosevelt.

While we were having coffee, General Eisenhower said rather diffidently, 'I don't know if it would interest you, Admiral, but my friends have persuaded me to spread out my various decorations so that they can be seen.' Having affirmed my interest, we went upstairs to a room adjoining one of the larger reception rooms used on formal occasions.

There, in a big glass case on the wall, hung the sashes of the many high orders which had been bestowed upon him, while in front were the insignia of the orders themselves. In the centre, by itself, was the Order of Merit bestowed by the United Kingdom, together with King George's personal letter which accompanied the award. In smaller cases around the room were the swords, scrolls of freedom and other gifts which he had received. I noticed in particular the solid gold hat which had been presented to him by Emperor Haile Selassie of Ethiopia. It was a remarkable collection the like of which cannot have been seen since that of the Duke of Wellington.

Eisenhower received three US Military Decorations, the Army Distinguished Service Medal with four oak leaf clusters, the Navy Distinguished Service Medal and the Legion of Merit, seven US Service Medals and fifty-five international and foreign awards. One of the 'freedoms' he had received in June 1945 was of the City of London.

The United States Naval War College at Newport, Rhode Island, is sited on a promontory overlooking the entrance to Narragansett Bay. On my first visit I travelled by train to Providence and thence to the college by car, enabling me to see the old town founded by Roger Williams in 1636. There is something very attractive about New England towns with their frame houses and redbrick churches with white towers and porticoed fronts. On another occasion I visited the library in Newport where the last Union Jack to fly over the town is still proudly preserved. I was also shown the mansions of the Vanderbilts, the Metcalfs, John Nicholas Brown and other well-known families, as well as the ruined house of a prosperous New York butcher who, because he was socially ostracised, wrote in his will that his house should remain for all time, without renovation, as an eyesore to the people who had refused his hospitality.

I was not surprised to find that the War College was more lavishly equipped than its counterpart at Greenwich, each student being provided with a typewriter, but contrary to what might be expected, language constitutes the main difference in the teaching of the two colleges. Confronted with any given situation, if the British appreciation covered two pages, that of the Americans would cover at least four, but the conclusions reached would probably be the same! When I asked for an explanation of the tendency towards verbosity, I was told that, being a mixed race with many different modes of thought, Americans find it necessary to express themselves very fully in order to be clearly understood! Yet no national can equal the Americans when it comes to coining *le mot juste*. One of the wittiest men I ever met was Admiral Robert 'Mick' Carney, wartime chief of staff to Admiral Halsey and who, for most of my time in Washington, served as deputy chief of naval operations. As an exponent of the succinct phrase he was without equal in men of my acquaintance.[8]

The signing of the North Atlantic Treaty on 4 April 1949, establishing the North Atlantic Treaty Organization (NATO), added to the responsibilities of the British Joint Services Mission. It was the first peacetime military alliance the United States entered into outside the western hemisphere. In addition to the US, founding signatories were Belgium, Canada, Denmark, France, Iceland, Italy, Luxembourg, the Netherlands, Norway, Portugal and the UK. I became the British representative on the North Atlantic Ocean Regional Planning Group and our first task was to evaluate the forces which each member nation was willing to make available and to match these with our estimates of what was required. When this had been done, we came to the question of command. Our job was to make proposals for discussion by the full meeting of the group, attended by the heads of the various navies or their representatives. At one such meeting the post of Supreme Allied Commander Atlantic (SACLANT) was accorded to the United States by unanimous vote in accordance with our recommendations. It was generally accepted as a fit and proper decision, having regard to the fact that the United States was contributing by far the largest share of the available forces. No one realised the storm which this decision was to evoke in Britain. While most naval officers were well aware that the sceptre of the sea which we had wielded for so long had passed inevitably to the United States, whose post-war navy was five times the size of ours, very few members of the British public were aware of this fact.

The selection of Eisenhower as the Supreme Allied Commander Europe (SACEUR), with operational headquarters in Paris, presented no problem, his appointment announced in December 1950. But the public opposition to the appointment of the Supreme Allied Commander Atlantic (SACLANT) meant that NATO's second operational headquarters at Norfolk, Virginia was not activated until April 1952. Until 2009 both positions were filled by Americans, a deputy coming from another NATO country.

During my time in Washington, among many places, I was glad to visit Charleston, South Carolina. As I stepped out of the long silver train which had carried me the 500 miles south overnight, I sensed a different atmosphere. This was the deep south of the cotton fields and the old plantations and the city was like a faded beauty of a bygone age. The American writer, John Gunther, who travelled the length and breadth of the forty-eight mainland states to write his informative book, *Inside U.S.A.*, refers to Charleston as a 'gem' but also as 'a kind of mummy... once it was the fourth biggest city in America, and probably the most brilliantly sophisticated; today much of its polish has worn off, though it still retains a cardinal quality of grace'. Certainly, the tempo of life seemed slower than that of the northern cities and herein lay its great attraction. Behind the iron grilles and porticos of the lovely old Georgian houses with their cool walled-in gardens of brilliant poinsettias, hibiscus and oleander there still existed a society as proud and select as any in the world.[9] A few miles outside the city, azaleas flourish in an area of peaty soil and pools of clear black water. They are a colourful sight and the wild and natural setting adds to their beauty. Paths and bridges have been constructed, making it easy for the visitor to wander amongst the bloom-laden shrubs, some of which have grown to a great height. A feature of the countryside is the way in which the trees and bushes are festooned with grey Spanish moss giving them the appearance of the gardens of Sleeping Beauty's palace before the arrival of the prince.

Historically, Charleston was where the American Civil War had begun in 1861 when, on 12 April, following the inauguration of President Abraham Lincoln, Confederate forces attacked Fort Sumter at the entrance to Charleston harbour. It also has the distinction of being the place where a submarine, the *H.L. Hunley*, was first employed in a warlike capacity (although in fact it was more of a submersible than a submarine).

With a crew of eight men, the H.L. Hunley *sank the USS* Housatonic *in Charleston harbour in February 1864. Named after its inventor, Horace*

Lawson Hunley, (who was killed in October 1863 during a training exercise) the Confederates' use of this 'secret weapon' was in order to break the Union naval blockade. During the attack, perhaps caught in the vortex of the sinking Housatonic, *the submarine also sank.*[10]

The principal hotel is named after Fort Sumter which stands in the approaches to the harbour. Outside the hotel is a signpost which informs the traveller that he or she is standing at a point 3,954 miles from the North Pole and 8,480 miles from the South Pole. The distances of such places as the Azores, Lisbon and Gibraltar to the east and Denver, Seattle and St Louis to the west are also marked, while, in a north and south line, the distances of Quebec, New York, Miami and Key West are shown. Altogether it is a most informative signpost!

I had visited the US Naval Academy at Annapolis on the shores of Chesapeake Bay several times, but my visit on Easter Day, 9 April 1950, with the First Sea Lord, Admiral of the Fleet Lord Fraser of North Cape, was the most memorable. He had been invited to take the salute at a march past of the midshipmen; the sun shone on the blue and gold uniforms of 3,000 young officers drawn up on parade and was reflected in the polished brass of the instruments of the band. Row after row of men, with highly commendable smartness and precision, filed past and up the steps into the chapel. The service was similar to that of the Church of England and, as a special tribute to their distinguished guest, the anthem chosen was William Blake's *Jerusalem*. Not since that historic service on board the *Prince of Wales* nine years previously had I felt so deeply moved as at hearing this particularly British hymn being so beautifully rendered by those massed American voices.

During the two and a half years I spent in Washington we were received with much kindness and hospitality. One unforgettable social occasion was the naval ball which took place in the old sail loft on the Gun Wharf. At the time the musical show, *South Pacific*, had just premiered on Broadway in New York and so the organisers of the ball had taken this as the theme of their decorations and entertainment. Hundreds of palm branches transformed the huge loft into a replica of a South Sea island and all lady guests were provided with leis which had come from Hawaii. Excerpts from the show were staged, compered by Commander Douglas

Fairbanks Jr USN whose wartime career had included service on the USS *Wichita* on escort duty during the disastrous passage of PQ17.[11]

On a tree-covered hill overlooking the Pentagon stands the white porticoed mansion built by George Custis, adopted son of George Washington and father-in-law of General Robert E. Lee. From this eminence there is a beautiful view of the city across the Potomac to the Lincoln Memorial and beyond to the Capitol. The wooded surround of this historic old house has been set apart as a resting place for the bodies of several thousands of America's illustrious dead of the Armed Forces, known as Arlington National Cemetery. Our own Field Marshal Sir John Dill, who died in 1944 while serving as head of the British Joint Staff (later Services) Mission, also lies there. He was so universally beloved and admired that a signal tribute was paid to his memory by the erection of a life-size bronze equestrian statue by his grave. The unveiling ceremony on 1 November 1950 was to be attended by President Truman, whom I had met several times and who had always impressed me as being a man who had the interests of his country and the peace of the world at heart. On this occasion, we were all surprised that one who was always so punctual in keeping his engagements should be late. It was not until after the ceremony that we heard how, as he was preparing to leave Blair House (his official residence while The White House was being renovated), an attempt had been made to assassinate him. His calm and unruffled appearance on arrival gave no indication of the threat he had just undergone.

The attempt was made by two pro-independence Puerto Ricans, Oscar Collazo and Griselio Torresola. Although they were stopped before they gained entry to Blair House, their actions resulted in the death of a White House police officer, Leslie Coffelt, and Torresola. Collazo was wounded; put on trial for treason, he was sentenced to death, which Truman commuted to life imprisonment. In 1979 President Carter commuted Collazo's sentence to time (thirty years) and he returned to Puerto Rico, dying in 1994.[12]

When, on 9 November 1950, it was time for me to leave the United States and bid farewell to so many good friends, I did so with a real pang of parting. I shall always be grateful for this opportunity in Washington which enabled me to meet and make friends with so many wonderful people. Joseph Addison was right, of course, when he wrote: 'Though we seem grieved at the shortness of life in general, we are wishing every period of it at an end. The minor longs to be at age, then to be a man of business, then to make up an estate, then to arrive at honours, then to retire.' When retirement actually knocks at the door, there are not many of us who accept it with any degree of satisfaction. But the measure of one's regret is that of one's affection for a truly great service and for the good company with which one has been privileged to sail 'o'er the glad waters of the dark blue sea, our thoughts as boundless, and our souls as free'.[13]

Appointed Companion of the Military Division of the Order of the Bath (CB) in the King's Birthday Honours on 9 June 1949 and promoted Vice Admiral upon his retirement on 1 December 1950, Schofield took a course in journalism and began to write, choosing as his subject matter his life's work, the Royal Navy. He died aged eighty-nine on 8 November 1984; his ashes were buried at sea off Portsmouth.

> *Here is my journey's end, here is my butt*
> *And very seamark of my utmost sail.*[14]

Abbreviations

ACM	Air Chief Marshal
Adm	Admiral
ADMF	Admiral of the Fleet
BBS	Brian Betham Schofield
BPF	British Pacific Fleet
C-in-C	Commander-in-Chief
Capt	Captain
Cdr	Commander
Cdre	Commodore
DSO	Distinguished Service Order
FM	Field Marshal
Gen	General
KGV	King George V
Lt	Lieutenant
Lt Cdr	Lieutenant Commander
Lt Col	Lieutenant Colonel
Lt Gen	Lieutenant General
Maj Gen	Major General
MRAF	Marshal of the Royal Air Force
PM	Prime Minister
Pres	President
RAdm	Rear Admiral
Regt	Regiment
RMS	Royal Mail Ship
RN	Royal Navy
RNR	Royal Naval Reserve
RNVR	Royal Naval Volunteer Reserve
TNA	The National Archives
US	United States
USN	United States Navy
USSR	United Soviet Socialist Republic
VAdm	Vice Admiral
VC	Victoria Cross
Visc	Viscount

Notes

Foreword

1 Shakespeare, *Henry IV,* Part 2, III, i.
2 Shakespeare, *As You Like It,* II, i.

Chapter One: *Disciplina, Fide, Labore*

1 Attributed to Vice Admiral Horatio Nelson, 1st Viscount Nelson, 1st Duke of Bronté KB (1758-1805).
2 Admiral of the Fleet John Fisher, 1st Baron Fisher, GCB, OM, GCVO (1841–1920); William Palmer, 2nd Earl of Selborne KG GCMG PC (1859–1942). See *Records by Admiral of the Fleet Lord Fisher,* Hodder & Stoughton, 1919 for an insight into Fisher's thinking. The outfitter is now Gieves & Hawkes.
3 Thomas Dodgshon Schofield (1859–1952) married Margaret Annie Bradley (1860-1953) in February 1889. They had three children: Phyllis, Brian, and Margaret (Peggy). With the exception of one letter dated 29 Jan 1915, BBS's correspondence to his parents has been lost.
4 Virgil, epic poet (70–19BC). The quotation is also attributed to John Dryden.
5 *Maxims and Moral Reflections of the Duke de La Rochefoucauld* from the French, George Nicholson, Ludlow, 1799. Maxim 39: 'Few things are impracticable in themselves; and it is for want of application, rather than of means, that men fail of success.'
6 *A King's Story, The Memoirs of HRH the Duke of Windsor KG,* Cassell & Co. Ltd, 1951, pp.62–63.
7 L. Lassimonne, Officier de l'Instruction Publique (French).
8 Canon Richard Shiers-Mason (1860–1933); Ethel (née Schofield) (1861–1932). In 1922 the mission's name was changed to the Mediterranean Mission for Seamen. In 2012 the Earl and Countess of Wessex visited the mission as part of HM The Queen's Diamond Jubilee celebrations.
9 See HMS Cornwall Magazine (8th Cruise), April 1913, Plymouth, for an account of the cruise, Schofield family papers.
10 Admiral of the Fleet Sir George Creasy GCB CBE DSO MVO (1895–1972).

Chapter Two: Pare Bellum

1 Captain Francis Kennedy to the midshipmen on board HMS *Indomitable*.

2 RMS *Lusitania* (and *Mauretania*) launched in 1906 and sunk by German torpedoes in 1915, had been fitted with revolutionary turbine engines.

3 Admiral of the Fleet David Beatty, 1st Earl GCB OM GCVO DSO PC (1871–1936). The 1st Battle Cruiser Squadron was formed as the 1st Cruiser Squadron in 1909, its name changed to the 1st Battle Cruiser Squadron in 1913. At the end of the war it became the Battle Cruiser Squadron.

4 Admiral F.W. Kennedy CB (1862–1939), Captain of HMS *Indomitable*, 1912–16. See HMS *Indomitable* Ship's Log ADM 53/22215, Feb 1912–Jun 1913; ADM 53/44828, Jun 1913–Feb 1914; ADM 53/44830 Mar 1914–Mar 1915, TNA. Caning is a form of corporal punishment which has been outlawed in most European countries, although not worldwide.

5 Admiral Sir (Archibald) Berkeley Milne GCVO KCB (1855–1938). At the beginning of WWI the Mediterranean Fleet consisted of 3 dreadnought battlecruisers, 4 large armoured cruisers, 4 light cruisers and 16 destroyers.

6 Lt Col W.P. Drury CBE (1861–1949), *The Passing of the Flagship and Other Stories*, 1933. He was a Royal Marine Light Infantry Officer, novelist and playwright.

7 Admiral Sir Ernest Troubridge KCMG CB MVO (1862–1926); the armoured cruisers were *Defence* (Troubridge's flagship), *Black Prince*, *Duke of Edinburgh*, *Warrior*; the light cruisers were *Chatham*, *Dublin*, *Gloucester*, *Weymouth*; Admiral of the Fleet Sir John Kelly GCB GCVO (1871–1936); Admiral Sir Howard Kelly GBE KCB CMG MVO (1873–1952).

8 Rear Admiral Wilhelm Souchon (1864–1933) had assiduously cultivated the Turks since hoisting his flag in the *Goeben* on 13 Oct 1913.

9 See Adm F.W. Kennedy, King's College Liddell Hart Military Archives, GB0099 KCLMA, Report, pp 1–61, 20 Oct 1914 & postscript 16 Nov 1914 and Kennedy 'Narrative from the Indomitable: Escape of the Goeben', *The Naval Review*, VII 1919, pp.110–126.

10 See Redmond McLaughlin, *The Escape of 'The* Goeben', *Prelude to Gallipoli*, Seeley Service & Co. 1974; Robert K. Massie, *Castles of Steel*, Jonathan Cape, 2004.

11 Vice Admiral Augustin Boué de Lapeyère (1852–1924).

12 See BB Schofield, Midshipman's Journal, IWM Documents.20947 for all relevant entries.

13 Admiral of the Fleet John Jellicoe, 1st Earl GCB OM GCVO SGM DL (1859–1935).

14 For the composition of the RN fleets and squadrons see http://www.naval-history.net/WW1NavyBritishShips-Locations5Contemp.htm.

15 BBS to Dearest Father & Mother, c/o GPO Jany 29th 1915. 189 survivors from the *Blücher* were picked up. HMS *Indomitable* mounted eight 12-inch guns in

four twin hydraulically powered turrets. The Zeppelin was not in fact harmed and returned to base.

16 Admiral of the Fleet Ernle Chatfield, 1st Baron GCB OM KCMG CVO PC DL (1873–1967). See Schofield, Midshipman's Journal, 16 May 1915, IWM Documents.20947.

17 Hell, Canto XVII in *The Vision; or Hell, Purgatory, and Paradise of Dante Alighieri*, tr. by the Rev. Henry Francis Cary, AM, William Smith, London, 1845, p.43.

18 Captain J.A. Moreton CMG DSO (1876–1920).

19 Admiral of the Fleet Sir Frederick Doveton Sturdee GCB KCMG CVO (1859–1925); Admiral Maximilian Graf von Spee (1861–1914). Sturdee's squadron consisted of 2 battlecruisers, 5 cruisers, and one armed merchant cruiser; they destroyed the German squadron of 2 armoured cruisers, 3 light cruisers, and 2 colliers; only one light cruiser escaped (sunk in 1915).

20 Sir Winston Churchill KG OM CH TD PC DL FRS RA (1874–1965), Prime Minister 1940-45, 51–55.

21 Lieutenant Commander Harold De Gallye Lamotte later received the DSO for services in minesweeping operations. https://www.thegazette.co.uk/Edinburgh/issue/13516/page/3447. See HMS *Seagull* Ship's Log ADM 53/59574–75, Oct–Nov 1915, TNA.

22 The Second Sea Lord and Chief of Naval Personnel 1914–16 was Admiral Sir Frederick Hamilton GCVO KCB (1856–1917).

Chapter Three: The Harwich Force

1 Shakespeare, *Henry V*, St Crispin's Day Speech before the battle of Agincourt, IV, iii.

2 Admiral of the Fleet Sir Reginald Tyrwhitt GCB DSO (1870–1951). See E.F. Knight, *Harwich Naval Forces*, Hodder & Stoughton, 1919 for a full account of the Harwich Force during WWI.

3 Captain E.W. Kirkby DSO (1885–1960). See HMS *Manly* Ship's Log ADM 53/ 48189–94, Feb 1916–Jan 1917; HMS *Torrid* Ship's Log ADM 53/63376–85, May 1917–Dec 1918, TNA.

4 Rear Admiral Sir Horace Hood KCB DSO MVO (1870–1916). Information from typed notes, undated, Admiral F.W. Kennedy, King's College Liddell Hart Military Archives, GB0099 KCLMA.

5 Based in Wallsend, Tyne and Wear, at its apex it represented the 3 major shipbuilding families of Swan, Hunter and Wigham Richardson. As Swan Hunter, the company continued to construct vessels on Tyneside until 2006.

6 BBS donated his carving of HMS *Torrid*'s ship's badge to the IWM on 25 Jun 1970, Catalogue no 5358. The Zeppelin referred to on p.31 was shot down on 11 Aug 1918. See the painting by Charles Pears (1918). Art.IWM ART 1357.

7 This was probably the Hull and East Riding Sports Club, where members can still 'enjoy a meal, drink at the bar, watch TV and attend all social events, which are usually free'.

8 The Palace Theatre was on the corner of Victoria St North and Corporation Rd. Opened on 10 Dec 1904 and built on the site of an earlier Theatre Royal, it continued as a Variety theatre until 1931 when it was refurbished as a cinema. Last used as a warehouse, it was demolished in 1979.

9 BBS wrote this quotation in the book of Common Prayer which he gave to his mother on her birthday on 9 Aug 1919. For statistics see spartacus-educational.com/FWWnavy.htm http://www.roll-of-honour.com/RoyalNavy/WarshipsLostWW1.html

Chapter Four: HMS *Renown*

1 'I Serve': motto from the Prince of Wales's heraldic badge.

2 Vice Admiral Sir Ernest Taylor CMG CVO (1876–1971).

3 M. Epitácio Pessoa (1865–1942), President of Brazil (Jul) 1919–22. See HMS *Renown* Ship's Log ADM 53/57633–40, Apr–Nov 1919.

4 To Dearest Papa, from Government House, Ottawa, 31 Aug 1919, *A King's Story, The Memoirs of HRH the Duke of Windsor KG*, p.142, p.139.

5 For an account of Crossing the Line, see 'Entering Neptune's Domain', by Vice Admiral B.B. Schofield, 'Maga' *Blackwood's Magazine*, Aug 1969, Vol. 306, no. 1846, pp.122–23.

6 Otto Hermann Kahn (1867–1934) was a German-born banker and patron of the arts.

7 Enrico Caruso (1873–1921) died of pleurisy.

8 Sir Ashley Sparks (1877–1964) had moved to the US in 1897; chief representative in the US of the Cunard Steamship Company (later Cunard-White Star Company Ltd, reverting to Cunard Line in 1950) 1917–50, during which period two of the largest liners, the *Queen Mary* and *Queen Elizabeth* were built.

Chapter Five: 'A most reliable Navigator'

1 The Poetical Works of Fitz-Greene Halleck (1790–1867), 'Marco Bozzaris', D. Appleton & Co., New York, 1865, p.7.

2 See HMS *Shakespeare* Ship's Log ADM 53/59903–04, Sep–Dec 1920, TNA.

3 Captain C.W.E. Trelawny DSO RN (1881–1965). See HMS *Godetia* Ship's Log ADM 53/78183, Mar–Apr 1922, TNA.

4 Admiral of the Fleet Sir Osmond Brock GCB KCMG KCVO (1869–1947). See HMS *Montrose* Ship's Log ADM 53/80880, Sep–Oct 1922, ADM 53/80886, Sep–Oct 1923; ADM 53/80887, Nov–Dec 1923; ADM 53/80888, Jan–Feb 1924; ADM 53/80889, Mar–Apr 1924, TNA.

5 General Sir Charles Harington Harington GCB GBE DSO (1872–1940).

6 Ismet Iönü (1884–1973), 2nd President of Turkey 1938–50.

7 Rear Admiral the Hon Edward Bingham VC OBE (1881–1939). https://www.
   thegazette.co.uk/London/issue/29751/supplement/9067.
8 Mehmed VI (1861–1926), 36th and last Sultan 1918–1922. He was succeeded by
   Mustafa Kemal Atatürk (1881–1938) 1st President of Turkey.
9 Captain Frank Slocum CMG OBE (1897–1982). In 1937 he joined the Secret
   Intelligence Service (SIS) from the RN's Tactical School. During WWII he ran
   agents to France from a forward base in the Scilly Isles.
10 Captain Bingham, HMS *Montrose*, 20 Mar 1924. 'This is to certify...' report on
   conduct of Lt (N) Brian B. Schofield, Schofield family papers.

Chapter Six: Of languages

1 Samuel Butler, *Satyr upon the Imperfection and Abuse of Human Learning, Part
   1st*, ll.65–69, ed. René Lamar, Cambridge University Press, 1928, p.69.
2 Admiral Philip Dumas CB CVO (1868–1948). He was advanced to the rank of
   vice admiral on 30 Jun 1924. Promoted full admiral 1928.

Chapter Seven: East of Suez in the *Enterprise*

1 Rudyard Kipling, *Barrack-Room Ballads*, 'Mandalay', v6, l1, Methuen & Co.
   Ltd, 35th ed., 1913, p.53.
2 Admiral Sir Herbert Fitzherbert KCIE CB CMG (1885–1958); Vice Admiral
   Stephen St Leger Moore CB CVO (1884–1955).
3 Sun Yat-sen (1866–1925), President of the Republic of China 1912 and President of
   the Kuomintang 1919-25. Chiang Kai-shek (1887–1975). Mao Tse-tung (Zedong)
   (1893–1976). There were five concessions: UK, Russia, France, Germany and
   Japan. Germany and Russia's concessions had ended in 1917 and 1920.
4 Sun Chuanfang (1885–1935).
5 Major General Sir John Duncan KCB CMG CVO DSO (1872–1948).
6 Eugene Chen (1878–1944); Sir Owen St Clair O'Malley KCMG (1887–1974).
7 Purgatory, Canto XVI in *The Vision; or Hell, Purgatory, and Paradise of Dante
   Alighieri*, tr. by the Rev. Henry Francis Cary, AM, William Smith, London, 1845,
   p. 99; dunnest i.e. thickest, murkiest.
8 Rudyard Kipling, *Barrack-Room Ballads*, 'The Ballad of the King's Jest', v3, p.98.
9 Ahmed Obaid bin Juma, Sheikh of Henjam, was the father-in-law of Sheikh Saeed
   of Dubai. In 1928 he was expelled from the island by the Persians, but reinstated
   following 'British efforts behind the scenes'. See Michael Quentin Morton, *Keepers of
   the Golden Shore, A History of the United Arab Emirates*, Reaktion Books, 2016, p. 104.
10 Admiral Sir Bertram Thesiger KBE CB CMG (1875–1966).
11 Sir Stanley Jackson GCSI GCIE KStJ (1870–1947). Known as the Honourable
   Stanley Jackson during his cricketing career.
12 George Goschen, 2nd Viscount GCSI GCIE CBE VD PC (1866–1952).

13 Adolf Hitler (1889–1945). The theme of many of his paintings included farmers' houses.

14 Sheikh Ahmad Al-Jaber Al-Sabah (1885–1950), 10th ruler of Kuwait, 1921–50.

15 Reza Shah Pahlavi (1878–1944), Shah of Iran, 1925–41. See Robert Higham, *Britian's Imperial Air Routes 1918–39*, Fonthill Media, 1960, 2016.

16 See HMS *Enterprise, Story of the First Commission, April 7th, 1926 to December 19th, 1928*, Gale & Polden Ltd; HMS *Enterprise* Ship's Log ADM 53/76966, 1 May 1927–30 Apr 1928 (mostly written by BBS); ADM 53/76967, 1 May 1928–25 Feb 1929, TNA.

Chapter Eight: 'The good ship *Malaya*'

1 Edmund Waller (1606–87), 'Panegyric to my Lord Protector', ll.115–16, *The Poems of Edmund Waller*, ed G. Thorn Drury, Lawrence & Bullen, London, 1893, p.142.

2 By Command of the Commissioners of the Lord High Admiral of the UK, &c, Admiralty SW1, 12 Nov. 1928; Vice Admiral Sir Nicholas Archdale CBE Bt (1881–1955). See HMS *Malaya* Ship's Log (much of which was written by BBS) ADM 53/80256–83, Jan 1929–Apr 1931, TNA.

3 Vice Admiral John Kelly relinquished command on 15 May 1929; Vice Admiral Howard Kelly came on board the *Malaya* 9 Jun 1929.

4 Fuad I of Egypt (1868–1936). Sultan 1917, King 1922 of Egypt.

5 Bodegas Humbert and Williams was founded in 1877 by Sir Alexander Williams, a connoisseur of sherry and Arthur Humbert, who specialised in international relations. The engineer commander was possibly R.C. Brown.

6 Captain Rory O'Conor (1898–1941), *Running a Big Ship on 'Ten Commandments'*, p.141, Gieves Ltd, 1937. While in command of HMS *Neptune* he was among one of 764 crew members who died on 19 Dec 1941 when the ship hit a mine off the coast of Tripoli. Only one man was rescued. See http://www.hmsneptune.com/history1.htm.

7 See Bruce Taylor, *The Battlecruiser* HMS *Hood, An Illustrated Biography 1916-1941*, p.63: 'The pulling regatta is the principal sporting event in the Fleet, and for good reason...in a big-ship Regatta a team of nearly three hundred officers and men goes forth in the boats to do battle for their ship.' HMS *Hood* had won the trophy in 1926–28 in the Atlantic Fleet Regatta.

8 See Alan Ereira, *The Invergordon Mutiny*, Routledge & Kegan Paul, 1981.

Chapter Nine: 'The bands of Orion'

1 Job 38, v31.

2 'By command of the Commissioners for Executing the Office of Lord High Admiral of the United Kingdom, &c'. Admiralty, SW1, 24 Sep 1934.

3 Admiral Sir Sidney Meyrick KCB (1879–1973); Vice Admiral Edward de Faye Renouf CB CVO (1888–1972) called BBS 'an extremely hardworking & capable Navigating Officer and as Staff Officer Operations has shown himself able to compete with difficult situations with equanimity and judgment', 31 Mar 1936, Schofield family papers.

4 Sir Kenneth Blackburne GCMG GBE (1907–1980). Governor of the Leeward Islands 1950–56 and of Jamaica 1957–62. Known now as Nelson's Dockyard, the harbour serves as a yachting centre and historical monument. The 2nd Cruiser Squadron was a formation in existence from 1904–19, 1921–41 and 1946–52. See HMS *Orion* Ship's Log (which includes entries written by BBS) ADM53/98439–50, Jan–Dec 1935; ADM 53/98451–62, Jan–Dec 1936, TNA.

5 The recorded death toll in 1902 was 1,680. The last recorded eruption was in April 1979 but prior warning meant there were no casualties.

6 Sir Thomas Alexander Vans Best KCMG KBE (1870–1941) was Governor of the Windward Islands 1930–35; his successor until 1937 was Sir Selwyn Macgregor Grier KCMG (1878–1948). Since the conversation took place in early 1935 it is likely that it was with Best.

7 Emperor Haile Selassie (1892–1975). Admiral of the Fleet William Boyle, 12th Earl of Cork and Orrery GCB GCVO (1873–1967).

8 *A King's Story, The Memoirs of HRH the Duke of Windsor, KG*, pp.325–26.

9 Rear Admiral Thomas Calvert CB CVO DSO (1883–1938).

10 The Non-Intervention Agreement was signed in Aug 1936 with the objective of preventing the Spanish Civil War escalating into a wider conflict. It had the agreement of 27 nations including the Soviet Union.

11 In Dec 1944 Admiral Hermann von Fischel (1887–1950) was taken prisoner by the Soviets and died in a camp outside Moscow. Ammiraglio d'Armata Angelo Iachino (1889–1976) had been awarded the Silver Medal of Military Valour for bravery in combat in the Northern Adriatic in Nov 1918.

12 Admiral of the Fleet Sir Roger Backhouse GCB GCVO CMG (1878–1939) became First Sea Lord in 1938; he reversed British policy of sending a fleet to Singapore, believing that the threat from Germany and Italy was greater than that of Japan.

Chapter Ten: Staff Officer on board the *Nelson*

1 Horace (Quintius Horatius Flaccus) (65–8BC). The Complete Works of Horace, tr by Various Hands, J.M.Dent & Sons.

2 See HMS *Nelson* Ship's Log ADM 53/105052–60, Apr–Dec 1937; ADM 53/105061–72, Jan–Dec 1938; ADM 53/109880–91, Jan–Mar 1939, TNA.

3 Admiral Sir Henry Ruthven Moore GCB CVO DSO (1886–1978). C-in-C, Home Fleet 1943–44.

4   Rear Admiral A.R. Dewar (1887–1972); his older brothers were Vice Admiral Kenneth Dewar CBE (1879–1964) and Captain A.C. Dewar CBE (1876–1969). They co-authored a controversial account of the Battle of Jutland, *Naval Staff Appreciation of Jutland.* Their other brother, Lieutenant Commander J.F. Dewar (1881–1942) suffered from acute alcoholism.

5   Admiral V.M. Orlov. From 1937–41 between 40–43,000 commanders of the Red Army were purged. Joseph Stalin (1878–1953) ruled the Soviet Union from the 1920s until his death, becoming de facto dictator from 1937.

6   See HMS *Rodney* Ship's Log ADM 53/105559–64, Apr–Nov 1937, TNA; King Haakon VII (1872–1957), Queen Maud (1869–1938).

7   Matthew Arnold's 'The Forsaken Merman' (1849) is the story of a merman who marries a young woman who later abandons him.

8   Christian X of Denmark (1870–1927). He was King Haakon VII of Norway's older brother.

9   John Gilpin was the subject of William Cooper's ballad, 'The Diverting History of John Gilpin', (1782) which relates how Gilpin became separated from his family and lost control of his horse.

10 Captain W.T. Makeig-Jones (1890–1939) took command of HMS *Nelson* on 13 Dec 1937. As Captain of HMS *Courageous* he went down with his ship when it was torpedoed by a German U-boat in Sep 1939. See Ch.12.

11 Admiral of the Fleet Sir Dudley Pound GCB OM GCVO (1877–1943).

12 Admiral Sir Guy Grantham GCB CBE DSO (1900–92).

13 António Óscar Carmona (1869–1951), 11th President of Portugal, 1926–51.

14 Admiral of the Fleet John Tovey, 1st Baron GCB KBE DSO (1885–1971); Admiral of the Fleet Andrew Browne Cunningham, 1st Viscount Cunningham of Hyndhope KT GCB OM DSO and two bars (1883–1963). Known as 'ABC' he became C-in-C, Mediterranean Fleet in Jun 1939. The 10th and last pre-war Captain of the *Hood* was Admiral Sir Harold Walker KCB CB (1892–1975).

15 Admiral of the Fleet Sir Charles Forbes GCB DSO (1880–1960) retired in 1943; Admiral Edward King CB MVO (1889–1971). In his report Rear Admiral Moore described BBS as 'a most competent and hardworking staff officer in whose judgement I have great confidence. He has carried out his duties in an exceptionally able manner', 12 Apr 1938 which Admiral Backhouse 'fully endorsed'.

16 Korvettenkapitän Günther Prien (1908–41). His U-boat, the *U-47* went missing in Mar 1941, probably sunk by British warships. Prien was among the 45 dead.

Chapter Eleven: Diplomacy before war

1   Thomas More (1779–1852), *The Sceptic: A Philosophical Satire*, London, 1809, p.12.

2   Vice Admiral Cedric Holland CB (1889–1950) On the outbreak of war he also became Head of the Naval Mission to the French Admiralty.

3 Sir Eric Phipps GCB GCMG GCVO PC (1875–1945); Sir Ronald Hugh Campbell GCMG PC (1883–1953); Sir Charles Mendl (1871–1958); Elsie de Wolfe (1859?/65–50); Hermann Göring (1893–1946).

4 Jacqueline Delubac (1907–97) was Sacha Guitry's third wife. They divorced in Apr 1939 and she was briefly married to Leslie Hore-Belisha, Britain's Secretary of State for War 1937–40.

5 Amiral François Darlan (1881–1942) served in the Vichy government, before switching his allegiance in 1942. He was assassinated in Dec 1942. See Ch.13.

6 Formerly known as the Jardin de l'Acclimatation Anthropologique so Parisians could understand different lifestyles and customs, it exhibited foreign people, especially Africans, but was closed down in 1931.

7 Virginia Cowles OBE (1910–83). Having begun her career as a fashion writer, she covered the Spanish Civil War and both the outbreak and duration of WWII. She died in a car crash.

8 Lieutenant Colonel W.L. Gibson MBE (1899-1987) had served in the Royal Artillery in WWI and in Berlin 1920–26; Sir Nevile Bland KCMG KCVO (1886–1972) escaped internment in 1940, leaving with the Dutch government to exile in the UK; he returned to Holland after the war, serving as ambassador until 1948. Captain Shutei Tonaki (1902–93) supported the Emperor's brother, Prince Takamatsu, in opposing Japanese aggression.

9 Admiral Maarten Tromp (1598–1653): Admiral Cornelis Tromp (1629–1691); Admiral Michiel de Ruyter (1607–76).

10 Baron Louis Guichard (1893–1979). From 1941–42 he served in the Vichy government under Amiral Darlan.

11 Eelco van Kleffens, *The Rape of the Netherlands*, Hodder & Stoughton, 1940, p 49.

12 Sir Nevile Henderson GCMG (1882–1942), *Failure of a Mission, Berlin 1937–1939*, Hodder & Stoughton Ltd, 1940, pp.290–91.

13 Henderson, *Failure of a Mission*, p.265.

14 Vice Admiral Richard Shelley CB CBE (1892–1968); Lieutenant General Sir Noel Mason-MacFarlane KCB DSO MC and two bars (1889–1953) had proposed assassinating Hitler but the offer was rejected by his superiors; Henderson, *Failure of a Mission*, pp.291–92.

Chapter Twelve: 'The race is not to the swift'

1 Shakespeare, *Henry IV*, Part 2, III, i, ll.50-52.

2 Captain John Pelham, 8th Earl of Chichester (1912–44) succeeded to the Earldom aged 14 on the premature death of his elder brother. He too died young, in a road accident aged 31.

3 Lieutenant Colonel Richard Stevens (1893–1967). Head of the Passport Control Office (PCO), The Netherlands. He spoke Arabic, Hindustani, Malay, French,

German, Russian. He was promoted from major to lieutenant colonel during his imprisonment.

4 W. Somerset Maugham, *The Traitor*, quoted in (ed.) Bob Blaisdell, *World War One Short Stories*, Dover Publications Inc, Courier Corporation, 2013, p. 56.

5 Admiral Johannes Furstner (1887–1970).

6 'The race is not to the swift...', Ecclesiastes 9, v11.

7 Major General J.W. van Oorschot (1875–1952) was dismissed from his position for overstepping his authority after the Venlo incident of 9 Nov 1939.

8 33 men were killed including the commanding officer.

9 Captain W.T. Makeig-Jones was captain of HMS *Nelson* 1937–39, while BBS was serving as staff officer; HMS *Courageous* was on anti-submarine patrol.

10 Captain Sigismund Payne Best OBE (1885–1978), *The Venlo Incident*, Frontline, Pen & Sword Books, 2009, pp.7–14, (first published in 1950 by Hutchinson & Co.). In his introduction to the 2009 edition, Nigel Jones emphasises that instructions to enter into discussions with the Germans came from the highest authorities, i.e. Chamberlain, who was still 'putting out desperate feelers seeking a compromise peace with Germany before too much blood had been shed'. Schellenberg prospered becoming head of Germany's foreign intelligence service; the second 'malign consequence' was that Venlo permanently inoculated the British, especially Churchill, who had been suspicious of the contacts with the Germans in Holland from the outset, against having any dealings with the German opposition to Hitler for the rest of the war; Heinrich Himmler (1900–45).

11 Payne Best, *The Venlo Incident*, pp.16–17. See also Eelco van Kleffens, *The Rape of the Netherlands*, for Dutch point of view, pp. 64–67.

12 Sir Lancelot Oliphant KCMG CBE (1881–1965), Ambassador to Brussels and Minister-Plenipotentiary to Luxembourg Dec 1939. He was interned by the Nazis 1940–41; Colonel F.A.A. Blake OBE (1897–19??) served in the Royal Artillery during WWI. He was military attaché in Brussels from Feb 1939–May 1940.

13 Leopold III (1901–1983) was King of the Belgians 1934–51; Admiral of the Fleet Roger Keyes, 1st Baron GCB KCVO CMG DSO (1872–1945) was Special Adviser to King Leopold 10–27 May and then Director of Combined Operations July 1940–Oct 1941; Winston Churchill, *The Second World War*, I, Cassell & Co. Ltd, 1948, p.440.

14 Eelco van Kleffens (1894–1983), *The Rape of the Netherlands*, p.93.

15 Admiral Sir Gerald Dickens KCVO CB CMG (1879–1962). Sir Nevile Bland to the Rt Hon The Viscount Halifax, 20 Feb 1940, Schofield family papers.

Chapter Thirteen: HMS *Galatea*

1 Lucian, *Dialogues of the Sea Gods*, 'Doris and Galatea', I, tr. H.W. and F.G. Fowler. Doris is ridiculing the figure and manners of Polyphemus, Galatea's lover. H. Williams' translation reads: 'Don't sneer, Doris, for he is Poseidon's son, whatever he may be like', Bohn's Classical Library, p. 61.

2 Admiral Sir George Frederick Edward-Collins KCB KCVO ADC DL (1883–1958). HMS *Galatea* Ship's Log ADM 53/112278–88, Feb–Dec 1940; ADM 53/114300-02, Jan–Mar 1941, TNA.

3 See Robert Pearson, *Gold Run: The Rescue of Norway's Gold Bullion from the Nazis, 1940*. Casemate Books, 2015.

4 Kleffens, *The Rape of the Netherlands*, p.153; Psalm 34, v19.

5 Winston Churchill, *Never Give In!* ed. Winston S. Churchill, Pimlico, 2003, p.218.

6 Admiral Sir Alban Thomas Buckley Curteis KCB CVO DSO (1887–1961).

7 Mary Borden (1886–1968), novelist and poet. She married Brig Gen (later Sir) Edward Spears in 1918.

8 Marshal Philippe Pétain (1856–1951); Amiral Lucien Cayol (1882–1975). See http://www.naval-history.net/xDKWW2-4007-20JUL01.htm.

9 Vice Amiral Guillaume de Toulouse-Lautrec (1902–1985). Henri de Toulouse-Lautrec (1864–1901). See Maurice Pasquelot, *Les dossiers secrets de la marine: Londres–Vichy 1940–44*. http://ecole.nav.traditions.free.fr/officiers_detoulouse_guillaume.htm.

10 Admiral of the Fleet Sir James Somerville GCB GBE DSO DL (1882–1949): Force H was hurriedly assembled to fill the vacuum of French naval power in the Mediterranean after France's armistice with Germany; Amiral Marcel-Bruno Gensoul (1880–1973). See Churchill, *History of the Second World War*, II, Cassell & Co. Ltd, 1949, pp.206–11. The sinking of the French fleet at Mers el Kebir remains controversial to this day.

11 Hesiod (c.750–650 BC), Greek poet, a contemporary of Homer, 'Theogony'; tr from the Greek, there are various translations depending on edition, circa ll.680–90.

12 Alfred Tennyson, 'The Charge of the Light Brigade', V, l.5. The verse begins: 'Cannon to the right of them, Cannon to the left of them...'

13 Plutarch (46–120). He continued: 'Life itself decays, and all things are daily changing.'

14 Captain E.W.B. Sim (1899–1941), 21 officers and 447 ratings lost their lives; some 100 survivors were picked up. Less than 48 hours later the U-boat which had sunk the *Galatea* was rammed by an Italian torpedo boat thinking it was a British submarine and sunk with all hands.

Chapter Fourteen: 'Sail on O ship of State!'

1 *The Poems of Henry Wadsworth Longfellow*, 'The Building of the Ship', J.M. Dent & Sons Ltd, London, 1930, pp.344–45. Churchill received this passage in a message from President Roosevelt in Jan 1941; he quoted it in the House of Commons on 9 Feb 1941 and concluded: 'Give us the tools and we will finish the job', Winston Churchill, *Never Give In!*, ed. Winston S. Churchill, Pimlico,

2003, p.262; See H.V. Morton (1892–1979), *Atlantic Meeting*, Methuen & Co Ltd., London, 1943, frontispiece and p.7.

2 Admiral Sir Maurice James Mansergh KCB CBE (1896–1966); Paymaster Lieutenant Commander Claude Egarr Millson RNR (1904–1980).

3 Admiral Sir Robert Raikes KCB CVO DSO (1885–1953).

4 Captain George Allen CBE (1891–1980), deputy director of Trade Division 1939–42.

5 King Peter II of Yugoslavia (1923–70) was deposed by the Yugoslav Communist constituent assembly in 1945.

6 A total of 59 bombing attacks against Plymouth were made killing over 1,000 people and wounding nearly 4,500.

7 Captain Ralph Kerr CBE (1891–1941) had been present at Jutland in 1916.

8 A.V. Alexander, 1st Earl Alexander of Hillsborough KG CH PC (1885–1965). Churchill, *History of the Second World War*, III, p.282.

9 Burkard, Baron von Müllenheim-Rechberg (1910–2003), whose *Battleship Bismarck: A Survivor's Story* (1980) describes his experiences. In 1980 he launched the UK edition in London on board HMS *Belfast* where he met BBS and they became regular correspondents.

10 Commander Norman Holbrook VC (1888–1976).

11 See Reports of interviews with Survivors from British Merchant Vessels attacked, damaged or lost by enemy action, Shipping Casualties Section, Trade Division, ADM 199/2130–48, TNA.

12 Sir William Elderton KBE PhD (Oslo) (1877–1962), actuary & statistical adviser to the Ministry of War Transport.

13 Frederick Alexander Lindemann, 1st Viscount Cherwell CH PC FRS (1886–1957) was scientific adviser to Winston Churchill 1940–45 and again in 1951–52.

14 Rear Admiral Michael Goodenough DSO CBE (1904–55); Supplement to *The London Gazette* of 26 July 1940, Issue 34907, dated 26 July 1940.

15 Field Marshal Sir John Dill GCB CMG DSO (1881–1944); Air Chief Marshal Sir Wilfrid Freeman GCB DSO MC FRAeS (1888–1953); Sir Alexander Cadogan OM GCMG KCB (1884–1968).

16 Franklin D. Roosevelt (1882–1945), 32nd US President 1933–1945.

17 Captain John Leach DSO MVO (1894–1941). His son, later Admiral of the Fleet Sir Henry Leach GCB DL (1923–2011), served with BBS on board HMS *Duke of York* in 1943. Winston Churchill, *History of the Second World War*, III, Cassell & Co. Ltd, 1950, p.381. See HMS *Prince of Wales* Ship's Log ADM 53/114891, Aug 1941, TNA.

18 Captain Sir Richard Pim KBE VRD DL RNVR (1900–87).

19 H.V. Morton, *Atlantic Meeting*, p.60.

20 Also starring in the *Santa Fe Trail* (1940) were Errol Flyn, Olivia de Havilland, Ronald Reagan and Alan Hale. Raymond Massey (1896–1983) also played John

Brown in the 1955 film *Seven Angry Men*. Thomas 'Stonewall' Jackson (1824–63). After attempting to seize the arsenal John Brown was hanged on 2 Dec 1859. In American history the surrender at Harpers Ferry is less well remembered than the John Brown incident.

21 Fleet Admiral Ernest King USN (1878–1956) retired in 1945, suffering a debilitating stroke in 1947.

22 Admiral Harold Rainsford Stark USN (1880–1972).

23 Churchill, *History of the Second World War*, III, p.384. Churchill says he chose the hymns.

24 See Martin Buell, *Master of Sea Power*, Little, Brown & Company, 1980, p.573.

25. Commander P.Q. Roberts (1904–1977); see B.B. Schofield, *The Arctic Convoys*, Macdonald & Jane's, 1977, p.11, pp.1–2.

Chapter Fifteen: 'The peril of the waters'

1 Shakespeare, *The Merchant of Venice*, I, iii.

2 Winston Churchill, *History of the Second World War*, IV, Cassell & Co. Ltd, 1951, p.237. Shakespeare, *Hamlet*, IV, v.

3 Churchill, *History of the Second World War*, IV, pp. 112–13.

4 Churchill, *History of the Second World War*, V, Cassell & Co. Ltd, 1952, p.11; Sir Amos Ayre KBE (1885–1953). BBS says the suggestion came from a member of his staff, Commander (later Captain) Godfrey Brewer DSO (1901–88). The idea had initially been proposed (although not followed through) in 1940 by the Director of Air Material, Captain M.S. Slattery. See Schofield, 'The Defeat of the U-Boats During World War II' in *Journal of Contemporary History* Vol. 16, No. 1, Jan 1981, p. 125; Kenneth Poolman, *Escort Carrier 1941-1945: An Account of British Escort carriers in Trade Protection*. Ian Allan, 1972, pp.73–74.

5 See Schofield, *The Arctic Convoys*, Macdonald & Jane's, 1977, App I, pp.141–43.

6 Admiral of the Fleet Sir Charles Lambe GCB CVO (1900–1960); Field Marshal Alan Brooke, 1st Viscount Alanbrooke KG GCB OM GCVO DSO and bar (1883–1963); Frederick James Leathers, 1st Viscount CH PC (1883–1965), Ministry of War Transport 1941–45.

7 Captain R.L. Hamer DSO (1884–1951), see HMS *Bulolo* Ship's Log ADM 53/117091, Jan 1943, TNA.

8 General Henri Giraud (1879–1949); General Charles de Gaulle (1890–1970), Prime Minister, President of France 1958–69.

9 Charles McMoran Wilson, 1st Baron Moran MC PRCP (1882–1977); Field Marshal Bernard Montgomery, 1st Earl Montgomery of Alamein KG GCB DSO PC DL (1887–1976); Field Marshal Harold Alexander, 1st Earl Alexander of Tunis KG GCB OM GCMG CSI DSO MC CD PC (1891–1969) was C-in-C Middle East Command; General Dwight Eisenhower (1890–1969), 34th US

President 1953–61; General George Marshall Jr (1880–1959) was US Chief of Staff 1939–45; Admiral of the Fleet Louis Mountbatten, 1st Earl Mountbatten of Burma KG GCB OM GCSI GCIE GCVO DSO PC FRS (1900–79) was Chief of Combined Operations 1941–43; Marshal of the Royal Air Force Charles Portal, 1st Viscount Portal of Hungerford KG GCB OM DSO and bar MC DL (1893–1971) was Chief of the Air Staff and was selected to co-ordinate the US and UK bombers in an offensive over Germany; General Henry H. (Hap) Arnold (1886–1950) was US Army Air Force (AAF) Commanding General; Harry Hopkins (1890–46) was Roosevelt's unofficial emissary to Churchill; Marshal of the Royal Air Force Sir John (Jack) Slessor GCB DSO MC (1897–1979) was assistant chief of the Air Staff.

10 Winston Churchill, *History of the Second World War*, IV, p. 621.

11 Brigadier Guy Stewart (1900–43); 11 were killed, 8 injured.

12 Pierre L'Enfant (1754–1825), French-American military engineer, whose design for Washington DC is known as the L'Enfant Plan (1791).

13 Admiral Sir Percy Noble GBE KCB CVO (1880–1955) had been C-in-C, Western Approaches 1941–42; Arthur Salter, 1st Baron GBE KCB PC (1881–1975).

14 Rear Admiral Ralph Metcalf USN (1913–2008).

15 See B.B. Schofield and L.F. Martyn, *The Rescue Ships*, Wm Blackwood & Sons Ltd, 1968.

16 Henry J. Kaiser (1882–1967); Captain Eric Brand (1896–1991); Paymaster Rear Admiral Sir Eldon Manisty KCB CMG (1876–1960). See David Twiston-Davies, *Canada from Afar, The Daily Telegraph Book of Canadian Obituaries* 1996, p.14.

17 Igor Sikorsky (1889–1972); Colonel John Llewellin, 1st Baron GBE MC TD PC (1893–1957).

18 Commander Harold Auten VC DSC RD RNR (1891–1964) was the author of *Q Boat Adventures*, 1919.

19 Lewis Williams Douglas (1894–1974) was an early member of the Committee to Defend America by Aiding the Allies. From 1947–50 he was US Ambassador to the UK.

20 Winston Churchill, *History of the Second World War*, IV, p. 621.

21 Captain William Derek Stephens (1898–1983) was director of Trade Division until 1945.

22 Captain William Beswick DSC RNR (1884–1959); Chairman of the Honours and Awards Committee to 'Dear Schofield', 3 Jun 1943, Schofield family papers. Five ships were lost in outbound convoys in 1944–45; between Aug 1941–May 1945, 40 outbound convoys (811 ships) and 35 homebound convoys (715 ships) sailed to the Soviet Union, of which 58 outbound ships (plus 5 lost in Kola Inlet) and 27 homebound ships were lost. See Schofield, *The Arctic Convoys*, App I, pp.141–43. Admiral Pound to 'My dear Schofield', 30 Jul 1943, Schofield family papers. Pound suffered two strokes and died 3 months later.

Chapter Sixteen: From *Duke of York* to *Dryad*

1   Rt Rev Jeremy Taylor (1613–67), *The Works of Jeremy Taylor, DD*, with some account of his life, summary of his discourse, notes, &c by the Rev T. S. Hughes, BD, A. J. Valpy, London, 1831.

2   Shakespeare, *Othello*, II, iii; Frank Knox (1874–1944) was an American newspaper editor and publisher. He was Secretary of the US Navy from Jul 1940–44.

3   Dame Vera Laughton Mathews DBE (1888–1959), director WRNS 1939–46, *Blue Tapestry*, Hollis & Carter, 1948, pp.214–16.

4   BBS's wife, Norah (widow of A.T. Handley), whom he had married on 12 Jul 1941, had become dangerously ill and he felt that he should relinquish his command to be closer to her.

5   Admiral Hon Sir Guy Russell GBE KCB DSO (1898–1977). Only 36 men were rescued from the *Scharnhorst* out of nearly 2,000. See HMS *Duke of York* Ship's Log ADM 53/117401–5, Aug–Dec 1943, TNA. She was laid up in 1951 and scrapped in 1957; a miniature of the ship's bell was given to BBS and remains in the Schofield family possession.

6   Colonel Evelyn Thistlethwayte (1861–1943); Major General Sir Francis de Guingand KBE CB DSO (1900–1979); see also Schofield, *The Story of HMS Dryad*, pp.89–92.

7   Group Captain James Stagg CB OBE FRSE (1900–75); see J.M. Stagg, *Forecast for Overlord*, Ian Allan, 1972 and BBS review in the Journal of the RUSI, Sep 1972: 'Had Stagg failed to hold the ring, the American view, confident, wrong, but backed by America's massive superiority, might well have prevailed – in which case D-Day would have been premature and a shambles. That all was well in the end was due to his clarity of vision, his patience, and his sheer intellectual strength'. Admiral Sir Charles Little GCB GBE (1882–1973); Admiral Sir Bertram Ramsay KCB KBE MVO (1883–1945).

8   Field Marshal Erwin Rommel (1891–1944) was known as 'the Desert Fox' for his early victories in the Western Desert.

9   Rear Admiral William Gordon Benn (1889–1962).

10   Frank Hugh Pakenham Borthwick-Norton (1877–1959); HMS *Dryad* later became the Maritime Warfare School; in 2004 it was moved to HMS *Collingwood* and the site handed over to the Ministry of Defence in 2005. It is now occupied by the Defence College of Police and Guarding, a training centre for the police services of the British Armed Forces.

Chapter Seventeen: The *KGV* and the Pacific

1   Sir Samuel Tuke (1615–74), *The Adventures of Five Hours*, Don Antonio: II, *A Select Collection of Old Plays in Twelve Volumes*, XII, Septimus Prowett, London, 1827, p.42.

2 Harry S. Truman (1884–1972), 33rd US President 1945–53.

3 BBS's wife's health had stablilised and so she encouraged him to take up the appointment. The BPF had been formed from the most powerful units of the Eastern Fleet with reinforcements from Europe; the remainder was re-mustered as the East Indies Fleet. See Tony Heathcote. *The British Admirals of the Fleet 1734 –1995,* Pen & Sword, 2002, p.90; HMS *King George V* Ship's Log ADM 53/121606–10, Aug–Dec 1945; ADM 53/123067–74, Jan–Aug 1946, TNA.

4 Admiral of the Fleet Bruce Fraser, 1st Baron Fraser of North Cape GCB KBE (1888–1981). First Sea Lord Sep 1948–Dec 1951.

5 Admiral Sir Bernard Rawlings GBE KCB (1889–1962). See Edwyn Gray, *Operation Pacific,* Leo Cooper, 1990, pp.245–54 for a discussion on operations including British-US tensions.

6 Canon James S. Bezzant BD MA (1897–1967), Chaplain RNVR 1940–46.

7 Fleet Admiral William Halsey Jr KBE USN (1882–1959). He had been in the Pacific since 1941.

8 Clement Attlee KG OM CH PC FRS (1883–1967), Prime Minister 1945–51. The Potsdam Conference, lasting from 17 Jul–2 Aug 1945, was also known as the Berlin Conference of the Three Heads of Government of the USSR, USA and UK.

9 Revised figures suggest between 70-120,000 civilians were killed at Hiroshima plus 20,000 soldiers and 39,000-80,000 were killed at Nagasaki.

10 The obi remains in the Schofield family possession. The visit to the British Embassy could have been on 3 September since both Vice Admiral Rawlings and BBS left the ship at 0915 and returned at 1305. They signed the book on 12 Sep 1945. See *The Times,* 5 Sep 1946 which records Admiral Fraser as being the first to sign the book.

11 William Adams (1564–1620). See 'Anjin-Miura', [the pilot of Miura] by B.B. Schofield, 'Maga' *Blackwood's Magazine,* May 1969, Vol. 305, no. 1843, pp. 404–10.

12 Vice Admiral Edward Ewen USN (1897-1959); Admiral Sir Peter Reid GCB CVO (1903–73).

13 'Melbourne Welcomes British Giant Battleship', By a Special Representative of *The Sun* who travelled from Sydney in *King George V,* Scrapbook, Schofield family papers.

14 'Britain's Powerful Battleship Has Rendezvous at Dawn', By A Special Reporter who boarded the Battleship from the pilot steamer, undated newspaper cutting, Scrapbook, Schofield family papers.

15 Captain R.T. White DSO (1908–95) was awarded his DSO in 1940, a bar in 1941 and a second bar in 1942. He was the youngest officer (aged 37) in the RN to be promoted captain in Dec 1945 at that time.

16 Additional information from 'Report of proceedings of HM Ship under my command, during the period 27th Oct to 10th Nov 1945 inclusive', 10 Nov 1945 and undated contemporary newspapers.

17 Major General Winston Dugan, 1st Baron GCMG CB DSO KStJ (1876–1951), Governor of Victoria 1939–49. Rainbird's jockey was Billy Cook.

18 Major General Herbert Lloyd CB CMG CVO DSO (1883–1957).

19 HRH Prince Henry, Duke of Gloucester KG KT KP GCB GCMG GCVO PC (1900–74), HRH Princess Alice, Duchess of Gloucester GCB CI GCVO GBE (1901–2004), HRH Prince William (1941–72), HRH Prince Richard, Duke of Gloucester KG GCVO GCStJ SSI (b.1944).

20 Founded in 1915 as the Blinded Soldiers and Sailors Care Committee; located in Bayswater Rd, it moved premises to Regent's Park. In 1923 the name officially adopted was St Dunstan's, its training and rehabilitation facilities moving to Brighton (and to Shropshire during WWII). In 2012 the name was changed to Blind Veterans UK. Additional information, *Sunday Empire News*, 3 Mar 1946.

21 Sir William Crowther (1887–1981) had a particular interest in the whaling industry, his grandfather, a former premier of Tasmania, having owned whaling ships. The bookends are in the Schofield family possession. Commander C.E.A. Cree (1911–2009); Sir Frank Gibson (1878–1965) was Mayor of Fremantle 1919–23, 1926–51.

22 The carved crest together with one of HMS *Duke of York*'s crest is in the Schofield family possession as are the wood carving tools.

23 Gideon Brand van Zyl, PC (1873-1956). Governor General of the Union of South Africa 1945–50. Field Marshal Jan Christian Smuts PC OM CH DTD ED KC FRS (1870–1950). PM of the Union of South Africa 1919–24, 1939–48.

24 In Sierra Leone, BBS received a letter from his wife's doctor saying that she could not withstand any more treatment. She died on 14 Mar 1946.

25 Admiral Sir Edward Neville Syfret GCB KCB (1889–1972). C-in-C, Home Fleet 1945–48. His flag was transferred from HMS *Nelson* which had been the C-in-C, Home Fleet's flagship in the 1930s.

26 Abdullah bin al-Hussein I (1882–1951) became king on 25 May the day the Treaty of London was ratified. It came into force on 17 Jun 1946.

27 The DUKWs were used for the first time in Europe during the Sicilian campaign. The initials are not an acronym but stand for D: Designed in 1942, U: Utility, K: all wheel drive, W: Dual tandem rear axles. Personal correspondence, May, Jul 1946, Schofield family papers.

28 Ed. note. In 2011 Lieutenant Colonel Roddy Riddell, Vice Chairman of The Black Watch Regimental Association, found a seating plan of the lunch held on board HMS *King George V* on 26 Jul 1946 when clearing out the desk of his mother, Deirdre – one of 'les' girls – after his father's death. Personal correspondence, 26 Jul 1946, from Oban, Schofield family papers and with Lieutenant Colonel Roddy Riddell, 3 Dec 2011 and 5 Jun 2018. See Victoria Schofield, *The Black Watch, Fighting in the Front Line*, Head of Zeus, 2017, p. 363.

29 Personal correspondence, 15 Aug 1946, Schofield family papers. BBS left HMS *George V* on 21 Sep 1946 going on leave pending re-appointment.

30 *The poems of Henry Wadsworth Longfellow*, 1823–1866, introduction by Katharine Tynan, J.M. Dent & Sons, 1909, 1930, 'The Secret of the Sea', v1, p.345.

Chapter Eighteen: Glad Waters

1 Shakespeare, *Richard II*, II, iii.

2 Admiral Sir John Edelsten GCB GCVO CBE (1891–1966). See Stephen Roskill, *Naval Policy Between Wars*. I: The Period of Anglo American Antagonism, p. 532.

3 BBS married Grace Mildred Seale (1909–2004) on 17 Aug 1946.

4 Admiral of the Fleet Sir John Cunningham GCB MVO DL (1885–1962).

5 George Jellicoe, 2nd Earl KBE DSO MC PC FRS FRGS (1918–2007); Patricia, Countess Jellicoe (1917–2012); Admiral Erhard Qvistgaard (1898–1980) was Chief of Defence 1950–62 and Chairman of NATO's Military Committee in 1953–54; Rose Qvistgaard (neé Laage-Petersen) (1900–98).

6 Admiral Thomas B. Inglis USN (1897–1984); Admiral Arleigh Burke USN (1901–1996) was CNO 1955–61. Admiral Louis Denfeld USN (1891–1972) was CNO 15 Dec 1947–1 Nov1949; Admiral Forrest Sherman USN (1896–1951) was CNO 1949–51.

7 Admiral Sir Frederick Hew Dalrymple-Hamilton KCB (1890–74) succeeded Moore in Sep 1948.

8 Admiral Robert B. Carney USN (1895–1990) was CNO 1953–55.

9 John Gunther (1901–1970), *Inside U.S.A.*, Hodder & Stoughton, 1947, p. 724.

10 In 1995 the submarine was located; in 2004 the 8 crew members, whose bodies were found still at their stations, were given a proper burial.

11 *South Pacific* (Rodgers and Hammerstein). The musical premiered on Broadway in 1949 and was instantly popular. Douglas Fairbanks Jr KBE DSC (1909–2000).

12 The first assassination attempt consisted of a letter addressed to Truman in 1947 by Zionist extremists containing powdered gelignite, a pencil battery and a detonator. It was diffused in the White House mail room.

13 Joseph Addison (1672–1719), Sat Jun 16, [1711], *The Spectator*, No 93, in *The works of the late Right Honourable Joseph Addison*, with notes by Richard Hurd, DD, vol II, Bohn's British Classics, 1856, pp. 411-12; Lord Byron, *The Corsair*, 1814, canto 1, stanza 1, ll.

14. Shakespeare, *Othello*, V, ii.

Biographical timeline

1895: born *11 October*

1908: entered RN College, Osborne

1910: entered RN College, Dartmouth

1913: **Midshipman**, HMS *Indomitable*

1914: outbreak of the First World War *4 August*

1915: *January*, Dogger Bank action; **Acting Sub Lieutenant**; HMS *Seagull*

1916: **Sub Lieutenant**; HMS *Manly*, Harwich Force; *May*, Battle of Jutland

1917: **Lieutenant**; HMS *Torrid*, Harwich Force

1918: *11 November* Armistice – end of the First World War

1919: HMS *Renown*, HRH the Prince of Wales's royal tour of Canada

1920: RN College, Greenwich; HMS *Dryad*, Portsmouth; qualified in Navigation; joined HMS *Shakespeare*, Home Fleet flotillas

1921: HMS *Godetia*, RN Fisheries Protection Squadron

1922: HMS *Montrose*, Mediterranean Fleet

1924: Qualified in Navigation and Pilotage for First Class Ships

1925: **Lieutenant Commander**

1926: Qualified as Acting Interpreter in French and Italian; Navigating Officer, HMS *Enterprise*, East Indies (and China) Station

1929: Navigating Officer, HMS *Malaya*, Mediterranean Fleet

1930: Navigating Officer, HMS *Malaya*, Home Fleet

1931: **Commander**; Tactical School, Portsmouth; Executive Officer, Navigation School, Portsmouth

1934: RN Staff College, Greenwich; Squadron Navigating Officer and Staff Officer (Operations), HMS *Orion*

1935: HMS *Orion* joins Home Fleet; review of the Home and Mediterranean Fleets by HM King George V in celebration of his Silver Jubilee

1937: HMS *Nelson*, Staff Officer (Operations) on staff of the C-in-C, Home Fleet, (HMS *Rodney* Jun-Nov). Royal review of the fleet in celebration of HM King George VI's coronation

1938: **Captain**

1939: Assistant Naval Attaché, Paris; Naval Attaché, The Hague and Brussels; outbreak of the Second World War *3 September*

1940: Fall of France; Winston Churchill replaced Neville Chamberlain as Prime Minister; BBS in command of HMS *Galatea*

1941: Director of Trade Division (Convoys) at the Admiralty

1943: Aug–Dec, in command, HMS *Duke of York* as Flag Captain to C-in-C, Home Fleet; appointed Commander of the British Empire (CBE)

1944: in command, HMS *Dryad*, (Southwick House Navigation School and Headquarters Normandy Invasion)

1945: in command, HMS *King George V*, flagship of British Pacific Fleet; Churchill replaced as Prime Minister by Clement Attlee (Labour); *8 May* VE Day, *15 August* VJ day; *7 September* BBS was awarded the Legion of Merit, Degree of Officer bestowed by the President of the United States of America

1946: Mentioned in Despatches for 'distinguished service during the war in the Far East'; at the Admiralty for compilation of *Fighting Instructions*

1947: **Rear Admiral**; Senior Officers' War Course, RN College, Greenwich

1948: Chief of Staff to Admiral Sir Henry Moore (later Admiral Sir Frederick Dalrymple-Hamilton), British Joint Services Mission (Navy), Washington DC

1949: Appointed Companion of the Military Division of the Order of the Bath (CB)

1950: **Vice Admiral** and retired

1984: died *8 November*

Acknowledgements

I should like to thank my sister, Elizabeth, who has not only given me her full support, but who also, in the twilight of our father's life, went through the manuscript with him in an attempt to fill out some of the missing names and dates. I am most grateful to Brigadier Henry Wilson, Pen & Sword Books, who recognised the value of publishing a memoir of a naval officer who may not have reached the highest rank and yet whose experiences give an insight into service in the Royal Navy during an exceptional time in history, both in war and peace; Rear Admiral James Goldrick, AO CSC, who met my father in 1979 during the course of his own research on the First World War at sea and kindly made many useful comments, Matt Jones, production manager at Pen & Sword, Irene Moore who copy edited the manuscript, Jon Wilkinson who designed the cover and Jamie Whyte who has drawn the maps which complement the narrative. I am, as ever, thankful to the London Library for its liberal lending policy and for being granted Thomas Carlyle membership, the British Library and The National Archives where I have been able to consult the logs of the ships in which my father served in order to verify facts and dates, as well as the Imperial War Museum and the Liddell Hart Centre for Military Archives, King's College, London. Finally, I should like to thank my friends and family, especially my husband, Stephen Willis, who, once more, has lived through seeing another literary enterprise come to fruition, and our children, Alexandra, Anthony and Olivia, who, although they never knew their maternal grandfather, were always fascinated by the stories of his life at sea.

Index

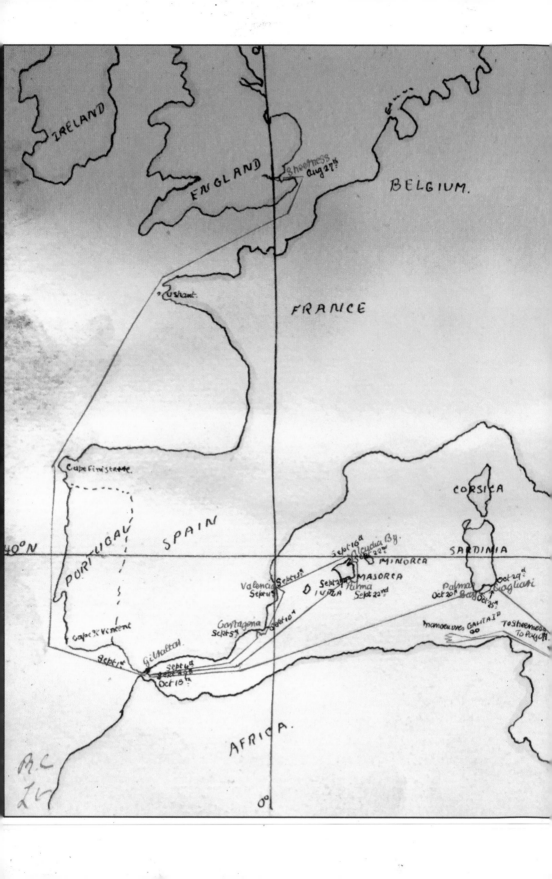